# GENDER AND AGRICULTURE IN TURKEY

# Gender and Agriculture in Turkey

## Women, Globalization and Food Production

Emine Erdoğan

**I.B.TAURIS**
LONDON · NEW YORK · OXFORD · NEW DELHI · SYDNEY

I.B. TAURIS
Bloomsbury Publishing Plc
50 Bedford Square, London, WC1B 3DP, UK
1385 Broadway, New York, NY 10018, USA
29 Earlsfort Terrace, Dublin 2, Ireland

BLOOMSBURY, I.B. TAURIS and the I.B. Tauris logo are trademarks of
Bloomsbury Publishing Plc

First published in Great Britain 2021
This paperback edition published in 2022

Copyright © Emine Erdoğan, 2021

Emine Erdoğan has asserted her right under the Copyright, Designs and
Patents Act, 1988, to be identified as Author of this work

For legal purposes the Acknowledgements on p.ix constitute an
extension of this copyright page.

Cover design: Adriana Brioso
Cover image courtesy of the author

All rights reserved. No part of this publication may be reproduced or transmitted
in any form or by any means, electronic or mechanical, including photocopying,
recording, or any information storage or retrieval system, without prior
permission in writing from the publishers.

Bloomsbury Publishing Plc does not have any control over, or responsibility for,
any third-party websites referred to or in this book. All internet addresses given
in this book were correct at the time of going to press. The author and publisher
regret any inconvenience caused if addresses have changed or sites have ceased
to exist, but can accept no responsibility for any such changes.

A catalogue record for this book is available from the British Library.

A catalog record for this book is available from the Library of Congress.

| ISBN: | HB: | 978-1-7883-1221-9 |
|---|---|---|
| | PB: | 978-0-7556-3934-2 |
| | ePDF: | 978-0-7556-1792-0 |
| | eBook: | 978-0-7556-1793-7 |

Typeset by Integra Software Services Pvt Ltd.

To find out more about our authors and books visit www.bloomsbury.com
and sign up for our newsletters.

*To my mother*

## CONTENTS

| | |
|---|---|
| List of Illustrations | viii |
| Acknowledgements | ix |
| Abbreviations | x |

Chapter 1
INTRODUCTION 1

Chapter 2
'THANKFUL' WOMEN FROM THE 'CENTRE OF THE WORLD':
   TURKEY AND HER PEOPLE 19

Chapter 3
THE BACKGROUND OF A TOMATO: CONTRACTING,
   RECRUITING AND ORGANIZING LABOUR 39

Chapter 4
'WE ARE ALL WOMEN UNTIL MONEY COMES': GENDERED
   LABOUR RELATIONS IN THE TOMATO PLANTING 49

Chapter 5
WITHOUT KURDISH FAMILIES THERE WILL BE NO TURKISH
   AGRICULTURE: FAMILIAL LABOUR RELATIONS IN
   THE TOMATO PICKING 63

Chapter 6
INSIDE THE 'KEMALIST' TOMATO-PROCESSING FACTORY 81

Chapter 7
*EL ÂLEM* SPEAKS: THE CONSTRUCTION AND PERSISTENCE OF
   RURAL PATRIARCHY 111

Chapter 8
'KEMALIST' AND 'TRANSITIONAL' PATRIARCHIES 139

Chapter 9
CONCLUSIONS 149

| | |
|---|---|
| Notes | 170 |
| References | 185 |
| Index | 196 |

# List of Illustrations

## *Graphs and diagrams*

| | | |
|---|---|---|
| 2.1 | CHANGES ON THE SIZE OF RURAL AND URBAN POPULATION | 23 |
| 2.2 | WOMEN'S EMPLOYMENT RATE BY URBAN AND RURAL AREAS BETWEEN 1988 AND 2013 | 25 |
| 7.1 | THE LANDOWNING FAMILY | 122 |
| 7.2 | *DAYIBAŞI'S* FAMILY | 128 |

## *Figures*

| | | |
|---|---|---|
| 6.1 | EXTERNAL ENVIRONS OF PLANT | 93 |
| 6.2 | THE FIRST AND SECOND PARTS OF THE SORTING LINES | 96 |
| 6.3 | THE THIRD PART OF THE SORTING LINES | 96 |
| 6.4 | THE UPPER AND LOWER PRODUCTION LINES | 97 |

## *Maps*

| | | |
|---|---|---|
| 1.1 | FIELDWORK SITES | 6 |
| 2.1 | REGIONS OF TURKEY | 22 |
| 3.1 | THE LOCATION OF MARDİN: THE HOMETOWN OF THE KURDISH SEASONAL MIGRANT WORKERS | 44 |

## *Tables*

| | | |
|---|---|---|
| 4.1 | TOMATO-GROWING STAGES AND GENDER AND ETHNIC DIVISIONS OF LABOUR | 50 |
| 7.1 | TYPES OF PATRIARCHY AND ASSOCIATED MASCULINITIES AND FEMININITIES WITHIN THE HOUSEHOLD | 117 |
| 7.2 | HIERARCHY IN MASCULINITIES IN RURAL HOUSEHOLDS | 118 |

# ACKNOWLEDGEMENTS

This book has begun its life when its cover photo was taken by my father, which shows me and my mother standing on my grandfather's tomato land. I have always been close and lucky enough to see how ordinary people can transform the world and also themselves with their labour. The book is, therefore, a reflection of what I have learnt and lived, thought and felt in the world of people making the 'life'. I appreciate all of them.

I am deeply grateful to *Carol Wolkowitz* and *Nickie Charles* for their labour making me more critical, emphatic and loving person over the past ten years. My way of thinking has been transformed with them; with their support and courage to think and to write as I am, so they are everywhere in this book.

During this study – and throughout my life – my mother, *annecim*, father, *babacım*, and my sister, *kardeşim*, have made me never feel alone wherever I am; *Çağrı* made everywhere I go feel familiar; and *Nehir* showed and taught me the way of making 'our own world'. I always feel incredibly lucky to have them.

Last but not least, I am deeply thankful to everyone who made this study possible – workers, farmers, managers, women, men, Turks, Kurds, young and old – whose lives coloured, shaped and transformed this story. Finally, to close the circle, I am grateful to veryone whose taxes have made it possible for me, through the support of the Turkish Ministry of Education, to complete this study which was funded as a PhD.

# ABBREVIATIONS

| | |
|---|---|
| AKP | Justice and Development Party (2001, currently governing party (2020)) |
| CHP | Republican People's Party (1923, currently the main opposition) |
| DEP | Democracy Party (1991–94) |
| FP | Virtue Party (1997–2001) |
| HADEP | People's Democratic Party (1994–2003) |
| HDP | People's Democratic Party (2012, currently a minority party) |
| İSGM | Worker Health and Work Safety Assembly (1969) |
| MEB | Republic of Turkey Ministry of Turkish Education |
| MHP | Nationalist Movement Party (1969, currently is the alliance of AKP) |
| PKK | Kurdistan Worker's Party (1978–present) |
| RP | Welfare Party (1983–1998) |
| TCKB | Republic of Turkey Ministry of Development |
| TCMB | Central Bank of Republic of Turkey (1930) |
| TEKGIDA-İŞ | Confederation of Food Workers Union (1952) |
| TEPGE | Agricultural Economic and Policy Development Institute (1996) |
| TÜİK | Institute of Turkish Official Statistics (1926) |
| TÜRK-İŞ | Confederation of Worker Unions of Turkey (1952) |
| TÜSİAD | Association of Industrialists and Businessmen of Turkey (1971) |
| YSMİB | The Union of Exporters of Fresh Fruit and Vegetables |
| ZMO | The Chamber of Agricultural Engineers (1954) |

## Chapter 1

## INTRODUCTION

*'Can you call what you write our Story'?*[1]

If the eye were not sun-like, it could not see the sun ...
Goethe

My first name is Emine. According to the Turkish National Office of Statistics (TÜİK 2017a), in the country of my birth, I am one of many thousands of 'ordinary' Emines, as the name has been constantly chosen as one of the top three woman names in Turkey. My name is Arabic in origin and was also the name of the Prophet Mohammed's mother. It was my grandmother, my father's mother, who bestowed this name on me; it was given to me not to carry the name of a prophet's mother, but to carry on a longstanding tradition in our family.[2]

The families of the other Emines could have had a traditional reason for choosing the name, as did my grandmother; presumably, they too have a rural background in the not-too-distant past. As such, they are at least familiar with the extended family structure from their mothers and fathers or maybe from their grandmothers or grandfathers. It is probable that most of them do not come from the upper class, nor are they the daughters, wives or mothers of the bourgeoisie, as the name is not very common among children of the upper classes. For the religious bourgeoisie the name is too traditional, and for nationalist[3] parents too much associated with Islam or Arabs. However, Emine is a safe name for Kurds in Turkey because until the 2000s, they could not give Kurdish names[4] to their children; thus, they chose names with a relationship to Islam.

Therefore, it is possible that almost all the women who we meet in this study could have been named Emine by their parents. This is because they are seasonal workers in tomato production and processing in Turkey who have rural backgrounds, do not come from upper-class families; among whom, few are Kurdish, and they are Muslims: this is their story. It is the story in which we could find the intersections of gender, ethnicity and class shaping the global food production. It is the story of whose parents would not have had any reservations about handing down a 'religious' name to their child. It is the story of whose mothers did not have a choice in the matter and simply gave their daughters the name of their mother-in-law. Hence, it is not surprising that I met seven Emines in the tomato lands and the tomato-processing factory where I worked during parts of 2013 and 2014. I have changed all of their names and used pseudonyms, choosing names common in the years in which those women were born; the only exception was the name of the young Kurdish seasonal migrant worker named Emine who worked in rural tomato production and who wished to keep her real name. She believes that she is unrecognizable, because the names of her family members have been changed, making it unlikely that people will figure out who she is. Furthermore, she also wanted to have the same name as mine in the study, as a sign of our close relationship.

She was the first Emine I met during the tomato planting time; she was a seasonal worker who had travelled approximately 1,500 km with her father and siblings and lived in a shack for six months in order to work. She had not been able to continue her education after primary school because there was no secondary school in the village that she and her family lived in at the time. She is also the eldest child in her family. When her brothers reached secondary-school age, her family migrated to the city with her uncle's family, not because of the boys' schooling but because of the conflict between the Turkish military and the *Partiye Karkeren Kurdistan* – Kurdistan Workers Party (PKK) in their area. As she said, although they did not choose to move to the city, her brothers now had the opportunity to continue their education at secondary school because they could travel by themselves; the girls, however, could not.[5] Emine's father worked in casual jobs in the city during the winter and in early spring. For most of the year, Emine and her two sisters would travel to the 'tomato land' with their father, while in the summers and during school holidays, her two brothers would join them. Her mother could not come because she had to stay in their hometown to look after her mother-in-law and father-in-law. Emine explained to me:

> My younger uncle did not have any school age children as my parents do; this means that they can go for seasonal work together as a family, so my *yenge*[6] (aunt by marriage) could not take care of my grandmother and grandfather, even though this should not be the work of the eldest *yenge* [her mother]. So, my mother looked after them for six months when we were here, then my younger *yenge* looked after them in the winter.[7]

When Emine's mother was not around during the tomato production season, Emine was responsible for domestic labour in the shacks; as the eldest girl in the family, she did the cooking and washed the laundry by hand. Her greatest dream of all was to marry Ahmet, who was a worker in the same group with us, but her father was completely against this relationship. After the season ended, Ahmet, along with his family, asked her father's permission to marry her three times, but he would not agree. They tried to elope, but Emine was afraid because it was too dangerous. Even though they were not followed, Emine explained that they would not be able to find a job or somewhere to live together in a big city because they did not know anyone there and did not have any money of their own. Also, it is a sin, she told me. 'Thinking about yourself but not your parents, as when you leave, they cannot look other people in the eye because of the shame'.[8] So, they could not manage to be together, and sadly, two years after I had worked with them, Emine married her father's uncle's son, as was her father's wish.[9]

Another Emine[10] is part of the family that owns the land on which the workers plant and pick tomatoes. She is married to one of the three sons of the landowning family, and she was able choose who to marry. Her father also did not want to let her marry her husband, but she eloped with him anyway. After a few months, her family made peace with her. If she had obeyed her parents, she would have lived her entire life with a man she did not like. She explained that she is glad to have disobeyed her parents. Emine, like her husband, is Turkish and has worked in agriculture since she was eleven years old, when she left school after five years of compulsory education.[11] Firstly, she worked on her grandfather's land, and then when her family sold off their lands, she worked on her neighbours' lands. Finally, she worked on her husband's family's lands. Although her husband's family has money, she can never spend this money as she chooses. In fact, she never so much as sees any of the money. Her dream is to educate her children. She believes that in farming, it does not matter how much you earn because you cannot spend it freely, as you have to be accountable to all the people you work with – this is what she and her husband experience. She wants her children to work in the public sector because she believes that a stable employment contract will give them the most security, as civil service contracts are permanent in Turkey and the wages are regular. For Emine, if her children do not grow up to be farmers, then they will not have to live with other people; 'I especially want this for my daughter – what could be worse than living with your husband's family?'[12]

Another Emine, the Emine I worked with at the factory,[13] unintentionally answered this question when she spoke about her relationship with her own mother-in-law.

> When I was living with her, I was sure that nothing could be worse than living with her. But I was wrong. When we were with them, my husband had to come home in the evenings, or at night at the very least. He had to sleep in the house. Now, he is free to do whatever he wants, sometimes he doesn't come home for several nights. How can I explain this to my daughters? I should have guessed that he would do something like this, as he had a bad reputation from when he was young. They – her husbands' parents – brought me in from another part of the world.[14]

This Emine was from a small village on the Black Sea coast of Turkey, an area with high unemployment and limited agricultural output besides tea and nuts. Fishing also comprises one of the main economic activities in the region. This limited diversity in economic output means that there is a high migration rate to western Turkey.[15] When I was working with women in the factory, I realized that many women were from the Black Sea region; they were *Laz*,[16] and most of them came to the region via marriage or their mothers came to the region via marriage. Emine explained the situation for me:

> When I was 16 years old, our neighbour showed me a picture of him [her husband] and asked me whether or not I would want to marry him. She told me that he has some land and property in the village. You know, when I thought about coming to Bursa, one of the biggest cities of Turkey, to marry a rich farmer, I was convinced that there could not be a better option than this. We were poor and if I stayed there, I would marry a poor man. I did not think too much about why they asked a girl from so far away. Our neighbour told me that one of her friends, who also went to Bursa for marriage, told my husband's mother about me. She said that she told her that I am capable and beautiful. Then they asked my mother for a photo of me, which she gave them. He loved me at first sight, now he wants to marry me. That moment, I fell in love with him.[17]

After she married him and moved to a village outside Bursa, she realized that her husband's family was not that affluent after all. She also learned that they did not own any property but had to work on other's lands. Even Emine had to work on the land.

Her new husband's family had paid Emine's family a dowry and some money for their neighbour's friend to be rid of their poor and troublesome son. Emine explained to me that 'rich' locals marry each other. She went on to say that when someone is not rich and has a bad reputation, there is only one option: finding someone else who does not have a better option. Later, having spent a few years in the region, she told me she could understand what happened to her because there are many brides like her and now there are a significant number of women like her in the factory. These workers were mostly the daughters-in-law or granddaughters of former smallholders who, as a result of the Turkish government's (the Justice and Development Party – AKP)[18] neoliberal economic policies over the past eighteen years, have been forced off their lands and into the factories.[19] Most of these families have become local, seasonal workers in food factories and have only had to move to their nearest towns as opposed to the 'big cities'.[20]

We will soon meet these three Emines and their friends who share similar life experiences, backgrounds and expectations. Indeed, any one of the Emines' friends could also have been called Emine. They and their friends, including the other 'possible' Emines, will be introduced in the following chapters, where I examine their work producing tomatoes for the Japanese market and the differences in their positions as seasonal migrant rural workers, members of a landowning family and as factory workers. Although their class positions, ethnicities and ages make their experiences within the global tomato production chain different, their experiences are nonetheless shaped by the same political, economic and cultural contexts. All three Emines have had to learn what it means to live with their mother-in-law and all three have had to learn how difficult it is to work on the land or in the tomato-processing factory. Furthermore, all three of their lives have been subject to change depending on changes within tomato production and changes to government economic policies. And, of course, what the government's decisions depend on is not always publicly known. However, at least these women know that the changes in tomato production depend on what the Japanese company wants. I, as another Emine and the narrator of this story, have attempted to uncover how the stories of these women are so deeply intertwined with national and global means of production and reproduction, not merely by virtue of being one of Turkey's many thousands of Emines, but by working with them on the tomato lands and in a tomato-processing factory as a 'participant witness' (Gordon 1995).

*Looking at tomatoes, finding People: Global commodity chain analysis*

Global commodity chain analysis (GCCA) has its origins in dependency theory's emphasis on the location of both rich and poor countries within the unequal but integrated international economy as the source of economic problems in the regions of the Global South. It was developed by Gereffi and Korzeneiwicz in 1994 to address contemporary forms of globalization in relation to the interaction between local and global initiatives.

The increasing trend of using GCC analysis for studying gender in global production has its roots in changes in the organization of the global economy, the political responses to these, as well as theoretical shifts in feminist theory. Firstly, in recent years, the spaces in which commodities are made have become more varied, more 'global' and more 'transnational'. As a result, it becomes increasingly necessary to focus on more than one location and to trace the transformation of labour by following the journey of a product in the global capitalist economy rather than studying either agricultural production with food processing or manufacturing separately. Moreover, while production of many goods mostly occurs in developing countries, it is very common for packaging or labelling to take place in the Global North, where consumption also takes place. Consequently, global tracing has increasingly become a crucial requirement for the analysis of global production and GCC offers one of the most promising frames to follow.

Secondly, many 'developing' country states offer limited social welfare rights or, sometimes, none at all. Indeed, quite the opposite is true; by reducing labour costs and not legislating against poor working conditions or by suppressing union activity, they often try to attract capital by cooperating with it (Williams 2013). In this sense, adopting a framework that emphasizes firms' success in socio-economic upgrading via their interaction with global capital rather than the responsibilities of the state has become more common.

Thirdly, the method of GCC of following commodities and seeing/finding the people's labour within them has overlapped with the increasing influence of postmodernism in social science (Marcus 1995). Focusing on one consumable item and tracking back how production (and in some cases reproduction) was organized have been an increasingly popular method for feminist studies of the global economy. Although GCC analysts do not necessarily identify their work with postmodernism (Barndt 2002; Chatterjee 2001; Dixon 2002; Ramamurthy 2004), they use 'multi-sited ethnography' (Marcus 1995) as a way of looking at the wider

Map 1.1 Fieldwork sites.

organization of social and economic relations at different sites in the commodity chain, as does this book. Here, I am following not only women's labour but also the journey of tomatoes. While working with the women of the tomato land and of the factory over two years (with intervals) in western and southeastern Turkey, I have encountered over 100 people during my fieldwork at three different sites.

However, I met more of my key informants on the land as a result of my longer fieldwork there; while the factory works for two months to process tomatoes, rural work lasts around six months. I worked on the land for two periods in 2013 and one period in the factory in 2014. My third fieldwork site is located in Mardin (showed on Map 1.1), which is the hometown of rural Kurdish migrant workers, whom I worked together with on the land in western Turkey. As Marcus (1995) suggested for multi-sited ethnographers, I intentionally chose these particular fieldwork sites. This mobile ethnography 'has produced refined examinations of resistance and accommodation – a concern with the dynamics of encapsulation, focused on relationships, language and objects of encounter and response from the perspectives of local and cosmopolitan groups and persons who, although in different relative power positions, experience a process of being mutually displaced from what has counted as culture for each of them' (ibid.: 96). Following the path of products can prove to be a very beneficial way of exploring the differentiations of the labour process and labour force. Furthermore, following the process exposes the circulation of capital as a whole and, hence, provides us with a clear picture of global capitalized labour (Rainnie 2013). This fuller picture of global capital also demonstrates that gender roles and relations play different roles in the labour processes of each of the different phases of production.

Although GCC analysis proposes looking at all the stages of a chain, my case of tomatoes does not include all the steps of a commodity chain; I do not include the consumption, marketing or retailing of tomatoes. Rather, I apply commodity chain analysis but focus only on the production, processing and reproduction of labour, similar to other GCC studies mainly focusing on production and/or reproduction (Collins 2014; Dedeoğlu 2014; Dunaway 2014; Ramamurthy 2004, 2014; Selywn 2012; Stewart 2015; Yeates 2014). Dunaway criticizes mainstream GCC analysis in her edited book, *Gendered Commodity Chains* (2014), by arguing that although the original concept included reproduction as well as consumption as parts of production, the focus of the evolving version ignores households. However, she argues, GCC analysis is still one of the most promising ways to include reproduction within global production analysis, thanks to its ability to show the flexibility of households in adapting to the global economy. Other feminist scholars have also increasingly pointed out the invisibility of reproductive work in GCCA and are successfully incorporating it themselves (Barrientos and Perrons 1999; Clelland 2014; Collins 2014; Ramamurthy 2004). In this sense, Stewart's study (2015) offers a very important account, as she makes the link between production and reproduction clear by focusing on the construction of South Asian gendered identities as part of the Global Care Chain. While doing so, she demonstrates that the care arrangements of the South Asian families who migrated to the UK are rooted in their familial relations, particularly in their marriage arrangements, which are clearly within the sphere of the relations of reproduction. In the current version of commodity chain analysis, there is no place for reproduction relations or identities, and thus, she, like other feminist scholars, proposes the reformulation of GCC analysis to take workers' identities and reproduction into account.

In a similar vein, this book argues that to undertake an analysis of the labour process of tomato production and processing as a commodity chain, it is necessary to analyse the construction of the gendered identities of rural women as part of this chain, and that this is not possible without focusing on the local regimes of production. As such, my analysis will focus on how rural gender identities are constructed and used as a factor for controlling labour, as well as how the construction of rural Turkish and Kurdish women and men makes tomato sauce in Japan possible. To understand this, I will deploy my locally developed terms, *'intersectional patriarchy'* and *'el âlem*,'[21] to understand the prevailing ideologies of the 'place' that I studied. Hopefully, the book integrates the relations of reproduction into the analysis of the global tomato chain in a novel, local way.

*Happy open relationship between patriarchy and intersectionality: 'Intersectional patriarchy'*

Second-wave feminists first adopted the term 'patriarchy' in the 1970s (Eisenstein 1979; Firestone 1971; Hartmann 1981; Millet 1977; Mitchell 1975). The idea underpinning the development of the concept was the argument that 'inequality between men and women was not just a creation of capitalism: it was the feature of all societies for which we had reliable evidence' (Rowbotham 1981: 72). The term literally refers to the 'rule of the father' and has been used to address the particular types of household structures and families in which an older male has authority over other members of the family, including women and younger males. However, depending on the answers to the question of what is the real basis of 'women's subordination', the concept has been used in many different ways (Bradley 1996). These include 'men's control of reproductive arrangements' (Firestone 1971), 'sexual hierarchy, which is manifested in the women's role as mother and "domestic labourer"' (Oakley 1974), 'kinship systems, in which men exchange women' (Mitchell 1975) or male control over women's labour (Cockburn 1983, 1991; Hartmann 1981; Westwood 1984). Furthermore, patriarchy has been criticized for being 'biologically reductionist' (Patil 2013; Rowbotham 1981), 'universal' (Acker 1989; Beechey 1979; Mohanty 1984; Rowbotham 1981), 'fixed' (Rowbotham 1981) and 'ignoring women's agency' (Acker 1989; Mohanty 1984; Pollert 1996).

While the concept of patriarchy began to lose its popularity in the late 1980s, the concept of intersectionality began gaining recognition in the 1990s. In 1989, Crenshaw used the term 'intersectionality' to emphasize that black women's oppression is situated at the intersection of racism and sexism. Since then, intersectionality has become an extensively deployed concept of feminist studies to highlight the matrix of domination (Crenshaw 1989) of different inequalities, such as ethnicity, age, nationality, sexuality, religion and disability (Bradley and Healy 2008; McCall 2005). There has been a long tradition in the study of work and employment relations, particularly within feminist scholars' work, of exploring the intersections of class, ethnicity and gender (Acker 2006; Cockburn 1983, 1985; Glucksmann 1982, 1990; Pollert 1981; Westwood 1984). However, according to McBride et al. (2015), as the majority of these works are informed by case studies and narratives, they run the risk of becoming essentialist by presenting their findings as representative of all people who might be positioned within the same intersectional categories. Although I do not agree with McBride et al. (2015) about the case studies of women's work becoming essentialist when applying the concept of intersectionality, this criticism can be interpreted in line with what Nash (2008) and Yuval-Davis (2006) argue that intersectional analysis ignores the articulation of identities and reaches unsubstantiated conclusions, such as 'all black women are the same' (e.g. Crenshaw's analysis (1991)).

Patil (2013) argues that both concepts, patriarchy and intersectionality, are incomplete. Although the focus of feminist studies has shifted from 'patriarchy' to 'intersectionality' over the last twenty years, Patil (2013) found, based on online research specifically in the World Cat, Article First and Eco databases for the year 2000 to the present, that 85 per cent of the studies that applied the concept of intersectionality focus on the Global North, while 60 per cent of those studies focus on the United States in particular. Patriarchy, on the other hand, tends to be used in studies that focus on women from the Global South or 'developing countries'. When we consider relatively recent studies on women's labour that adopt the concept of patriarchy, the same pattern is evident. While Ngai (2005), Lee (1998), Kabeer (2000), Cravey (1998), Dedeoğlu (2012, 2014) and White (2004) use the concept of patriarchy, Salzinger (2003) and Wright (2006) do not. Thus, Patil (2013) criticizes intersectionality in a similar way to how the concept of patriarchy has been criticized: its application is not sufficiently historical and transnational and it has not been applied to cross-border dynamics. For this reason,

Patil (2013) suggests that the term 'domestic intersectionality' is more applicable for the current use of the concept, which refers to within-nation relations.

This book proposes the term 'intersectional patriarchy',[22] which I define as a set of fluid and various forms of hegemonic masculinity with power over femininity and subordinate masculinities. Following Kandiyoti (1988), I retain the concept of patriarchy to indicate a structure of power and that women in some positions can exercise masculine power. Furthermore, I take from Connell (1987) the idea that there is a range of masculinities and femininities associated with different social positions and that these are fluid and changeable. An example of this is when older women govern younger women, they do so by asserting masculinity. I also use the term to refer to patriarchal household structures, which vary with the hegemonic masculinities and associated femininities constructed in the labour process. I relate patriarchy to intersectionality because gender, class, age and ethnicity affect the form taken by patriarchy in different households through creating different forms of masculinity and femininity. Indeed, the intersection of categories – gender, age, class, ethnicity, education and so on – creates fluid categories of masculinity and femininity. However, throughout, masculinity governs femininity.[23] I deploy the term *el âlem* to explain why everyone invests in the constructions of masculinity and femininity that lie behind these power relations (a more detailed discussion of this can be found in Chapter 7). *El âlem*, as an agential aspect of intersectional patriarchy, offers everyone a chance to exercise power over others – for the advantage of masculine power – but to a different extent.

I argue that intersectional analysis needs more engagement with studies that are based on lived experiences to escape from homogenizing women's experiences. This is because such studies can provide a chance to see how 'intersections' are fluid and changeable. Moreover, it can make the intersection of privilege and oppression that is so often missing from intersectional analysis more visible (Nash 2008). In this way, it can be argued that interaction with 'patriarchy' can offer space for intersectional analysis to explore the power relations between the privileged and the oppressed. Thus, to analyse the dynamic power relations between workers and managers, women and men, younger people and elders, mothers-in-law and daughters-in-law, I apply the term 'intersectional patriarchy' to show how the masculine-feminine hierarchy is reproduced through the construction of masculinities and femininities in the gendered division of labour. I illustrate this process by offering some of my own data. This data will take the form of excerpts from my field notes, which are denoted by the use of italics. By putting my own data forward, I emphasize the importance of lived experience for drawing together the concepts of intersectionality and patriarchy.

The differing formats of intersectional categories are evident in the differing responses of the people – workers, landowners and managers – that I worked with. For example, some male workers believe that *'they are doing a woman's job – implying tomato picking – since they are Kurdish'*. In this context, being Kurdish is feminized by the type of work and thus implies labour of low prestige. However, this does not mean that the men receive the same daily wages as the women. Women on the land are not paid directly but it is their husbands, fathers or brothers who receive their money because '*it is shameful for women to think or talk about money with a man, like a man*'. On the other hand, the factory manager shows preferential treatment to the women working in the warehouse because '*those women are doing men's jobs and he "hates" men who prefer not to work*'. He wants to find a man for the men's work, but '*men do not want to accept this men's work since it does not offer men's pay*'. Women working in 'proper women's work' – on the assembly line – explained that '*women working in the warehouse are not "women" since they are as wild* [implying physical strength] *as men*'. '*Educated women, however, can operate machinery with the men because they know both the language of men and that of machines*'. Therefore, it is evident that the categories of masculinity and femininity change in different contexts and are associated differentially with women and men and particular jobs; in other words, they are fluid.

To expand, let us consider how the reins of power are not fixed and can be changed across space and time. For instance, when ethnicity is given as a reason why men are doing women's work, being Kurdish is seen as feminized and 'less valuable' in the eyes of both the workers themselves and others. However, being a Kurd becomes more 'valuable' in the eyes of everyone in comparison to Syrians, who are increasingly searching for rural work in Turkey since the Syrian War began in 2011. According to UNHRC (2019), 3.6 million Syrian nationals live in Turkey. They mostly work unregistered and rural work therefore is an option for them. However, landowning families prefer Kurds, '*since Syrian men are as weak as women, but Kurds are really strong since they always eat meat products. Even Kurdish women can work like men*'. This demonstrates how the categories of masculinity are fluid and denote relative differences in social value and power. Here, I must also mention that alleged differences in physical strength are not the only reason why Syrians are not favoured. Landowning families claim that they do not know Syrians enough – '*at the end of the day, we have lived together with Kurds for hundreds of years*'. They can communicate with Kurds, but due to language barriers, they '*cannot speak with Syrians like men*'.[24] Here it is important to note that this is valid for when I did my fieldwork on the land in 2013. At that time, the Syrians were not a significantly sized group in Turkey and *dayıbaşı* did not employ them as groups. Instead, they took them on within other groups. However, Syrian workers have increasingly begun to be hired in group form.

Turning back to fluidity of categories, differences in physical strength are not the only reason given, but it often leads to the association that being Kurdish, in comparison with Syrian, leads to being stronger and more 'masculine'. However, in the context of doing 'women's work', being Kurdish is associated with femininity and weakness. As Salzinger points out, '"feminine" at one level can be "masculine" at the next' (2003: 15). Indeed, the intersections of gender, class, ethnicity, education and age that I focus on in this study are variously coded as 'masculine' or 'feminine', but it is apparent that masculinity always dominates. It is for this reason that I not only retain the concept of patriarchy but expand on it through the use of intersectionality, to include masculinities and femininities. I argue that the intersection of categories – gender, age, class, ethnicity, education – creates fluid categories of masculinity and femininity but that throughout, hegemonic masculinity governs femininity. The quotes taken from the people that I worked with not only give us clues about the shifting nature of masculinities and femininities, they also indicate the fluid nature of the gendered divisions of labour, which persist through the ideologies of masculinities and femininities. As I did here, throughout the book, I will rely on people's own voices to build my arguments.

### *Feminist ethnography*

She was sitting in the same corner of the garden under the tallest tree of my 'short' life, where she has sat for all of her 'long' life. When our eyes met while I was jumping down from the tractor in all of my awkwardness, I thought that I should be ready for a discussion, which was already racing towards me from her eyes. My childhood passed by with my 'childish' attempts to hide from her sight, however with time, I also began to learn to send my glances to argue with hers in silence. At the same time, she had begun to lose the power of her sight and to support her sight with words. Since I was already trained from birth to defend myself with words, thanks to this being my mother's area of specialty, at the moment when my grandmother was waiting to have an argument with me in her favourite corner, I was ready for a discussion. When she asked me to come to her side, I went to battle with all of my necessary equipment; looks, words and of course, my 'stable' thoughts about the necessity of continuing my fieldwork. When I arrived by her side, we began an ordinary discussion of each of my working days on the land. She asked me as always: why am I doing this? I have seen everything, tomatoes are the same, women are the same, why I am going continuously to the land, etc. And, I repeated the same answers, 'I will continue to go until the end of the season, this is my job, I am doing research about those women's lives'. Then, she asked me, 'Why can't you ask your questions directly to the women without going to the land? What are you hoping to achieve while by going to work on the land?' 'In order to understand them', I said to my eighty-six-year-old grandmother. At that, she began to laugh, 'You can't', she said. 'You can't understand people; I am almost dead but still don't understand myself. I lived with your granddad for 60 years and I didn't understand him. I don't understand my own children. Do you understand yourself? Just stop this research, otherwise you will not finish it' – [implying the impossibility of reaching an understanding of the women I worked with].[25]

Contrary to my grandmother's advice, I have not stopped my research. Rather, I continued to work in the tomato land and the following year at a tomato factory under my grandmother's disapproving gaze. Unfortunately, as my grandmother suggested, I am not at the point where I can assure you that I understand either the people I research or myself. My lack of understanding does not stem from the failure of my fieldwork, but rather the impossibility of fulfilling such a claim. However, I can assure you that I walked a long path to gain a better understanding of the women there and myself. Moreover, it became apparent that there was no better 'path' for me to seek to achieve a less fragmented understanding than the one I walked through: experiencing and being a 'participant witness' (Gordon 1995) to the conditions.

I situate this research within 'feminist ethnography' because of the differences Leavy (2007) notes in the focus between feminist ethnography and other kinds of ethnography. I focus on gender relations and seek to understand the relations between genders and other forms of power and difference. I also seek to conduct and write using feminist theoretical positions and ethics. Feminist ethnography offers a different version than orthodox ethnographies by placing women's own voices centre on the production of anthropologic knowledge (Behar 1995). However, as Behar points out (ibid.), while feminist ethnography revises the male gaze of the ethnography, it is not just about how 'male' ethnographers look at category of 'woman'. Feminist ethnography is a new way of looking at all categories of doing research including the field, the subject, the people, researcher's status, the relationship between researcher and participant, representation, the writing style (ibid.). Behar states for their own feminist ethnography project, *Women Writing Culture* (Behar and Gordon 1995), that feminist ethnography is different from traditional ethnographic traditions by 'its inclusiveness, its creative process, its need to combine history and practice, its humour, its pathos, its democratising politics, its attention to race and ethnicity as well as to culture, its engendered self-consciousness, its awareness of the academy as a knowledge factory, its dreams' (ibid.: 6). This book tries to follow the path of feminist ethnography as portrayed by Behar (ibid.). It has the largest scope involving people from many different backgrounds in the analysis of rural Turkey (i.e. Turks, Kurds, women, men, managers, farmers, landowning families, rural workers, factory workers, the educated and uneducated, religious and irreligious ones). It presents the findings of the deepest participant observation of work among rural women (on the land, in the factory and in the home) in global production carried out to date in Turkey. This deep and long engagement with participants offers that intersecting relations of gender, class and ethnicity. The book uses people's own voices as much as possible and understands their experiences on the combination of history and practice. It pays attention to Turkish and Kurdish identities in relation to both gendered practices of global production and their political stances in Turkey.

Apart from these, the book is applying feminist ethnography because I believe that to research 'someone' or 'something', it is necessary to become an insider, to feel as much as to see. Leavy (2007: 187) reveals that 'using the self as much as possible' is one of the most important aspects of feminist ethnography. This lies at the core of this ethnographic practice and refers to reflexivity. In feminist research, strong reflexivity is seen as a condition of strong objectivity (Harding 1986), which makes clear our vantage points and, hence, our 'situated knowledge' (Haraway 1988). Revealing under 'what conditions' our knowledge is produced also demonstrates how we researchers are transformed through our research.

Previous and pioneering studies of women's work also highlight the capacity of ethnographic methods to transform researchers themselves through producing academic knowledge (Glucksmann 1982; Kondo 1990; Lee 1998; Ngai 2005; Pollert 1981; Salzinger 2003; Westwood 1984). Salzinger (2003) emphasizes the advantages of ethnography to being an active/productive researcher:

> Thus, through ethnography, I was able to enter the gendered heart of global production, where the subjects who produce are themselves produced by their conditions. In consciously situating my idiosyncratic, theorising self in that space, I became capable of telling meaningful stories about the world beyond. (Salzinger 2003: 8)

By using ethnography, I seek to represent the stories of women, because a story[26] has the power to show us the conditions under which a phenomenon appears and also tells us about a process. Therefore, we can make the claim that everyone's world is a story and thus, it should be told as a 'story'. The women I have conducted this research with are also fans of stories. They mostly have no formal education, so books are not amongst the options for them to learn about others' worlds. Additionally, travelling is a fantasy for the majority of them and men most often choose the TV programmes that they watch at home. Hence, telling stories and even creating them is their main way to get to know about others' worlds. The actors in these stories are not always imaginary characters or imaginary events, but mostly real people. Some might say that they are gossiping and I would agree with this; yes, most of them are 'gossiping', but they are still telling stories. And, apparently, these are not 'boring' stories; 'gossiping' is enjoyable, 'eye-opening', sometimes depressing and even frustrating, but certainly not boring. Since it was what women wanted from me and since it also embodies their style, I have tried to write their stories as they tell them. To make this possible, I used a dictaphone to record my own voice each evening to recount what they told me earlier that day. During the day, I made quick notes to remind myself of the events of the day and then when I came home, I recounted the day's events to the dictaphone using everyday language.

One of the women informants' main concerns was about what I would say in my writing about them and thus, it became mine too. On many occasions in the field, women, especially the formally educated and relatively young factory workers, warned me about not writing something too boring for other and older women. To them, being an academic meant 'talking about boring stuff', similar to the debate programmes on TV. As such, they warned me about this: 'Don't tell people boring things about us', or, as another of them told me, 'Sometimes, when my husband watches TV debates, I hear some academics talk. I don't understand what they are saying to us. You seem "normal," we understand each other. But, are you like this normally, too?' (9 March 2014).

Clearly, the women I worked with had some concerns about how they would be represented in this book; they did not want to be treated distantly through 'technical' language, which they think of as boring and complicated. Pillow (2003: 180) notes that reflexivity is about 'whether we can be accountable to people's struggles for self-representation and self-determination, including ourselves'. Indeed, writing using complicated, technical language is neither their style nor mine. Thus, during the process of writing and in my analysis, I have attempted to keep the discussion as close as possible to the most authentic me and to the women as well. As I told them during my fieldwork, I will discuss what they like talking about: their daily concerns. I also seek to emulate their style of narration and I do this by avoiding piecemeal storytelling. Here, however, because of the 'obligations' of 'academic writing' – the practical concerns of writing an academic manuscript – I have had to stop telling the women's stories as pure narrative and instead, talk about them sociologically. Nevertheless, the women I worked with know that when work requires us, we must stop telling stories. Here, I am not suggesting that our stories are not part of our work on the land, in the factory and within these pages; on the contrary, they are embodied in our work, they are the motivations for our work, they shape our way of working and so shape us, but not merely under the title of production.

The people in this book transformed me during the research and because I also 'touched' their lives, this book, to some extent, has become a more collective enterprise. My values, opinions, feelings and knowledge changed during my fieldwork as a result of my interactions. They know me, we met, we shared and we produced tomatoes together. Even if this is different from writing a book, producing something together in our work on the land or in the factory enabled them to see my way of producing something. They always made jokes about the seriousness with which I took the job or tomatoes or people, so they knew that I was taking the things that I do seriously. They always made jokes about how I cannot write about depressing things without crying, so they know that my emotions are also here. They saw me while I was taking notes and looking over books sometimes during breaks and made fun of how I was studying even during work, so they know that during work, I see things in a different way to them, that I write things that are different from what they think. Despite this, the women have an insight into what I do and how I do it. In this way, my research experience itself is a subject of theorization (Bott 2010; Stanley and Wise 1991) and my status in the field, therefore, is more like a 'witness' rather than an 'observer'. 'A witness is less an observer than a teller – that is, one who translates what s/he sees and hears for an audience' (Gordon 1995: 383). 'In participant witnessing, the lines between ethnographer and informant blur as each hears the other in a way that encourages self-representation' (ibid.). My being of 'participant witness' (Gordon 1995) is also related with my background. Although I have never worked on the land before my fieldwork and met the people on the study, I know them from my grandmother, mother, aunt, grandfather, uncle and father. I know them from my 'home'. I know them as being one of the ordinary Emines.

## Synopsis of the book

The book begins by exploring the state's role in shaping global food production and processing in Turkey, as well as the history of women's employment in the country, with a particular focus on Kemalist ideology and its gender categories

(Chapter 2, 'Thankful' Women from the 'Centre of the World': Turkey and Her People). Kemalist ideology, which could be seen as Turkey's official ideology since the early 2000s (White 2012), refers to the official national commitment to the vision of the founder of the country, Mustafa Kemal Atatürk (1881–1938), which revolved around modernization, secularization, Westernization and cultural unity (ibid.). These principles made the position of women central to his proclaimed values. I explore how Kemalism tries to construct and sustain these principles in Turkey through accolades for two types of women, including the 'Daughters of the Republic' and 'Anatolian Women'. In contrast was a third type, the 'Backward Religious Woman', which emerged in the early years of the Republic. She was seen as an obstacle to the modernization of Turkey. Chapter 2 is also important to look at Kurdish identity within the Kemalist and recent state policy. To pull together my account of the current socio-political and economic context in Turkey, I deploy the 'sociological imagination' (Mills 2000 [1959]) and 'sociological autobiography' (Merton 1988 cited in Stanley 1993) as tools to write Chapter 2. Social autobiographies utilize 'sociological perspectives, ideas, concepts, findings, and analytical procedures to construct and interpret a narrative text that purports to tell one's own history within the larger history of one's times' (ibid.: 42). Sociological imagination (Mills 2000 [1959]) also refers connecting the individual to social forces – biography and history – that illustrate beyond the individual experience to understand social realities. Since I mainly use people's own stories to build this book, I express 'feminist responsibility' to the people in the study by using my own story to construct context in the chapter.

Chapter 3, 'The Background of a Tomato: Contracting, Recruiting and Organizing Labour', offers the background of the organization of tomato production. It is divided into three sections. In the first section, we will see how the factory decides on the conditions of their agreement with farmers, how they reach and choose the farmers, how they control them and how they control other factories in the region. The second section presents the landowning families' – farmers – perspective in getting into contract farming. Then, the final section tells the organization of the Kurdish migrant's recruitment through the gang-master's story.

Chapter 4, '"We Are All Women until the Money Comes": Gendered Labour Relations in Tomato Planting', explores how the labour process of tomato planting is shaped by class, ethnicity and also the locality of women. The chapter consists of five sections, which are dedicated to different women whose identities reflect their different positions in the organization of the production of the land. The first section is mine; I am offering the wider picture of the organization of work. The second section is based on *Fatma*; she is the wife of one of the landowners, a housewife and an unpaid worker on the land for the past twenty-five years. The third section is on *Melek*; she has been a seasonal worker for the past fifteen years and is married to the gang-master. The fourth section is focused on *Hazal*; she is a fifteen-year-old Kurdish migrant worker and this is her second year of working. The final section reports from *Mefaret*, a local Turkish woman who has worked in agriculture for the past forty years.

Chapter 5, 'Without Kurdish Families There Will Be No Turkish Agriculture: Familial Labour Relations in Tomato Picking', reveals the social relations underpinning, or what workers call the 'bloody' story of tomato picking. Workers use this metaphor to link the colour of tomatoes to the difficulty of the job. This chapter, however, goes beyond demonstrating the difficult working conditions of tomato picking and demonstrates to us how capitalist tomato production depends on capitalizing on the familial features of Kurdish families. It also illustrates the ways in which capitalist production generates control, deskilling and creating new hierarchies of power among the workers themselves, as well as how families can be a tool for the construction of both control and resistance of the workers. The importance of this chapter lies in emphasizing Kurdish seasonal migrant workers' labour as an indispensable part of the Turkish economy, as well as global production. While doing this, the chapter does not portray Kurdish families as passive victims but evokes their capability of shaping the system.

Chapter 6, 'Inside the "Kemalist" Tomato-processing Factory', focuses on where female members of the small farming families end up in the employment ladder during the transformation of Turkish agriculture: in the food factory. Drawing upon participant observation in the factory in 2014 for a season, along with in-depth interviews with the factory's general manager and women workers, this chapter illustrates how the gender ideologies of the Kemalist regime are manifested on the shop floor of the tomato-processing factory, as well as how they operate in the management of women's labour. The importance of this chapter is based not only on its revealing of the articulation of gender and global factory production on the shop floor, but also on its demonstration of how the ideologies of political Islam and Kemalism have a direct effect on organization on the shop floor.

Chapter 7, 'El Âlem Speaks: The Construction and Persistence of Rural Patriarchy', draws on observations made at the landowning family's home and at the seasonal agricultural workers' homes – both the shacks the latter live in while working on the land and at their own homes in their hometowns. I identify two different forms of rural patriarchy that occur in parallel with the actors' different relations with tomatoes. The term 'intersectional patriarchy' reveals how patriarchy has taken different forms in the landowning family's household and in Kurdish migrant workers' households as well. Moreover, drawing on informants' own explanations of their reasons for contributing to the reconstruction of patriarchal relations, I conceptualize (the) *el âlem* as a particular form of social order – in this particular context – serving as an agential aspect of intersectional patriarchy.

In Chapter 8, '"Kemalist" and "Transitional" Patriarchies', I discuss two further forms of patriarchal household structure that characterize the factory manager's and the women factory workers' homes, and which I identify as 'Kemalist' and 'transitional' patriarchies. In doing this, the chapter demonstrates the interweaving relationship between production and reproduction relations similar to the previous chapter. This chapter also offers the changes on gender relations by revealing how daughters become more important/useful for factory women than sons.

Finally, the conclusion presents the main arguments of the book and discusses the importance of thinking 'globally' from the perspective of the 'local'. Indeed, the book reveals how the local dynamics of rural Turkey has been effected by the global economy and vice versa. This concluding chapter summarizes what can be learned from the book through the stories of women – that global tomato production is gendered, and this process of gendering can be best understood from the mouths of the mostly female workers. Local concepts, in this case, the 'intersectional patriarchy' and *el âlem,* are vital for this understanding. Accordingly, it is explained here that the application of these concepts and the stories of the mostly female respondents help in understanding how and why people – both men and women – invest in the construction of the governing masculinity and, in a similar way, to the sustainability of this unsustainable economic system.

## Chapter 2

## 'THANKFUL' WOMEN FROM THE 'CENTRE OF THE WORLD': TURKEY AND HER PEOPLE

To introduce Turkey, I begin by drawing from the world that surrounded me when I was growing up there. I believe that talking about the social, political and economic patterns of a country can be comprehended more deeply by tracing its impact on people's lives (Mills 2000 [1959]). This chapter primarily attempts to highlight the changing patterns of women's labour and the socio-economic transformation of the rural population in relation to the Kurdish question through exploring two main ideologies of the Turkish Republic: Kemalism and Political Islam.

In the following sections, I first identify the ideological process of creating the 'Turkish' citizen through Kemalist ideology, drawing on my own experiences and interpretations of the Turkish education system. This is being done in the hope that it will provide background information about how people are expected to perceive the social, economic and political changes that have occurred in the country, especially in relation to participants of the factory in the factory and on the land. I highlight the experiences my mother had as a 'housewife' to introduce the possibilities and limitations facing uneducated, rural women's labour in an urban context. Through relating my educated father's experiences in paid employment, as well as offering insights from his disputes with my paternal uncle, who has an opposing political perspective, I will trace the economic and political transformations that have shaped the country until the 2000s. Then, I will offer an account of the Turkish political economy under the current Turkish government (Justice and Development Party – AKP) rule (2002–20), which underpins the capitalization of Turkish agriculture.

### Kemalism and its women

At first glance, this section might seem strange in a book on gender relations and women's work. However, to better understand the experiences of Kurdish women, especially those with whom I worked, as well as their relationship with local Turkish women workers, looking at the construction of and changes in the hegemonic ideology of Turkey, Kemalism is vital. Therefore, I start from the place where most Turkish citizens begin to learn about Kemalism officially: state schooling.[1]

I began my schooling when I was five years old and continued until the age of seventeen when I went to university. My education was in keeping with other students in the centralized Turkish education system, whose main aim was to instil the principles established by Mustafa Kemal Atatürk, the founder of the Turkish Republic. These principles are 'nationalism', 'populism', 'secularism', 'republicanism', 'statism' and 'revolutionism' (MEB 1983) and are the kernels of Kemalist ideology. Furthermore, I was taught that Turkey possessed the most precious geographical location in the world, and everything bad that had happened there was due to other countries coveting her 'perfect' position, which is at the nexus between Asia and Europe. This 'perfect' geographical position is also the reason why Turkey has many 'enemies'.

Imagine that your 'perfect' country is surrounded by 'enemies', all of whom are waiting for a fatal opening through which to strike.[2] To illustrate this thinking, Turks have a popular saying: 'There is no friend of a Turk, apart from another Turk.' Indeed, there is no other option but to hold together as fellow Turks. 'Fortunately', Mustafa Kemal Atatürk says, 'a Turk is worth the world'. That is why, each morning of the school day, I proudly shouted along with the other students, 'My existence shall be dedicated to the Turkish existence. How happy is the one who says "I am a Turk!"'[3] When I learned coincidentally from my father that I was not a Turk but a Bosnian ethnically, however, I cried to my teacher, saying that I couldn't take the oath with my friends anymore[4] since I am not a 'Turk'. 'Fortunately', my teacher consoled me by saying, 'Of course, we are all not Turks, but we all feel like Turks.' The only thing I should do is to be 'thankful' to Turkey for accepting me. To demonstrate my thankfulness, I had to study as hard as I could to be a good Turkish citizen, and through this, I could automatically pay my debt to the country for accepting my family's presence.

What my teacher told me was a reflection of Kemalist nationalism ('Atatürk nationalism'), which is the official nationalism discourse of Turkey (Bora 2003).[5] It is identified mainly as being bound up with Atatürk's statement that 'the nations who build up the Turkish Republic belong to the Turkish nation', despite their different racial backgrounds. However, as Bora suggests (2003: 437), 'the official ideology may well be in line with nationalism based on the principle of the citizenship; but in foreign disputes, in "national causes," and even, for instance, in the domains of popular culture such as international sports competitions, an ethicist, "essentialist" aggressive language of nationalism can easily make itself felt'. As thought in my school, I can locate myself 'on the side of the nation' and hence escape the aggressiveness of official nationalism by internalizing the Kemalist ideology, which entreated people to be faithful followers of Atatürk's principles and reforms. Mustafa Kemal's reforms refer to a series of changes in the social, legal and political system of the country to create a 'modern' and 'western' Republic. As Göle (1997: 84) suggests, 'The Turkish way of modernization is an unusual example of how indigenous ruling elites have imposed their notions of a Western cultural model, resulting in conversion almost on a civilizational scale'. For example, the caliphate was abolished in 1924; the state declared secularism in 1928; and in 1926, French and Swiss penal codes were adopted as part of the constitution. Similar to other nation-building projects,[6] women are central in the construction process of Kemalist ideology via its modern – 'egalitarian' – reforms (Kandiyoti 1991). In Kemalist ideology, the outlook of women symbolizes the outlook of the nation and thus, they must be modernized[7] (Kandiyoti 1987, 1991, 1995; Sancar 2012). For instance, Western clothing for women was encouraged, while veiling was discouraged. Furthermore, women were given the right to vote in 1934 (one of the earliest dates for women's voting in Europe). The Kemalists attempted to construct Turkish women as 'modernised, westernised, educated and secular', thereby erasing all other femininities (Durakbaşa 1998). Turkish scholars call this particular women's image of Kemalism 'Daughters of the Republic' (Arat 1998b; Durakbaşa 1998; Kandiyoti 1996, 1997). To achieve this ideal, Kemalists tried to increase women's participation in public life: the proportion of women working in highly skilled jobs, such as law and medicine, was the highest in Europe (Abadan-Unat 1991; Acar 1993). Motherhood and marriage were de-emphasized and women were expected to adopt more masculine character traits. Durakbaşa (1998) suggests that although some called the early years of the republic feminist because it allowed for some middle-class, educated women to enter the public domain, Kemalist ideology did not alter the patriarchal norms of morality (Kandiyoti 1997; Tekeli 1990). Rather, it mostly maintained the basic cultural conservatism about male and female relations (ibid.). Additionally, it did not propose the erosion of asymmetric power relations between the sexes; rather, it tried to asexualize the public domain through emphasizing women's masculine traits. Moreover, this was mostly applied to educated, secular, republican, urban women.

Kemalists were aware of the fact that Turkey was still a rural country when the republic was established and that the majority of women were rural and uneducated. Therefore, they created another image of women, which is the 'physically and emotionally strong, rural but wise women of Anatolia[8]' (İncirlioğlu 1998: 200) – *Anadolu Kadını* – 'Anatolian Women'. Kemalism portrays a powerful image of rural Turkish women as the carriers of the pre-Islamic spirit of the 'authentic Turkish' culture (ibid.: 200), in which women are always shoulder to shoulder with men while working or in the political arena. Thus, these wise, powerful and confident rural Turkish women are mostly portrayed as mothers of the nation (White 2012).

On the other hand, it was evident that not all segments of society supported the Kemalist regime and its reforms. Kemalist ideology, therefore, constructs those 'other' rural women as 'backward', 'submissive', 'traditional' and 'primitive' (İncirlioğlu 1998). These adjectives are mostly associated with Islam, which has become the core of the counter-hegemonic struggle against Kemalism in Turkey in recent years and is symbolized by the use of the headscarf. The constitution of 1982 that was drawn up following the 1980 coup banned the headscarf in the public domain. As a result, the headscarf has become a means of resisting dominant Kemalist discourses (Göle 1991, 1997; Kadıoğlu 1994; İlyasoğlu 1994). The bodies of the 'traditional and backward' women who wear headscarves have become the central focus in this arena of struggle to reassert their own femininities.[9]

Although the power blocks are shifting in Turkey, the idea of being thankful to the country stays the same. One still has to be 'thankful' and 'proud of' the country not only because you have to internalize the idea of paying a moral debt to the country, but also because being marked as 'being ungrateful' has serious consequences, even dangerous ones. Moreover, the country is not the only thing one should be thankful for; women must be grateful to men, while workers must be grateful to their employers. Such gratefulness is fundamental to the capacity of the state to govern more than 80 million people, seeming to offer citizens the opportunity to survive in very basic conditions. Citizens should be grateful to the state because it gives them a place to live and the right to earn their living; workers should be thankful to employers because they earn money, thanks to the jobs that employers offer them; women must be grateful to male members of the family because men earn the money to live, as well as protecting women from being sexually harassed by outsider men. Thus, the rule of life in Turkey, in that sense, is very basic: one cannot 'live' in this country without being grateful.

## *Some 'ungrateful' residents of an apartment in İstanbul: The 'Kurdish problem' in Turkey*

Until 1997, my parents and I lived in one of the most crowded neighbourhoods of İstanbul, 'Bağcılar', with a population of around 754,000 within an area of 22 km$^2$ (TÜİK 2015). This neighbourhood was home to migrants from all around Turkey and was an ideal place to see the lives of rural migrants and their city-born or grown-up children. In our fifteen-flat apartment building, none of the adults were born in İstanbul. My parents had come there from one of Bursa's villages (in the same region as İstanbul – 'Marmara region' – the most industrialized and wealthy region of Turkey; see Map 2.1), while others came from villages on the eastern Black Sea coast of Turkey, one of the regions with a very high unemployment rate,

**Map 2.1** Regions of Turkey.

second only to the southeastern region. Kurds came from the southeastern region mainly because of the military conflict between the Turkish Army and the PKK during the 1980s and 1990s. With this profile, our apartment reflected the two main social phenomena of Turkey since the 1950s: 'excessive' immigration from rural to urban areas[10] and the 'Kurdish problem'.

Until the 1980s, the reason for migration was mostly related to the mechanization of Turkish agriculture. And it was also due to the development of highways and rapid population growth (Gürel 2011). Small-scale farmers who could not buy the agricultural machinery could tended to move to big cities. Additionally, Karpat (1976) also pointed to the increasing availability of employment opportunities in industries in urban areas. Thus, while around 60 per cent of the population was living in rural areas in the 1970s, this proportion had decreased to approximately 41 per cent by the 1990s, as seen in Graph 2.1 (TCKB 2012; TÜİK 2015). The consequences of mass migration from rural to urban areas in Turkey have been widely discussed in the literature as increasing urban sprawl, *Gecekondulaşma*,[11] and leading to difficult working and living conditions for migrants, as well as related issues pertaining to adaption and assimilation (Karpat 1976; Keleş 1983).[12]

These early studies of migration[13] as well as rural transformation did not take into account migrants' different ethnicities or the differences in agricultural dynamics in the country, as Kurds and Turks had been living in different agrarian systems (Yalçın-Heckmann 2012). In southeastern Turkey, Kurds had largely lived under a system called *Aşiret*,[14] in which the lands in a particular region are owned by a very large extended family that includes many smaller extended families. A group of mainly senior men from these families govern the people in the region, who are bound up with each other through kinship ties. Most of the time, the area in which the extended family has power is bigger than the village. As such, kinship relations and economic organization are intertwined with each other in these communities (ibid.). It is also evident that Kurds were not the only ones working on lands under

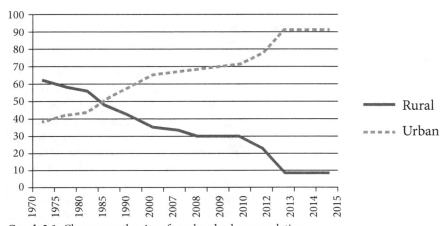

**Graph 2.1** Changes on the size of rural and urban population.

the rule of a senior man. Turks also worked for an *ağa*, a senior man who owns the majority of land in a village. This system, deriving from previous feudal systems of landownership, began to decline in central and southwest Anatolia as a result of increasing employment opportunities in urban areas in the 1960s.[15] The important difference between these 'feudal' agrarian systems is mostly the place of kinship ties in constructing the group. While the former one – *Aşiret* – consists of people who have kinship ties with each other and whose class positions depend on their positioning in the hierarchical ladder, in the latter one – *Ağalık* – most of the time, there is one local landowning family who controls most of the lands and there are no kinship relations between this family and rural 'peasants'. Boratav (2004) makes a distinction between these two agrarian systems and 'wealthy landowning families'. For Boratav (2004), 'wealthy landowning families' are more prevalent in western Turkey, where the majority of the villagers also own plots of land to varying degrees. Furthermore, Boratav (2004) emphasizes the differences between *ağa* (of *aşiret* or of a village) and members of a 'wealthy landowning family' by pointing out that labour operates differently under these two systems. He shows that under an wealthy landowning family, both landowning families and local workers work the lands together.

Turning back to rural–urban migration, Turkish scholars have mostly preferred to focus on trends in migration rather than concerning themselves with the rural environment from which migrants come (Özuğurlu 2011). Rural migrants were constructed as people without a history; they have mostly appeared in academic works only in relation to the problems they create, such as urban sprawl or their 'adaptation' to urban life. Therefore, such studies mostly focused on *hemşericilik*:[16] local networks between people who were born in the same place, people who arrived from the same place and people who have a tendency to live in the same places when they migrate (Karpat 1976; White 2004). Apparently, the neighbourhood in which we lived in İstanbul also exhibited this trend. My father's cousins lived in the next apartment, and our neighbours' relatives or *hemşerileri* (plural) also lived in close proximity to us. There was no one from central Anatolia or the south coast of Turkey, but mainly from the Black Sea coast and from southern Anatolia.

In the 1990s, 'Bağcılar', the neighbourhood in İstanbul where we lived, did not consist of slums but of newly built and cramped apartments. The official website of the district describes 'Bağcılar' in the 1990s as 'a big village with no infrastructure, streets and roads full of mud'. This improper urbanization meant that our municipality (referring to 'Bağcılar') faced many great difficulties in the process of modern urbanization, beginning in 1992. The population of this big village was categorized as 'working class'. However, there were no industries in the neighbourhood. None of the women in our apartment building worked outside the home and it was not common for other women in the district to work either. Although official statistics do not tell the entire story, the district mainly consisted of a conservative population. My mother, who never previously donned a headscarf, began to wear one while she was in and around the district. She would put on her headscarf and when we got within forty minutes walking distance of my aunt's house, she removed it. My aunt did the same when she came to our house.

'Bağcılar' was a typical example of the conservative neighbourhoods in which rural women were controlled within their 'familial' and 'localistic' networks. Thus, this situation can explain the low rate of paid employment of female workers in Turkey in these areas. Indeed, this form of urbanization can be seen in the dramatic decline in women's employment; in the 1970s and 1980s, women's employment decreased from around 50 per cent in the 1960s to 30 per cent (see Graph 2.2 (TÜİK 2011)).

This seems to mirror what Boserup (1970) forecast for women in developing countries when they first migrate from rural areas. She offered a 'U'-shaped model to understand the trends in women's employment. The bottom of the 'U' shows the shift from female majority farming systems to urban employment opportunities for women when they migrate to towns and cities. However, later, after such a sharp decline as a result of foreign investment's drive for cheap labour and new opportunities in urban areas to obtain resources, such as education, she argued that the women's employment rate would increase dramatically. While evidence from other developing countries, especially in Southeast Asia and Latin America, confirms her book's findings (Pearson 2000), Boserup's model cannot be applied to the case of Turkish women (Buğra and Yakut-Cakar 2010; İlkkaracan 2012; Toksöz 2007, 2011). As seen in Graph 2.2, their employment rate in urban areas has increased by only 8 per cent since 1988, while also during this time, foreign investments increased from 19 per cent in 1988 to 28.3 per cent in 2012 (TCMB 2012). Moreover, this participation in the labour market is also limited to certain sectors – essentially, 'socially approved' occupations (Makal and Toksöz 2012). Women are still directly excluded from some jobs because of *el âlem*, as other people do not find these jobs to be 'appropriate' or 'respectable' for women.

Official statistics and academic studies of women in Turkey confirm that in the 1990s, rural, uneducated women were confined to the home even when they moved to urban areas, much like my mother. Furthermore, educated women in urban areas were more likely to be employed in paid employment (Acar 1993). Many

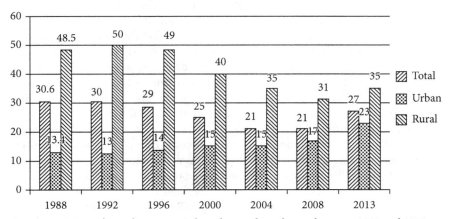

**Graph 2.2** Women's employment rate by urban and rural areas between 1988 and 2013.

rural women living in the city, on the other hand, tended to fear the outside world. My mother, for example, was not fond of the world beyond the apartment. Indeed, she adored the inside world of the apartment block, particularly her neighbours. They organized *gün*; this is a direct translation of the word 'day' and refers to regular gatherings of women in the home for tea and home-made aperitifs, such as bulgur salad (*kısır*[17]), pastry (*börek*[18]), biscuits and so on. They also exchanged gold or money (also foreign currency; in my childhood, the German 'mark' was mostly used). These gatherings are a way for women to save money for household goods and expenditures (White 1994). When women came together for tea or coffee, they always had their lacework to hand. Some of the women did lacework to sell to others, while some made elaborate lace tablecloths and other such home wares for their sisters' or daughters' dowries '*çeyiz*'.[19] My mother also made lace items to sell in Germany. One of our distant relatives had migrated to Germany years before. When she came to visit Turkey during her summer holidays, she took back with her what my mother had made during the year and sold it in Germany to Turkish women who did not have the time for lacework, as they were busy working in paid employment, mostly in German factories. When, each year, my mother's money arrived, she bought a gold bracelet as a way to save to buy a house in the future. Lacemaking was a popular way of earning money for 'housewives' in Turkey (Çınar 1991, 1994; Lordoğlu 1990; White 1994). This is similar to other 'developing' countries, such as India (Lessinger 1990; Mies 1982; Vera-Sanso 1995) and is still common practice.

The harmony that the women experienced in the apartment block did not exist in wider society. The 1990s were the years when the conflict between the Turkish army and the PKK reached its peak.[20] This is also the reason for most of the Kurdish people in this study lacking the formal qualifications that might have enabled them to seek work beyond seasonal migrant agricultural labour. They were mostly children or teenagers during the 1980s or 1990s, at a time when continuing compulsory education was difficult, especially in the rural southeast (Akın and Danışman 2011).

There are different explanations for the Kurdish rebellion and the emergence of 'Kurdish nationalism'. The Turkish state promoted the idea that 'international powers' were sponsoring the PKK and trying to divide the country. Some other explanations focus on the asymmetric economic relations experienced in all the regions of the country and emphasize that Kurds live in the most disadvantaged regions of the country (Strohmeier and Yalçın-Heckmann 2013). However, history tells us that the Kurds' uprisings date back to the establishment of the modern Turkish Republic. Kurds have lived in the region, called Kurdistan, for centuries, which is now partly located in Turkey. Arabs, Armenians, Seljuk Turks and finally Ottomans have invaded the same region for centuries. After the collapse of the Ottoman Empire, the Kurdish region was divided into four sections. Kurds are now living in Turkey, Syria, Iran and Iraq. Studies have proposed that as the assimilation policies of the Turkish state increased over the years, the movement for Kurdish freedom in Turkey became stronger (Besikçi 1969 cited in Aydın 2005). The military, following coups in 1960, 1971 and 1980, did not hesitate to persecute anybody showing any sympathy with the Kurdish movement (Aydın 2005). In the period between the 1960s and early 2000s, the Turkish state changed the names of Kurdish villages to Turkish names; it banned speaking and publishing in Kurdish, education in Kurdish, defending oneself in Kurdish in court and giving Kurdish names to children. Indeed, according to scholars, the emergence of the PKK was related to these traditionally heavy-handed state policies against Kurdish self-expression (Yeğen 1996). Apart from the peak of the conflict with the PKK in the 1990s, the Kurdish crisis was also a big part of the agenda of Parliament. In 1994, for threatening the unity of the Turkish state, three Parliamentarians of the DEP (Kurdish 'Democratic Party') were arrested in Parliament and sentenced to eleven years in prison.

These events took place largely beyond the four walls of our apartment in 'Bağcılar'; however, one day, a 'husband' brought the conflict into our homes. After watching the news on TV, our top-floor neighbour, Sevim's husband, began swearing at Kurds from his balcony. Unfortunately, they lived next door to a Kurdish family and they heard his rant. Their conversation began on the balconies and continued into the corridors of the apartment. The fight became even larger when relatives or *hemşeri* from other flats in the apartment also became involved, as well as people from the streets. In the end, three men were stabbed. While they were fighting, alongside the swearing and crying of women and children, the words 'traitors' and 'tyrants' were heard flying through the air. After this, my parents decided to go back to their home city of Bursa, the fourth biggest city in Turkey, which did not receive nearly as many migrants as İstanbul.[21] There, many people 'were like us'; they had migrated from the Balkans during the last fifty years or they were already there. That is to say, they were locals. The one explanation my father gave me about our moving was, 'İstanbul was too crowded with lots of different people', and, as he hoped, I stopped seeing Kurds around me for a long time.

### *For a day, my mother stops being 'thankful': Turkey's first direct 'homeworking' project*

Moving to Bursa did not make structural changes to my mother's 'working life', which I look at in detail in this section to show the available forms of women's labour for global production in Turkey.

Like many Turkish 'housewives', my mother continued to do domestic tasks and to make her lacework in Bursa. However, she also looked after my paternal uncle's son and my paternal aunt's daughter, both of whom came from our village to Bursa for their schooling. Looking after the children of your husband's brothers and sisters was a very common practice in the 1990s if parts of your husband's family were still living in the countryside. My mother was no exception, as my other aunts living in the city were also looking after their husband's siblings' children, and many of our neighbours were too. My mother did not 'work' in paid employment until one day in 1997, when my father came home with a brochure with a headline stating, 'a factory in every home'. After reviewing the documents, he convinced my mother that they could earn money with this 'opportunity'.

A national company was selling Swedish knitting machines with a three-year job guarantee, providing women with free training courses with the promise that as soon as they finished the course, the company would provide fabrics and patterns so women could work at home to produce the goods. My mother and paternal aunt accepted, and they became part of Turkey's first large homeworking scheme (Koç 2001). They bought the machines by borrowing money from our relatives in Germany. When my mother and aunt finished their course, they immediately received patterns and materials and the company told them that they had to finish an exact number of arms (of a sweater) by an exact time; otherwise, they would be paid less. The company paid workers by piece rates. To reach the quota, my mother was working almost sixteen hours a day, and as my father had found this 'perfect' job opportunity, he also worked on the machine when he came home.

With time, the company began to give out more difficult patterns, which were time consuming, and reaching the quota in the agreed time became increasingly difficult. Furthermore, the company did not bring the yarn and other materials or collect the completed work from our home. Instead, my mother had to collect the materials and take the finished items to their offices in person. These loads were heavy and the office was far from our house. One day, I went with my mother to drop off what she had produced. A woman checked every piece my mother had done, and then she reduced the price to be paid for almost all pieces by claiming that the quality of the work was poor. Thereafter, she counted them and gave my mother some money. My mother didn't want to accept the amount, as she thought it was too low. The woman was saying to my mother, 'Take the money and give me your blessings' – *hakkını helal et!*[22] They began to argue and my mother began to cry. She repeatedly said that she would not accept the amount, as it was not fair to her. Since she refused the money, the woman forced me to take it. My mother took my arm and we left the place almost at a run, my mother still crying. That day, she was not thankful; she gave up the job. However, the machine was still at our home and, as she had not completed the three-year working period as agreed, my parents had to pay for the machine or find someone else to take on the agreement to purchase it. My aunt managed to find someone who had recently married and had moved to the city from the village. She took the machine and my mother just broke even without making any profit.

The project that my mother worked on was the first direct homeworking scheme, operated by a national firm acting as a subcontractor for a Swedish company. According to Koç (2001), previous examples of homeworking were more like genuine self-employment. However, in this case, the company had made a legal contract with the women and this contract also involved buying the machines. So, some of the women who joined the project applied to the courts because of the conditions of their agreement, which, although similar to an employment contract, did not specify the amount of pay or working conditions. Although they were successful in some respects, they did not get any of the money back that they had initially invested in the machines.

Koç (2001) says that home employment subcontracted by companies in Turkey, in contrast to self-employment at home, began to systematically increase in the 1980s. This form of employment was encouraged by the media as well as by the government.[23] Çınar (1991) conducted the first detailed research on women's homeworking in Turkey, highlighting the relationship between patriarchy and capital in using women's labour in the home. Apparently, women and the male members of their family chose to become involved with this kind of work because women could work in their 'own' homes. Thus, it enabled them to do housework and to work in a de facto gender-segregated environment. In another study, Lordoğlu (1990) interviewed around 500 women, again in Bursa, and pointed out that the main homeworking tasks included knitting, lacemaking and embroidery. Lordoğlu further noted that women in this form of employment worked without social insurance or job security. Moreover, the employers provided the materials and women were paid piece rates.

Lordoğlu (1990) also highlights, as does Çınar (1991, 1994), how homeworking is favoured by women, as it enables them to do housework and have childcare, while preventing them from working outside of the home. According to TÜİK (b), in 2014, 57 per cent of women who were not in active paid employment cited their role as a housewife as being the reason behind them not looking for paid work outside the home. This figure draws parallels with the 58.6 per cent of respondents in the same survey who cited their responsibilities in the home, both household chores and childcare, as being the primary reason for them not seeking out paid work (TÜİK 2014b). As such, more than half of the women who are not in paid employment state that this is because they are housewives (TÜİK 2017b).

Besides traditional gender roles and norms, the mechanization of agriculture and consequent migration to cities as well as the conflict between the Turkish Army and the PKK were the main reasons driving the exploitation of women's labour through homeworking in the 1990s. Women who migrated from rural areas had not traditionally been sufficiently qualified to gain better-paid skilled jobs, while working in factories was considered taboo. In the 1990s, women working in factories were mostly those who had come from the Balkans in the 1980s and had settled in big cities rather than women of rural origin within Turkey (Nichols and Suğur 2004).

While the large direct homeworking project failed and gained a bad reputation nationally, the ateliers (*atölye*) kept their popularity as appropriate workplaces for women. Thus, it is likely that the majority of women workers in Turkey first encountered global capital through small textile enterprises, mostly located in the basements of buildings in residential neighbourhoods, which are called *Atölye* (ateliers) (Dedeoğlu 2012). Therefore, it is unsurprising that ateliers were also common in the neighbourhood where we lived, even in the flat beneath our home. Our neighbours had their own small atelier, which employed only their nuclear family and close relatives. They were close friends of my parents and had also migrated from the Balkans,[24] though more recently. Although my family did not know them personally before my parents moved into their block of flats, a common friend had introduced them and they asked around to find us a flat when we were coming from İstanbul. They found a flat for us, even though it did not belong to them, as well as providing a spoken reference for my parents. Finding a home for your kinfolk,[25] *hemşeri*, or member of your 'imagined community',[26] is a very common practice. Similarly, this was also shown by White (1994) in her study of İstanbul. This provided the basis for a relationship with my family and, as a 'requirement' of this friendship, my mother helped out in their atelier when the number of working people decreased for any reason. The most commonly articulated reason was that their children were busy preparing for their exams. During high school, they worked in the atelier when they came home from school but could not do so during exam season. In those days, my mother became a 'helper', as did her other friends. None of them earned any sort of remuneration other than the owners' prayerful thanks (*hayır duası*[27]).

Dedeoğlu's (2012) study of the ateliers of İstanbul demonstrated how familial or kinship networks shape production relations in these family-run establishments. She showed how, in a patriarchal society such as Turkey, it is difficult to bring women to the export zones, and hence, global capital seeks to utilize Turkish society's most treasured concept: 'family'. Global capital has incorporated sub-contracting family firms, and they have primarily employed female labourers in the textile and garment sectors ever since. 'Ateliers' are seen as 'proper' places for women to go to work because they are not located in industrial zones, but rather in neighbourhoods. The ateliers of do not employ men, only women, and the women workers do not have to travel on public transport to get to work. Although my mother did not receive any money, ateliers are the main employment opportunity for many women in Turkey. Women's familial commitments (Suğur and Suğur 2005; Gündüz-Hoşgör and Smith 2008) and the need for the recognition of the workplace as 'honourable' and 'safe' by their social environment (Dedeoğlu 2012; Ecevit 1991; Nichols and Suğur 2004; White 2004) shape ateliers by two interrelated concepts: 'family' and 'patriarchy'. Women's roles as mother and/or wife in their family also shape their employment trajectory in Turkey. This apparently enables to see the interweaving relationship between production and reproduction: the paid and underpaid work. These women are invisible in the official statistics, as they mostly work without registration and, hence, they do not obtain any of the benefits of paid employment (Dedeoğlu 2010).

## Unemployed fathers, offended uncles: Economic and political instability in Turkey

While my mother was spending her days trying to find the best price to sell her lace at the market during the last years of the 1990s, my father worked as an account manager at various different companies. His salary was good enough to pay for rent, food and private tuition for my sister and I, as well as to send money to his parents and brother in the countryside. In the countryside, farmers were struggling due to the instability of the economy, and they were constantly looking for opportunities to earn extra income. However, none were successful in the long term. Between 1990 and 2000, my extended family in the village built a poultry farm (which operated for only two years), opened a small stand at the entrance of the village to sell some vegetables they produced to people passing in their cars (this operated for five years) and built a 'dark room' to grow mushrooms (which lasted for just six months).[28]

On the other hand, my father was always saying that he could be fired from his work at any moment. My parents' main goal was to buy a house, and in those days there was no mortgage system. People borrowed money from their relatives, friends or people from their 'imagined communities'. However, our only 'rich' relative, who lived in Germany, was fed up with giving loans to all her distant relatives. Therefore, my parents bought a building plot outside of the city, and my mother began selling the bracelets she had bought with her lacemaking work. They also took loans from our other relatives and began building a house in Bursa. Before they managed to finish it, my father was fired and we had to move to our unfinished home without electricity or water. This was in 1999, during the last of the Turkish economic crises of the 1990s. So, while we were sitting by the light of a candle with our other unemployed neighbours, the economic crisis and its bedfellow, political crisis, were the main subjects of discussion amongst the adults.

Yalman and Bedirhanoğlu (2010) describe Turkey in the 1990s as a crisis-ridden country. One economic crisis after the other followed from 1994 to 1998–9, and these had serious political reverberations. Coalition governments consisting of political parties from polarized ideological positions were in government during these years. Furthermore, while the conflict between the Turkish Army and the PKK reached a climax at this time, there were also tensions between religious and secular groups over a religious political party, the Virtue Party (*Fazilet Partisi*), which had won the largest vote in the elections. People were also polarized; my father and paternal uncle – *amca* – stopped talking over a woman Parliamentarian called Merve Kavakçı. She was elected a member of Parliament in 1999. However, members of the Democratic Left Party (DSP) prevented her from taking her oath of office in the opening ceremony because of her headscarf. She became a symbol of the struggle against attempts to ban the headscarf in public places, including at universities and in Parliament. While my *amca* was a fervent supporter of headscarf freedom in public places, my father advocated secularism. Unsurprisingly, each accused the other of being 'ungrateful'. My father was accused of being ungrateful to his family values, of which respecting religious identities is an important part, while my uncle was accused of being 'ungrateful' to republican values and even to Atatürk himself. They were both stubborn in their beliefs and the polarizing political environment brought these issues to the fore. The events that caused my father and his brother to fall out were also the reason why there has been tension between the country's religious and secular movements since the establishment of the Turkish Republic.

The Republic of Turkey not only makes the existence of other ethnic nationalities invisible, but also aims to make religion invisible. The Caliphate[29] was banned in 1924, while all Islamic circles were also disbanded. Not only did they ban all activism, but the state also suppressed basic Islamic education by unofficial actors in the 1930s and 1940s. Tuğal (2009: 36) has stated that 'secularist hegemony was built on a specific party system, the establishment of bureaucratic authority, the construction of the Turkish nation, the secularisation of Islam, the making of urban identity, and the development of corporatism'. He continues by asserting that the creation and sustainability of the secularist project were based on the unintended 'balance' between the Turkish centre left and centre right; they differ from their equivalents in the West but express the internal divisions within the power bloc in Turkey. According to Tuğal, 'The rigidly secularist bureaucracy, the officially protected bourgeoisie, and rigidly secularist intellectuals and professionals constitute the dominant segments of the power bloc, and favour a regime of relative exclusion and repression of the subordinate sectors of the bloc' (ibid.: 37). They are 'the conservative wing of the bureaucracy, the internationally oriented bourgeoisie, merchants, mildly secularist and liberal intellectuals and professionals, and some pro-modernisation provincial notables' (ibid.).

Since the 1990s, the subordinate power bloc has successfully mobilized workers, peasants, artisans, the semi-employed and unemployed, religious intellectuals and professionals in their struggle against the dominant sectors (Tuğal 2009). This struggle became more apparent in the 1990s following the election victory of the Islamist Welfare Party, *Refah Partisi*. This party had a chance to be part of the coalition government as well as gaining some municipalities in local elections. However, the military perceived their practices and policies to be a threat to the secularist system. Consequently, in 1997, the military intervened in the party in a process known as a 'postmodern coup' in Turkey. After the intervention, in 1998, the Islamist politicians established a new party, called the Virtue Party. However, this party was closed down in 2001 due to being perceived as a threat to the secular republic. This was the fourth and last political party closed by the *anayasa mahkemesi*[30] – Supreme Court – due to being perceived as a threat to the secular state.

## Social neoliberalism and AKP

From this point forward, I depart from my family's experiences to write about the context of the country after the 2000s. The 1980s and 1990s had been their story; they were the main actors of the 'social transformation' of the period and they had migrated from a village to İstanbul and then back. However, Turkey in the 2000s was a different world, one in which my parents were merely part of the audience.

## AKP, political Islam and women's work

In 2001, Recep Tayyip Erdoğan, the current (2020) president and former prime minister (2003–14) of Turkey,[31] was released from prison following four months' imprisonment for reading a poem at a demonstration – perceived as a threat to the secular Turkish state – and established the AKP. The party won a majority in its first election in 2002 after another economic crisis in 2001. Since then, Turkey's current government has embraced a full neoliberal agenda for the country and has largely been given free rein to pursue this agenda, thanks to its position as the country's majority party for last the eighteen years. As expected, the *anayasa mahkemesi* also tried to close down the AKP, but was unsuccessful.

Öniş (2012) offers a brief account of the political economy of Turkey post-2001 and underlines that the strong economic performance of the Turkish economy has led to the durability of the AKP's electoral success. The AKP was elected just after the 2001 economic crisis, in which unemployment had reached a peak, output collapsed and there were negative distributional consequences. This situation forced the coalition government to make new regulatory reforms under the impetus of the IMF and European Union, while the AKP inherited neoliberal development plans that it subsequently applied successfully. During the early years of the current government's control, Turkey enjoyed its strongest period of economic growth since 1950. According to Öniş (2006, 2012), besides this economic growth, the AKP also secured its electoral support through applying informal and formal redistributive tools. In other words, social welfare became accessible only for groups which came under the scope of informal communities or networks associated with the AKP. However, because they also continuously invested in health and education, this has impacted the middle and poorer segments of society, even those who were excluded from the party's associations (Öniş 2012). What is important in the present context is that the AKP's 'social neo-liberalism' allowed it to transcend the boundaries of class politics and construct broad-based cross-class coalitions of political support that would not have been possible under the old style, 'classic neo-liberalism' (Öniş 2012: 144). Thus, the AKP's adoption of neoliberalism is different from 'classical neo-liberalism', which is focused more on free-market trade (Yalman and Bedirhanoğlu 2010). Therefore, the current Turkish government has a crucial role in the construction and regulation of the institutions that enable market forces to properly come into play. This 'social neo-liberalism' enables the AKP to gain supporters from different segments of society.[32] This was also the result and the reason for the military coup in 1980, which put an end to class-based politics in Turkey via an authoritarian constitution that put limitations on trade union movements (Adaman et. al. 2009) and replaced it with identity-based politics. In doing so, the AKP has successfully married social neoliberal economic policies to the ideology of 'political Islam'.

Examining the Turkish political economy is not possible without considering the adaptation of 'political Islam' to the neoliberal economy. Tuğal (2009) offers a thought-provoking analysis of how neoliberal capitalist economic policies have absorbed 'Islamic' thinking. Drawing on research from his longitudinal fieldwork in one of the religiously conservative neighbourhoods in İstanbul (Sultanbeyli), Tuğal shows how radical Islamists who believe in the necessity of an Islamic state have become 'moderate' through their 'integration' into the system under the AKP's policies, while also drawing on the self-perceptions of ex-radicals. A few years ago, Islamic politicians and their supporters campaigned against both 'communism and capitalism'; however, now they have shifted their economic policy agenda to include 'some elements of capitalism but no elements of communism' (Tuğal 2009: 217).

In his ethnographic study, Tuğal (2009) offers a snapshot from ex-radicals' daily life. He shows how their daily conversations in tearooms have changed from discussions about struggles and Islamic rule to the daily routines of their own enterprises. As such, Tuğal argues that the moderation and integration of Islam into the current economic and political system have also shifted the gender regime in the neighbourhood. He mentions that it is more common to witness women on the streets of this neighbourhood, that the number of unveiled women has increased and that, even if they are veiled, women choose more colourful veils and wear heavy make-up. Moreover, he states that the number of women working in the neighbourhood has exploded when compared to the situation before the AKP government. Based on this, it is possible to argue that the integration of Islam into the neoliberal economy has opened a new door for religious women, for whom working in paid employment has become more acceptable within their social networks. Moreover, it might be said that the AKP's Islamic ideology does not aim to prevent women from working at the bottom of the employment ladder, and to be the targets of the 'friend' of the current government: global capital. Thus, the AKP does not constitute as an obstacle to their paid employment; rather, its moderate Islamic ideology makes 'conservative' women employees' work more acceptable. Nonetheless, they are concerned about women who seek to access the upper echelons of the employment ladder, which they consider to be the exclusive realm of men, or about women who are not working in socially 'approved' occupations.

## *The AKP and its 'cooperative nationalism' on the Turkish lands*

The neoliberal policies of Turkey's current government were first applied to agriculture, and the liberalization of the agricultural sector has directly led to an increase in investment in food processing from foreign investors. A special report published by the Turkish Central Bank on the food and beverage industry stated that foreign investment in food processing increased by almost tenfold between 2006 and 2011 (TCMB 2012). The report also emphasized that this resulted directly from 'developments' in the agricultural sector in Turkey. According to the report, the food and beverage industry has become the biggest industrial sector in Turkey.

While the Turkish Ministry of Industry refers to the liberalization of agriculture as 'development', many Turkish scholars see this process as 'forcing the capitalisation of agriculture', the 'proletarianisation of the rural' (Keyder and Yenal 2013) and 'the death of small farmers' (Aydın 2005; Keyder and Yenal 2013; Özuğurlu, 2011). Inevitably, the 'Seed Law' and the 'Land Law' have had a significant impact on capitalizing and opening 'Turkish agriculture' to 'global capital'. With the 'Seed Law' (2006), the government put restraints on growing domestic crops by forcing farmers to use the 'registered seeds' that are sold by 'international agricultural companies'. The 'Land Law' (2007), on the other hand, seeks to regulate the size of land holdings.

New legislation has compelled farmers to either sell or buy land, resulting in the rapid extinction of small farmers and the continued growth in the holdings of larger farmers and landowning families. Although 80.7 per cent of Turkish agriculture is carried out on land holdings smaller than 25 acres and the average land holding per farm is around 3 acres (TÜİK 2016), the rural population, which made up approximately 25 per cent of total population in 2016 (TÜİK 2018), was reduced from 35 per cent at the beginning of the 2000s (TÜİK 2014b) and only 7.5 per cent of the population lived in villages in 2018 (TÜİK 2019b).[33] However, as Keyder and Yenal (2011) point out, this time migration has not occurred from rural areas to big cities, as in the 1960s, but rather to 'rural towns'. Farmers with nothing to gain from employment in the big cities prefer to migrate either to towns with factories or to other villages, where they can work as paid agricultural workers. Seeking work outside agriculture is a common consequence of this process. Some villages, which have developed town-like characteristics in recent years, owing to the availability of a wide spectrum of income-earning activities, ranging from small-scale production in labour-intensive commercial agriculture to seasonal employment in tourism, have also become key destinations for rural migrants (Keyder and Yenal 2011). Some of these migrations feature entire families looking to re-establish themselves in new locations, but some can also be described as seasonal migrations of workers living away from their family for short periods of time. For the most part, it is men who migrate to larger towns and villages seasonally. On the other hand, contract farming has remained a survival strategy for farmers in Turkey (Keyder and Yenal 2011). Under contract farming, farmers have to produce the crops for agri-business firms and, whilst this guarantees a market for farmers' produce, such contracts give them less money in exchange for the guarantee of earning money. Moreover, under such contracts, farmers lose some degree of control over their land and decisions about their agricultural productivity.

While almost half of the population working in agriculture in Turkey is female, women rarely figure in the scope of Turkish scholars' studies about the transformation of the rural population. However, the transformation of their number in the agricultural workforce – the only information I could find about their work in agriculture – demonstrates how they are directly affected by these changes. In 1970, 90 per cent of women in the labour force were working in agriculture; in 1980, the figure was 87.9 per cent; in 1990, 82.3 per cent; in 2000, 75.7 per cent (TÜİK 2011a); and in 2013, 32.9 per cent (TÜİK 2014c). The figure that stands today is 28.3 per cent (TÜİK 2017b). Although agriculture has lost its place as the main employment sector of women in Turkey in the last five years, taking the informal statistics into consideration, it can be asserted that agriculture is still a large sector to employ women in Turkey. In agriculture, women are generally responsible for the manual, labour-intensive tasks and their labour is attributed no value and no return by rural people (Toksöz 2011). While male labour mostly concentrates in work that entails the use of machinery, women undertake highly labour-intensive work, such as sowing, weeding, hoeing and reaping (Toksöz 2011). In addition, women in agriculture today are mostly Kurdish seasonal migrant workers because most agricultural labourers consist of Kurdish seasonal migrant families. Moreover, it is apparent that the conditions of Turkish agriculture have worsened due to neoliberal policies. Landowners are under pressure from the companies that purchase their produce; they therefore need to increase productivity by making workers work harder and for less remuneration. Local women do not accept work in low-paid strenuous jobs and prefer to work for the food factories in nearby towns. Consequently, in the past ten years, Kurdish seasonal migrant workers have increasingly been employed in the western, north and south coast of Turkey (Duruiz 2015).

Seasonal migration of Kurdish labourers is also result of the 'reconciliatory' politics of the AKP government. Tuğal (2009) states that the AKP emphasized unity between Kurds and Turks, but focused on democratic values rather than Islam as the bedrock of unity. To solve the Kurdish crisis, the AKP government engaged in dialogue with Abdullah Öcalan, the PKK leader who has been in prison since 1999. In 2013, when I worked with Kurdish seasonal workers on the land, the government announced the beginning of the 'reconciliation process', which proposes to work towards an agreement between the Turkish state and the PKK to reach a 'peace process'. The Kurdish movement began to achieve peak political representation through holding an intermediary role in meetings between the Turkish state and Abdullah Öcalan. Bans on speaking and publishing in Kurdish were removed and the state media established a Kurdish TV channel. The AKP has been supported by a majority of the Kurdish population from its establishment until the election of June 2015 when HDP (People's Democratic Party) won seats in the parliament. This caused the AKP lose its majority in parliament. Afterwards, the ceasefire between the Turkish state and the PKK ended. Since 2016, few political representatives of HDP (People's Democratic Party) – leaders, parliaments, mayors and members – have been imprisoned (some of them are still (2020) in prison awaiting their hearing). The ending of ceasefire caused tensions between Turkish local employers and Kurdish workers, and some of the latter left their workplaces (BBC 2015). Although farmers have tried to find other workers, it has been reported that locals will not accept the conditions, so they had to go to refugee camps to conscript Syrian workers. This result conforms to what Tuğal (2009) has said about the nationalist ideology of Turkey in the 2000s. The 'hegemonic nationalism' of the 1980s and 1990s, which aimed to assimilate minorities, has been replaced by 'corporate nationalism' that 'locks them in disadvantaged urban locations, restrictive cultural identities, and low-paying jobs' (ibid.: 101), which is clearly the situation first of Kurdish seasonal migrant workers and now of Syrian migrants.

## Historical change under the 'official feeling'

In this chapter, I historicize the transformation of rural women's labour in Turkey, including their migration into cities and towns. While doing so, I have focused on the broader polarizations in the country: men–women, rural–urban, Turkish–Kurdish, secular–religious. These divisions underpin the meanings that my informants attach to their own and others' actions. I showed what it means to be a Turk or a Kurd in Turkey through focusing on how these identities are constructed in schools, on TV, in apartments and on the land.

I focus first on the education system, not only as a place where national identities are constructed, but also as one of the important institutions in which Turkish citizens learn the 'official feeling of the country': thankfulness. Without talking about thankfulness, it is difficult to understand women's acceptance of their relations with men, workers' appreciation of their employers or citizens' gratitude to politicians. Everything about relations between people in Turkey hangs in the air without emphasizing the importance of 'gratefulness'; we are unable to understand my mother's unpaid work for the neighbours who found us a house to rent, her looking after my cousins, or some people labelling Kurds as traitors simply because they want to speak Kurdish. To understand this book, it is important to bear in mind the 'official feeling of the country' and the political and economic history which most of the people I worked with have lived under until now.

## Chapter 3

## THE BACKGROUND OF A TOMATO: CONTRACTING, RECRUITING AND ORGANIZING LABOUR

*Entering the world of tomatoes*

We are just producing tomatoes. We are not like businessmen or policemen or politicians. But a tomato is something too. Everyone eats tomatoes. (Former farmer, 4 May 2013)

In 2015, two years after this statement, a political crisis with Russia over a downed fighter jet by the Turkish military service occurred and people in Turkey learned that a tomato is actually 'something': an important thing. The sudden embargo of the biggest importer of fresh Turkish tomatoes caused the Turkish tomato producers to earn almost 40 per cent less in 2016 than the previous year (TZMİB 2017). Turkish citizens began to see resentful tomato producers in the daily news, talking of 'serious' politicians, such as Vladimir Putin or the current [2020] Turkish President, Recep Tayyip Erdoğan. They discussed tomatoes in their 'serious' joint press conferences,[1] which is not surprising because tomatoes have the highest export rate among both fresh and processed vegetables in Turkey (TÜİK 2016). Furthermore, the country is ranked fourth as the biggest fresh and processed tomato producer in Europe and seventh in the world. Considering almost half of the population still works in agriculture, approximately 30 per cent of working women are employed in agriculture, as the agro-food industry is the second biggest manufacturing sector, it is safe to say that many thousands of women in Turkey make money from tomatoes.

This is not the first study paying attention to the power of tomatoes in shaping the social fabric of a country. Brandt's (2002) extensive work, *Tangled Roots*, also considers the gendered work of tomato production by following women's work and the production of tomatoes as far as Canada. She makes it very clear that global tomato production makes women's work more insecure, more difficult and more poorly compensated. Brandt does not, however, clarify the impact of women workers on globalization, which may be attributed to her underestimation of the importance of relations of reproduction in her analysis. Although she offers an account of the double burden women workers face due to their familial responsibilities, she pays no attention to how production relations shape and are shaped by women's lives outside of work, as this book does. Similarly, another influential study on tomatoes, *The Force of Irony*, by Torres (1997), also neglects the relations of reproduction and solely focuses on workers' productive labour to understand their struggles. While it inspiringly brings to light the struggles of workers engaged in tomato production, the issues of gender and reproductive labour are not addressed in the analysis.

*Exploring the Tomato* by Harvey et al. (2002) also analyses tomato production to understand the changing contexts and conditions in economics, politics and culture, while the tomato itself is approached as an object of fascination. However, the book does not adopt a GCC analysis, arguing rather that tomatoes cannot be considered commodities themselves, as they need other objects or goods to make them into commodities. For example, tomatoes are not the sole ingredient in tomato ketchup. In this regard, this study treats tomatoes not as the subject of analysis, but rather its object. Here, in contrast, tomatoes are considered subjects along with the workers – mostly women – engaged in their production. By following both of these elements simultaneously, I emphasize that one of them is not the determinant of the other, but rather that they create each other as part of a continuous process.

This chapter looks at how this continuous process of tomato making is organized, as well as how the labour force is contracted and recruited. It will be divided into three sections. The first section demonstrates how the factory decides the conditions of their agreement with farmers, how they reach and choose the farmers, how they control them and how they control other factories in the region. The second section presents the landowning families' (farmers) perspective in getting into contract farming. Then, the final section explores how the Kurdish migrants' labour force is constructed by the *dayıbaşı*[2] (gang-master) through his connections with his kin.

### *The factory negotiates in 'winter': Conditions of tomato agreement*

According to their producers, there are two types of tomatoes: 'factory tomatoes' and 'tomatoes for eating'. Workers and farmers refer to the tomatoes that are produced for the factory as 'factory tomatoes' and to those that are produced for national supermarkets and sold 'fresh' as 'tomatoes for eating'. The story I tell is mainly the story of 'factory tomatoes', not 'tomatoes for eating'. This is because I focus on global production and the 'factory tomatoes' are 'global' enough to travel as far as Japan. Thus, let us start with the role of one of the biggest tomato-processing factories in Turkey: Red.[3]

The structure and operation of Red, the factory that purchases the tomatoes that I helped produce on the land, have benefitted indirectly from many of the policies of the current Turkish government (AKP), which has been in power since 2002 and has encouraged the internationalization, liberalization and privatization of the Turkish economy, as discussed in Chapter 2. The factory was established in the 1960s in Bursa, which produces 68 per cent of the processed tomatoes in Turkey (ZMO 2014). As such, Red is one of Bursa's five major factories. It produces tomato purée, tomato paste, chopped tomatoes, peeled whole tomatoes and ketchup. Moreover, since 2007, the company has had Japanese shareholders. On its website, the company introduces itself as pioneering the establishment of the export-oriented agricultural industry in Turkey. Official reports on processed tomato exports also support this claim. Over the last fifteen years, Red has increased its export range to forty different countries, including Japan, the United States, Germany and the Netherlands. The website and the general manager assure me that all phases of tomato production and processing, from seed to canned tomato products, are under the company's control. Furthermore, as a result of this control, they claim that they are able to offer products of the desired quality and freshness to their consumers. The company's control, from seed to canned tomato, is reflected in agricultural production and how the desired quality of the product affects the construction and composition of the agricultural labour force, as well as its working conditions.

The factory's main method for establishing control over farmers is 'contract farming'. After harvesting, the factory and farmers agree upon a fixed price per kilo of tomatoes for the next year. Then, the factory gives farmers the seeds and fertilizers they need or advance payment to them to buy particular seeds and fertilizers. According to this agreement, a farmer has to produce an exact amount of tomatoes for each hectare of land planted. If farmers cannot meet their production targets, then it is considered to be their fault. In cases such as this, the farmer receives a lower price for the crop. The same goes for cases in which the quality of the tomatoes is lower than expected.

Farmers often complain about how the factory reduces the 'fixed price' by accusing farmers of not using fertilizers or pesticides correctly. During harvest time, there are regular fights between farmers and quality controllers outside of the factory gates at any given time, on any given day. 'Once you get involved with the factory [implying contract farming], you cannot escape. If you want to stay in your job [implying farming], you have no choice but to keep producing for the factory, as they are the ones providing seeds and fertilisers'.[4]

Turkish agriculture consists of mainly small-scale farmers; around 80.7 per cent of farmers have properties smaller than 25 acres and average landholding per farm is around 3 acres (TÜİK 2016). The factory manager states his dissatisfaction with this:

> We have to deal with lots of people. It takes all winter and far too much time. A man has 10 hectares [around three acres]. When he comes to us, you should see him, he believes that he is a king; you know that those peasant[5] men think that they create the world. Their women are not judicious, so they always tell their men that they are the best. Then, we have to grapple in order to reach an agreement. The farmers think that they have endless fields that are more fertile than any other. But, farmers do not know how to manage their fields, they are not aware of technology, new fertilisers, nothing, absolutely nothing. The government should do something about it, if they want to compete with the world. They

[the farmers] drive me crazy. We have tools but don't have competent people. Imagine trying to produce for the Japanese market with people like them.[6]

Although scholars see the current neoliberal policies of Turkish agriculture as heralding the 'death of small farmers' (Keyder and Yenal 2013; Özuğurlu 2011), the factory manager thinks that the government's regulations geared towards organizing agriculture in a more export-friendly way are insufficient. It is evident that the factory manager desires the end of smallholder farming. His scorn for farmers and preference for the extinction of small-scale farming or peasant production are very similar to what Wright and Madrid (2007) found in the Colombian cut-flower industry. There, peasants were seen as backwards, hazardous and undisciplined, and thus, unable to cope with changes in agriculture. In a similar vein, the factory manager of Red sees peasants as responsible for Turkey's inability to advance in capitalist agricultural production and sees modernization as a tool to 'heal' them.

On the other hand, the factory manager's claim about the farmers' lack of knowledge appears to ring true. It is clear that farmers have relatively limited knowledge about the application of new seeds, fertilizers or new technologies, including irrigation systems. However, the manager appears to ignore the fact that there is no source from which farmers can learn about these new demands and requirements stemming from the transformation of agricultural production. Neither effective unions nor official training programmes exist for farmers. Ironically, official reports also agree that farmers are totally alone under the new system and that they do not know how to cope (TEPGE 2014).

Not knowing how to use fertilizers is not the only problem that farmers have to contend with. The obligation to use registered seeds (Seed Law 2006[7]) is their biggest problem, as before they did not have to pay for seeds. Because registered seeds are hybrids, they cannot be used year on year.

> You can borrow a tractor from your neighbour, but you cannot borrow seeds from someone. You have to buy seeds and the only way you can get money for seeds is by going to the banks. In order to borrow from the banks, you need valuable property to give to the banks in the form of a loan. So, if you have many acres of land, you can apply for credit from the banks. If you don't, you won't have the money to buy seeds, fertilisers etc. So, most of our neighbours are giving up farming and looking for other jobs [in the last 10 years, around a million farmers have given up farming (TÜİK 2013). They [former smallholder farmers] no longer work in the villages because they are not satisfied with what we offer them. You know we cannot afford to employ workers in tomato picking with a daily wage in hours. It is impossible! We are producing more tomatoes than before, so we need a larger workforce. But, we cannot employ more workers since we also do not have money.[8]

Under these conditions, farmers try to reduce the cost of labour to try to guarantee a profit. Thus, the cost of labour is the only thing the factory does not have direct control over.

## Farmers: Always in between

As can be expected, with the cost of production tied to the whims of global capital, working conditions on the land where 'factory tomatoes' are grown have consistently deteriorated. Working hours are now longer and wages are based on group performance. As the factory pays the farmers depending on the amount of tomatoes they bring to the factory, the farmers also pay the workers depending on the amount of tomatoes they pick. Both farmers and farm workers are paid depending on the aggregate weight of these tomatoes, with the plum ones weighing less. When some tomatoes are overripe, the factory pays the farmers less and the farmers subsequently pay less to their workers. In this sense, both farmers and workers share a common interest: they both want to pick as many tomatoes as possible before they decrease in weight. Based on this, farmers try to find workers eager to work very long hours each day, because the dividends from the tomatoes decrease as the picking season wears on.

Local women workers work on the tomato land during the planting season (see gender and ethnic division of labour regarding the tomato growing stages in Table 4.1). They are paid a daily wage based on eight hours of work per day. However, local women do not accept work during picking season, when working hours rise to sixteen per day and payment is based on group performance. Instead, in the summer, local workers often choose to work in the factory or picking 'tomatoes for eating', which are produced for national supermarkets. The working conditions are far better on the lands of 'tomatoes for eating' than the lands of 'factory tomatoes'. In this way, the cheapest way and often the only option available to farmers is employing Kurdish migrant families to pick 'factory tomatoes'. Kurdish migrant rural workers do not have regular employment and their main source of income is seasonal rural work. This is the lowest paid, most insecure and least prestigious work in Turkey. However, this is in line with Turkey's nationalist ideological position, which has become more prominent since the 2000s. This form of 'corporate nationalism' (Tuğal 2009) locks Kurds into disadvantaged urban or rural locations, restrictive cultural identities and low-paying jobs. The extended family structure of Kurdish families also fits in perfectly with the conditions of rural tomato work; they can work on a group performance–based payment system within their extended family groups. Also, their lack of alternative employment opportunities makes them more willing to acquiesce to long working days and a performance-based payment system.

Kurdish workers, therefore, become the most reasonable option for farmers. While they are not reluctant to employ them, they do so for the purpose of lowering costs. However, employing Kurdish workers has been a source of trouble for most of the farming families in the village that I conducted the study on, including the family I worked for, because of the reactions of local villagers. Locals do not want Kurds in their villages, believing that they are 'lazy', 'hazardous', 'dirty' and 'traitors'.

## Waiting for the call to 'work': The dayıbaşı and his 'familial labour force'

Existing literature on the 'feminization' of agricultural work in the Global South shows the prevalence of low-paid work, poor working conditions, precariousness and seasonal migration (Barndt 2002; Barrientos and Perrons 1999; Barrientos et al. 2003; Chant 1991; 1997; Chant and McIlwaine 1995, 2009; Whitehead 2009). Thus, it is not surprising that when we think about rural tomato production, we mostly imagine women workers working for long hours in 40-degree heat. This is the quintessential image of the tomato lands in Turkey. To tell the story of the tomato lands, however, I will begin with the view from the window of one Kurdish migrant woman's house, as it is in the homes that labour is first constructed. This house is around 1,500 km away from tomato lands in a village near the town of Mazıdağı, near the city of Mardin, Turkey.

The population of Mardin is 809,719 (TÜİK 2017a). According to official statistics, the level of unemployment in Mardin is 20.6 per cent, which is the second highest rate of unemployment across Turkish cities (TÜİK 2017a). Because of this, seasonal rural work is an important source of income for the people of Mardin, including the workers I worked with in this study. Mardin, Mazıdağı – the town – is located in the Mesopotamia region, which, as part of the Fertile Crescent, has gone down in history as the birthplace of settled agriculture. However, for almost a century, the fields that Hatice's house overlooks have lain fallow. The 'emptiness' of those fields and, consequently, the pull of migration to western Turkey, both seasonally and permanently, are seen by some to be a cause of the Kurdish–Turkish conflict and the result of it by others. Although Hatice does not appear to care about whether the conflict is the cause or the consequence of economic deprivation in her region 'anymore' (*in her words*), it still seems absurd to look out of one's window onto the fields of the 'famous fertile Mesopotamia' and talk of travelling 1,500 km for seasonal rural work.

**Map 3.1** The location of Mardin: the hometown of the Kurdish seasonal migrant workers.

I got really angry when they asked us whether there really is no work in our village. They think that we are going in for this torture eagerly. Do they think we are crazy? Why would we want to leave our houses and live in the dirt for months? There is nothing else for us. We could go into cotton but they pay us very little and it's in just two weeks. So, we have to go for this tomato job in the spring. When the weather begins to get warmer, I know that Yahya [her husband] will come one day and say to me, 'get ready, we're going to work'. For me, it is okay, but the children do not want to go. When the weather gets warmer, they become upset because they know that we will leave for work soon. It is getting more difficult now that they are older.[9]

The children do not want to go for seasonal work, as they have to leave school before the term finishes (all educational establishments in Turkey break for summer in June and work on the land starts in April). Although the children of migrant workers can technically complete the school year by temporarily enrolling in schools in the places their families migrate to, this is not always possible because of the discrimination directed towards Kurdish migrant children in schools in western Turkey. Mehmet (twelve) told me his story, leading him to not continue his education when they migrate to the west:

I want to finish school and go to university. But, we have to move when my parents start working in the spring. Because of this, I can't pass the school year [In Turkey, if a student is absent for more than 20 school days, they are unable to pass and are held back a year]. I tried to go to school in Bursa. But, I didn't get on well with the others. They called me a 'terrorist' and 'dirty', and when I said that I was not, they beat me up and trapped me in a wheelie bin [here, Mehmet is to referring heavy-lidded, steel wheelie bins, which are common on the streets of Bursa but in the UK, are more commonly associated with large-scale commercial waste]. I will never go to school in Bursa again.[10]

'When the weather gets warmer, Mehmet becomes extremely withdrawn and introverted because he knows that we will have to move. He does not want to go there, he is afraid. I am also afraid sometimes. Especially, if we don't know where we will be going. In some places, they really hate us. Fortunately, we are going together [implying her husband's extended family and distant relatives]'.[11]

Although there are plenty of options for seasonal rural work in western Turkey, Kurds often want to remain with the same employer over a number of years. Melek reports that this makes them feel safer in a place. On the other hand, although they cannot trust 'strangers', they can migrate, work and live with their familiar and 'trustworthy' relatives. 'All I can ask from God is that we migrate together as a family and work for someone we have worked for before'.[12] Unfortunately, this is not always the case:

Leaving home to become seasonal workers requires a quick decision', says Yaşar [Hatice's husband]. 'You do not have very much time to decide, as the farmers will not wait for you. When they call you, you should directly respond with 'yes' or 'no'. The agreements are mostly made at the end of the season every year. If you're happy with the farmer you already worked for during the year, your *dayıbaşı* has to very quickly promise that you will work for him the following year. As you know, we will not be working for the same family this year,[13] so our *dayıbaşı* [Hatice's husband's brother] will find us a new landowning family because we do not have a prior agreement. That's why he has gone to 'Bursa',[14] he has gone to find a new family for us to work for. When he finds someone, he always calls me and tells me to gather 'our lot' [meaning his extended family members, who always migrate together seasonally] and, if there aren't enough of us for the landowning family, I will ask our distant relatives to come with us, or our relatives' distant relatives. Here, everyone is some kind of relative, you just have to find out how you're related.[15]

Being related in some way is a basic condition for becoming a member of the group. While the *dayıbaşı*'s elder brother tries to reach the numbers of workers the landowning family wants, in the meantime, the *dayıbaşı* waits in the hope that the others will come to work. Last season, whilst we were working on the land, I asked the *dayıbaşı* how he found employers, and he told me that he did so with the recommendation of their previous landowning family. When I asked him how he first established connections with the region's landowning families, he replied that his military service provided the opportunity to meet the first landowning family he worked with. While he was doing his military service in the northern part of Turkey (in Turkey, military service is compulsory for all Turkish male citizens over eighteen years old. However, in some terms, you can pay instead of going to the military), he became close friends with a farmer's son. After they finished their military service, he visited his friend's hometown and worked with him on his father's land. By working on the land, Osman gained the trust of his friend's father, who then asked for Osman's relatives to come to work on his lands. So, Osman initially invited his two brothers to work on the land with him, and they later started to migrate seasonally as an extended family. They worked for his friend's family for six years.

> We called him 'father'. Unfortunately, he died, and his children divided the land between them. Then, they got smaller and did not need us anymore, but because we worked there for many years, now farmers in the region knew us and we knew them. Because of this, it is easier for us to find a job in this region. However, there is no one like him. He treated us just as he would treat his family. Now, the others treat us like we are their slaves. After him, we did not find regular employers, we had a lot of troubles, but still, this region is the place we know the best.[16]

Before Osman established connections in Bursa, the family were migrating to İzmir – Turkey's third biggest city; interestingly, they only began to go to İzmir after Osman's elder brother completed his military service there. Like Osman, he became familiar with the city and later invited his other brothers to join him. As seen, although Osman is not the eldest male member of the family, he arranges their working contracts with employers and this gives him a more privileged position in the decision-making process in the family than his elder brothers. He controls not only his younger sisters' and brothers' labour, but also overall his elder brothers except the eldest. This shows us how managing the public relations of the family – the public face of the family – is one of the main components of (hegemonic) masculinity in rural Turkey (see Table 7.1).

Kurdish women have only entered the migrant labour force later and this is very similar to the literature suggesting that women elsewhere are only able to enter the workforce alongside their male family members (Kabeer 2000; Lessinger 1990; Vera-Sanso 1995). Initially, Osman's family did not migrate seasonally as an extended family; the women and children initially stayed at home whilst the men migrated for seasonal work in tourism, industry or agriculture. 'There were no jobs for our women in those times. All of the "landowners' women" [inverted commas added] were working on the land but now that they are richer, their women do not want to work on the land. But, this is good for us now because we are getting richer' (7 September 2013). If leaving the land and becoming workers in factories or in the service sector are considered to be an indicator of becoming richer (official sources also consider this to be indicative of 'economic development'), then Osman is right. However, people who migrate are more in debt than ever before. Often, these debts are accrued by former smallholder and subsistence farmers selling their land to raise a deposit for mortgaged flats or houses in towns and cities. However, once families have bought houses in these towns and cities, they not only lose their means of subsistence (their farms) but they are also effectively stripped of their land. These people's conditions are explored in greater detail in Chapter 8.

## Chapter 4

## 'WE ARE ALL WOMEN UNTIL MONEY COMES': GENDERED LABOUR RELATIONS IN THE TOMATO PLANTING

I always believe that numbers are cold and distant from named individuals. People cannot cry for Turkey's millions seasonal workers but they can cry for Pınar, just one of them. I am not suggesting that the intention of this book is to make people cry for somebody. Here, I only use the word 'cry' to empathize with someone and I write this with the intention of making readers 'witness' to the women workers' experiences on tomato land. This chapter answers the question of how the agricultural labour process is organized in Turkey, using the example of the production of tomatoes with mostly Kurdish seasonal migrant workers for the Japanese market. In the chapter, we can see what they see and come to understand how the relations of capitalist production, kinship, ethnicity, class, age and gender intertwine in the agricultural labour process of tomato production and how these intersections create masculinities and femininities within the division of labour in tomato production.

The chapter is divided into five sections. Each section is dedicated to different women whose identities reflect their different positions in the organization of production on the land. The first section is 'mine' and covers what I experienced while we are planting tomatoes in terms of our working conditions and the organization of labour. The second section is *Fatma*'s; she is the wife of one of the landowners, a housewife and an unpaid worker on the land for the past twenty-five years. The third section is *Melek*'s; she has been a seasonal worker for the past fifteen years and is married to the *dayıbaşı*. The fourth section is *Hazal*'s; she is fifteen years old; this is her second year of working. The final section reports from *Mefaret*, who is a local Turkish woman who has worked in agriculture for the past forty years.

### *Spring through my eyes: The inequalities of 'female' tomato land*

In the planting season, there were no men but only women on tomato land. This is why I call tomato land during the planting season 'female tomato land'. Men – from the landowners' family – come to the land first, when the women are not there, in order to prepare the land for planting by ploughing breaks up the soil and

**Table 4.1** Tomato-growing stages and gender and ethnic divisions of labour

| Stages of tomato growing | Gender and ethnic division of labour |
| --- | --- |
| Buying tomato seedlings and pesticides | Oldest son (second generation) of Turkish landowning family |
| Preparation of land for planting Ploughing (by tractors) Setting up irrigation pipes | Male members of Turkish landowning family |
| Planting the seedlings | Female members of Turkish landowning family Kurdish women seasonal migrant workers Turkish local women workers |
| Checking and servicing irrigation pipes | Male members of Turkish landowning family |
| Applying pesticides | Male members of Turkish landowning family |
| Tying trusses and pinching out (between planting and picking) | Female members of Turkish landowning family Kurdish women seasonal migrant workers |
| Picking tomatoes | Seasonal Kurdish male and female migrant workers |
| Filling trucks | Seasonal Kurdish male workers |

laying pipes to irrigate the tomatoes (see Table 4.1). Then the women come to the land prepared for planting and they plant continuously all day. The landowners' wives[1] and daughters[2] live, work and spend their time with the Kurdish seasonal migrant workers on the land. Sometimes, local women work on the land too. The landowners' wives work both as workers and as managers. Fatma, the landowner's eldest daughter-in-law, is the manager. Regardless of their seniority, all the women workers must wake up around 6 am. Firstly, they serve breakfast, wash the dishes and prepare lunch for themselves and other family members. This is also applicable to the landowning family's wives and daughters. Despite their wealth, the landowning family do not hire domestic workers. This is because in rural communities, hiring a domestic servant is seen as shirking one's responsibilities and duties as a 'proper woman'. This is why all workers regardless of their social status and wealth wake up at the same time and get ready to go out to the land by 07.15.

The women's different class identities are evident from the very start of the day. The first instance of class divisions manifests itself in transportation. The landowning family's wives and daughters sit in the cabin of the truck, whereas the ordinary workers, including me, sit in the open air at the back of the truck. Most of the time, the truck driver is one of the landowning family's sons. If no one from the landowning family is available to drive, one of the male migrant workers will. As soon as women step onto the land, they start planting, even if they are from the landowning family. During the day, they are unlikely to see or interact with any men unless something urgent happens such as someone falling ill or running out of clean drinking water.

Planting is a monotonous task. First, the women bring boxes of tomato seedlings from the edges of the land, where the men leave them, to where they will be planted. Carrying fresh drinking water and boxes of seedlings is a job usually reserved for younger women or inexperienced women like me. Throughout the day, the women have to plant the seedlings. They do not need to dig holes for the seedlings, as the earth is softened by water that is fed into the soil through pipes. The drip irrigation method pre-softens the soil and makes the process of planting a relatively simple one. None of the women see the process of irrigation or ploughing. As seen in Table 4.1 these are entirely men's jobs, as application of pesticides. Women do not have any knowledge about using pesticides. As these tasks require driving tractors or other special machines (for instance, for applying pesticides), both men and women normalize this gendered division of labour. Existing literature elsewhere on the gender division of labour in using machines has already demonstrated how technology is seen as men's area in both agriculture and manufacturing (Boserup 1970; Cockburn 1983, 1985; Phillips and Taylor 1980).

Turning back to women's work on the land, working in the capitalized rural tomato-planting process is not dissimilar to working on an assembly line, although here neither tomatoes nor lines move. While it is the women who move continuously, there is substitute organization. Tomato work, over time, has become both repetitive and unskilled. Tasks are divided and largely automatic, with no thought required; women are simply responsible for pushing seedlings into the soil all day. The women do not have any knowledge of or control over what they are producing. Before the capitalization of agriculture, the previous year's crops were used to fertilize new seeds. So, workers needed to be able to tell healthy seedlings apart from the unhealthy ones. The introduction of hybrid seeds, however, has meant there are no visible differences between seedlings and hence no difference in planting them. In this way, the women are further alienated from their work: global seed corporations control their planting methods and they have no autonomy over the production process.

Although the process of planting is very similar to assembly line production, unlike in the factory, women working in the fields are able to freely talk to one another. They can gossip or listen to music together more freely. As I noted in my fieldwork diary:

> Today I thought that maybe I can write a headline about planting season: 'We are all women until we are divided by money'. We all enjoy each other's company until one of the landowning family's wives (especially Fatma) comes and warns the women about their slowness or long breaks. I am really not sure whether workers take an advantage of the good atmosphere and slow their work as she claimed or not. I am not sure and probably can't be sure at any time. But I know that breaks became an obsession for both sides and all the bad and good feelings revolve around breaks. All the best and worst moments of the day happen during break time. It is a nightmare for me when landowning's wives and workers start to argue about the start and finish times of breaks because they always ask me to arbitrate. Actually, both can be right at different times. Generally the landowning's wives do not want to give breaks on time, and workers do not want to start working on time. I stopped bringing my watch to the land because I didn't want to take sides in this endless argument. I sometimes think that trying

to have longer break is in the 'nature' of being worker, and making the break shorter is the 'nature' of the being landowning. Anyway, the thing of which I am sure is that when we talk about men, we are more likely to reach consensus. Both the workers and the landowning family's wives like to tell dirty jokes and make sexual innuendoes. These are "universally" enjoyed. When some men come to the land for hoeing, the women say that the day will not be enjoyable because they cannot talk freely when men are on the land. Even though their sisterhood collapses sometimes because of their different classes, they still have very much common ground arising from their gender and I like these moments on the land.[3]

When it is just the women, workers can talk freely and listen to music. These are the enjoyable activities that are permitted during the working day. They can go to the toilet whenever they want, but if they go to toilet in the breaks, they earn the accolade of star worker. Most, however, prefer to go to the toilet in their working time since working on the land is backbreaking work. Going to the toilet is seen as a welcome break. There are however no toilet facilities on the land. Women have to use the edge of another field hidden by brushwood as a toilet.

The tasks on the land are the same for all the women, but there are slight differences in responsibilities based on social status. If they belong to a landowning family, they will have the dual role of worker and manager. They have to keep other women under control to guarantee that they 'deserve' what they earn. 'Deserving what you earn' is very subjective. Because of this, different women from the landowning family have different attitudes towards controlling workers.

In the following section, I will introduce Fatma. She is the wife of the eldest son of the landowning's family and is known for being the strictest and most controlling landowner/worker.

### Through the eyes of the employer:
### 'The obsession with controlling young workers'

'When Fatma does not come to work, I feel more comfortable. She is always watching me, so I panic when she is with us.'

(Pınar, 5 May 2013)

Fatma's controlling behaviour towards Pınar is because Pınar is the youngest worker (14). Even though Pınar takes shorter breaks and tries to work faster than the others, Fatma always shouts at her. As Fatma explains to me, her problem is not with Pınar personally but with her father and the *dayıbaşı*. The landowning family do not want to employ workers younger than sixteen because they are not capable of long toil and heavy manual labour. Fatma says that they do not want to pay child workers the same wages as adult workers. She says that landowning family told the *dayıbaşı* that they did not want young workers on the land but the *dayıbaşı* brought young workers in anyway. Fatma further explains that the *dayıbaşı* threatens to break up the work groups if the landowning family do not agree to pay younger workers at the same rate as adults. In the planting season, there are about fifteen of us working on the land. Of the fifteen of us, five workers are under the age of sixteen. Fatma told me that the *dayıbaşı* and his workers threatened to stop work if they did not agree to hiring children and that the landowning family were forced to capitulate because of how difficult it is to find thirty boarding workers once the season has begun. Fatma explained that situations such as this arise every year.

Studies on global commodity chains argue that global production leads to improved regional and local development outcomes (Barrientos and Kritzinger 2004; Selwyn 2012). Selwyn (2012) demonstrates that this has been achieved through improved working conditions won through the actions of organized labour. In Brazil, the Rural Union of Brazil (STR) has successfully improved working conditions. In Turkey, there is no effective rural union. However, workers often find their ways to cope with relations of capitalist production and create their own 'organised unions': their families. They act collectively under the leadership of the *dayıbaşı* and can threaten the landowning family with wildcat strikes and work stoppage. Membership of these unofficial unions is compulsory rather than voluntary.

Fatma says that she feels pity for those young girls who are made to work by their families. Her perception of coerced labour is in part true, as Pınar told me that if she had a choice, she would not work. Fatma's attitude to Pınar was contradictory; sometimes she shouted a lot, but I have also seen Fatma in tears after shouting at Pınar. She said that she knows that mistreating the young girls is a sin but that she is in a situation where she must ensure production output by controlling workers but is powerless to prevent the use of child labour. Fatma explained that she could not simply put an end to their employment by talking to either *dayıbaşı* or the girls' families. She says that this is because if she raised the issue, the workers would threaten to down tools and would leave the land altogether.

The landowning family are also angry because they claim that although the *dayıbaşı* brings young workers to the land in planting season, he does not in picking season. Fatma and other members of the landowning family argue that this is because they know that during picking season, when wages are paid based on group performance, young workers will not be able to 'pull their weight'. During the picking season, young workers stay at home to take care of the younger children. Fatma told me:

> I guess that you will write something about me and my harsh attitudes towards the younger ones, so please say that we are losing 175 TL (around £45 – at the time of the study) every day because of the young workers and 175TL is the same cost as a box of tomato seedlings. And, say that I am more concerned about them than their families are.[4]

Fatma's perplexing reactions regarding Pınar mirror the conflicting relations of capitalist production and these are reflected in my fieldwork diary as follows:

> Honestly, I want to become angry with someone; I want to become angry with Fatma or the girls' parents, but when I talk to them, I find myself empathising

with them. I am not angry with their families because I know that they need their girls to work because they need money. I have learned from the land that it is almost impossible to blame one side. They all have their reasons to blame others. I am not sure whether I can say that the structure causes both sides to behave unethically or not. I do not want to underestimate people by saying that the system is to blame but the situation reminds me of Adorno's saying that 'the wrong life cannot be lived rightly'. In my mind, the structure is the 'wrong' one, and the 'people' are very limited in their means to live 'rightly' in this structure.[5]

When I hear Fatma's remonstrance about what she sees as workers' attitudes towards the landowning family, it is difficult to say that she is wrong:

They [the workers] do not understand that earning money is difficult for us as well. I am working here just like them, we do the same job, my children do the same job with their children, and my husband does the same job with their husbands. When they see the large lands, they automatically think that we are rich; they are not aware of how much we have to pay for seeds, land, gas, irrigation and workers. They only think that I am a happier woman than they are since my husband is richer than their husbands. They do not know that I have to live with my husband's siblings to survive. Otherwise, we get smaller by sharing what we have, and we can't cope with the factories. They do not think that we have financial problems too. Recently, Sinan [their neighbour in the village] killed himself because of bankruptcy. Many of our neighbours have already migrated to towns. Workers only think that they earn less and ignore that we do not earn much either. They do not see that we do the same work as them under the same conditions. My position is worse than them since I am also responsible for the quality of work, if these do not grow well because of bad planting, my husband will blame me for not controlling the work and for cooperating with workers rather than him. Also, if our employees work slowly, I am again responsible for this and directly lose money by having to extend the amount of time worked. I have to do something to speed up their work.[6]

The landowning family consists of two brothers' and their sons' nuclear families (see Diagram 7.1). The wives of all of these sons work on the land in the planting season, but none of them behave like Fatma. All of them agree with Fatma's thinking about workers and work, but their reactions are very different. They all have different reasons for behaving differently towards the workers. For example, Nezahat is the workers' favourite among women from the landowning family. Her husband's family employed her as a seasonal migrant worker some years ago, and this is how she met her husband, Recai. Although they come from different economic backgrounds, their marriage was not shocking news for anyone in the village they lived in or possibly around the region. They are both 'peasants' and 'Turkish', and in rural western Turkey it is more acceptable for a woman to marry someone from a higher socio-economic background than it is for a man[7]. Nezahat explains her reason for being a 'nice boss' to me:

Before I married Recai, I was one of the seasonal workers on 'his' land.[8] So, I know what workers think about their lives because I thought like them. I thought that if I can marry him, I can save my life but as you see nothing has changed for me, I am still a worker on land, but it belongs to us. I hope that my children will not have to work on the land. I know that they [the workers] think that our life is perfect, and that we are lucky because we are richer than they are. I am not angry with them because I know that that's how it looks from the outside.[9]

Not only is Nezahat the workers' favourite, but Fatma has problems with her because she thinks that Nezahat is always on the side of workers. 'Nezahat cannot understand me because she still thinks and acts like one of the workers'.[10] I am not sure if Nezahat understands Fatma's concerns. Although she understands what Fatma worries about, she does not think in the same way as Fatma. Nezahat understands the *meaning* of work better than Fatma does. On the other hand, Fatma thinks that Nezahat is as lazy and as slow as the workers. Even though both workers and landowning family see Nezahat as being on the workers' side, I do not think that Nezahat is totally on the side of either the landowning family or the workers. For the women I worked with, not strictly controlling the workers automatically puts Nezahat on the workers' side. From my point of view, she is the only one from the landowning family who shows concern for both groups. Maybe, the position of the *dayıbaşı*'s wife, Melek, can be likened to Nezahat's position.

## Through the eyes of the 'middle woman': 'No one likes me'

Melek is twenty-eight years old, the wife of the *dayıbaşı* and mother to four daughters. She has a similar position to the forewoman in the factory in that she is not only a worker but also a manager. Her job is called a *çavuş* (sergeant); this is similar to the way in which ranks are assigned in the factory. On the land, however, unlike in the factory, workers call Melek by her name. She was five months pregnant in the planting season. Although she does the same work as other workers, she is paid twice as much as the other workers because she is the *dayıbaşı*'s wife. She has known the landowning family for three years; her husband has brought a different group of workers for three years to the same land. Her biggest problem is not having a son, and her greatest hope is that her current pregnancy will result in one. If she does not have a son, her husband will have the 'right' to take another wife.[11]

Her situation was very perplexing for me since I am totally against the idea of preferring boy children, but I have found myself hoping that Melek has a boy. This confusion persists in my interactions with Melek and it is not only tied to the sex of her child but also with her attitudes towards her work and the workers. Melek means 'Angel' in Turkish but most of the workers call her a 'devil' because they say that she is always on the side of the landowning family. Seeing Melek on the land, I am forced to agree. For instance, it is Melek's responsibility to announce the start of break time but she shortens breaks by delaying her announcements. She also shouts at workers when the landowning family complain about them. Despite this kind of behaviour, the daughters-in-law of the landowning family are still not happy with her. They think that her attitude towards the workers is too soft.

Melek told me that unless she behaves in this way, none of the workers will be able to work on the land the following year. She says that they will not even be able to return to the same region because then they will be perceived as lazy. She said to me:

> If I am on 'our' [the workers'] side, we will all lose our jobs for next year. They [the landowning family] will not call us next year, and they also will complain to all of their neighbours [other landowning families], saying that we are not working fast enough. This bad reputation even affects people from our hometown. They will say that people from Mazıdağı [where they come from] do not work properly. It is always like this.[12]

Awarding or punishing workers collectively is a very common way of managing labour, especially when it is constructed through localistic or familial networks (Dedeoğlu 2010, 2012; Ecevit 1991; Erdogan 2016; Lee 1998; Kabeer 2000; White 2004). Kabeer demonstrates how factories in Bangladesh manage women by comparing them with each other with reference to their neighbourhood. These studies also show that being a good worker depends on not agitating for your 'own' rights such as breaks or starting and finishing work on time. The same applies on tomato land. I have heard lots of conversations in the village about the definition of a good worker. It mostly includes obeying the wishes of the landowning family. For example, one of the women from the local village whose family also employs seasonal workers came to me and said 'make your research about our workers. This year we have perfect workers. They start work at 7.00, and they do not stop until we want them to'.[13] Where I worked, the landowning family thought that 'Melek' spoiled her workers because she followed exact start and finish times. On the other hand, the workers said that she does not follow exact start and end times; they always start early and finish late. Apparently, Melek mostly overlooks the agreed finishing time in favour of the landowning family but she did not do this because she was a 'devil', but because she tries to be an 'angel' for the others in the long term.

## *Through the eyes of a Kurdish seasonal worker*

Hazal, who is fifteen years old, is Pınar's aunt. Pınar's father is married to Hazal's elder sister. Hazal comes to land with her three brothers. She hates Fatma and Melek because of their attitudes towards Pınar. Although Hazal is Pınar's aunt, their relationship is more like one between two sisters. Hazal always works on the next row to Pınar, and they are the slowest, so Fatma and Melek always send me to help them finish their line. Pınar and Hazal like me because I help them. I can see that they are struggling to keep working all day. Hazal is ten years younger than I am. Although this is clear to see from our faces, if you were to compare our hands, it would be easy to think that Hazal was many years my senior. Working on the land is very strenuous, particularly for someone who is fifteen. Hazal, however, told me that she is not that young. She explained that she started working on the land two years ago and that she once found the work a lot more difficult. She also told me that working on the land is sometimes more enjoyable than staying at home. She has said that the most enjoyable part of the work, apart from talking with Pınar, is having a chance to socialize with other women and compete with them. For me, the competition between workers is one of the most irritating things at the work because Fatma uses competition to cheat and manipulate the youngest workers into working faster. Fatma says she will give a reward to the fastest worker; she says that she will reward them with an ice cream, a Coca-Cola or permission to finish work ten minutes early but this never actually happens. Hazal works really hard to win rewards and she often 'wins', but ultimately, she is never able to claim her rewards. Even when she wins the 'reward' of stopping early, Fatma creates a new job for her such as burning empty seedling boxes. I find this really upsetting. It is depressing to see a 'child' deprived of the ice cream has worked so hard to earn. Fortunately, Hazal is also aware that 'Fatma' cheats them by offering false promises, and she told me 'I know that she will not buy me ice-cream, but I can motivate myself by making myself think that I'm going to win something at the end of it'.[14] Ice cream is not the only thing to ease the work for her; the gang master, 'Osman', is also another reason for her to come to the land.

Osman, the *dayıbaşı*, does not work with the women during planting season, but he comes to the land to see whether everything is all right. The *dayıbaşı*'s visits are the only time when fellow workers from the landowning family are not the only ones to evaluate the seasonal workers' output. When he comes to inspect the workers, the *dayıbaşı* always comes to Hazal's side first instead of coming to his wife, Melek's side. When I realized this, I could not believe it since although I know that there is a possibility of Hazal being taken as a second wife, I did not imagine it actually happening. Now I see how Osman's attention makes Hazal happier and how it makes Melek more desperate. Being someone's second wife is not common among women from the landowning family, whereas this is seen as an active possibility for Kurdish women. Fatma has not missed this opportunity to use this 'delineation' between Kurdish and Turkish women as a means of exercising control over Hazal's work by trying to irritate her:

> Today, I was upset. Fatma was angry with Hazal because she is always at the back when we are planting. She is really slow, and Fatma told her 'Pray that your father doesn't give you away as a second wife. The other wife will kill you because you are so incompetent. While she said this, she looked at 'Melek' (she did so directly since everyone knows what Osman thinks). I couldn't believe how cruel Fatma is. How can she pick on a fifteen-year-old girl in this way? But, fortunately, Hazal only smiles since she views this as an opportunity. I know that Fatma said this just to hurt Hazal because Fatma views Hazal becoming a second wife in the same way that I do. The women in the landowning family always make jokes about how Kurdish women's husbands or fathers marry more than one woman. I could not imagine what would happen if Osman flirted with Fatma's

daughter, who is only three years older than Hazal. There would be no possibility for the workers to make fun of it. You simply cannot make fun of women in the landowning family.[15]

Hazal appeared to be happy with Osman being interested in her since she thinks that he is a good option for her to marry.[16] She told me: 'He likes me, and I don't have any chance to marry someone I like [she already likes someone but her family are totally against this relationship]. So, he is a real option for me, he owns land in his hometown, and he does not have any sons'.[17] I did not say anything since I felt that she would know what I would say and do in her position. We, however, live in entirely different worlds; they are even not parallels or opposites; they are on different planets.

### Through the eyes of a 'resentful' local worker

Mefaret is a fifty-eight-year-old, ethnically Turkish and is one of the most 'resentful' workers on the land. She has been working in the same village for as long as she can remember. Now at the age of fifty-eight the landowning family, her neighbours, do not offer her a job but prefer Kurdish seasonal workers.

This is how she perceives the transformation process in Turkish agriculture, and this is why she is 'resentful' towards the village landowning family:

> In old times, they would come to us and offer us work. Now we want to work but they have Kurdish workers for a whole season. They just call us when they need extra workers in planting season. In the picking season, it's only Kurds who work on the land so there are no jobs for us. If I were younger, I would work in the factory, but now, I am much too old to work in the factory.[18]

She is not the only one who feels let down by the landowning family. During my two years of fieldwork, I often had the opportunity to talk to local village women both in the day and in the evenings. Although local women feel betrayed because the local landowning family choose to employ Kurdish workers, they do not show their dissatisfaction to the landowning family, only to the migrant Kurdish workers. Local workers believe that if Kurds would not accept working in those conditions – group performance–based payment, long working hours, living in shacks – they could continue to work on the land as before. As a result of this belief, local women do not have any reservations about expressing their anger towards Kurdish migrant workers on the land.

The landowning family employ local women during the planting season but this is usually for less than half of the planting season, when there are concerns about ensuring that the seeds are planted before heavy rain. These women come from the nearest villages or the nearby town. The women who come from the nearest town are usually recent migrants from nearby villages who move to access job opportunities or for their children's education.[19] Mefaret is the unofficial and aggressive leader of this group. She has a good relationship with the women in the landowning family, especially with Fatma, and she does not have any hesitation about acting like a member of the landowning family in terms of managing the workers. She continuously criticizes Kurdish women workers and complains to Fatma about them not 'working properly'. In my diary, I wrote:

> Today when I saw Mefaret on the shuttle in the morning, I became anxious. This is because I know that whenever she's on the land, the day does not pass smoothly. She always bullies Kurdish workers, especially the younger ones. She starts quarrels with the Kurdish workers and with the landowning family's wives. Unfortunately, she didn't surprise me today. After an hour of working, she asked me to give her water. And when I went to her, she whispered to me 'look at their lines' [she pointed to the Kurdish workers' lines and said that they had not been weeded properly] and look at my daughters' lines [she pointed to the work of the local Turkish women]. Honestly, I could not see any difference between the different lines of seedlings but she insisted she was right and she began to tell them off. Fortunately, the Kurdish women did not seem to take her seriously and they did not respond to her. Mefaret did not react well to being ignored and she complained to Fatma about the women not working properly. Fatma called Mefaret 'abla' [older sister][20], she took her complaints seriously and began shouting at the Kurdish women. Melek could not remain silent and she said to Fatma that the women had been working in the same way that they usually do. Melek then said that Mefaret was looking for a fight. When she said this, Mefaret began to shout at Melek. She shouted: 'they [the Kurdish women] know how to fight better than everyone ... you're terrorists', she said. Mefaret's words reflect the hegemonic discourse surrounding the Turkish-Kurdish conflict that labels Kurds as 'terrorists' because of their possible support of the PKK. I could not believe how she could develop such a tenuous link, especially when we were all on the land together planting tomatoes. Nobody else seemed surprised by the seemingly ridiculous link that Mefaret made. Melek's response was also unexpected; she said 'you are the real terrorists, you are real murderers'. When she said this, all of the women were shouting at each other in a matter of seconds. Fatma panicked and raised her voice. 'That's enough; I don't want to hear anymore politics!' Maşallah [Praise be!], you are worse than men talking about politics. If they hear you, they will divorce you!' This was enough for women to stop fighting. I was relieved that Fatma put an end to the fighting. Despite this, I was hurt by the way she put an end to the fight, by implying that women should not be talking about politics. I think that most of the women felt guilty and ashamed for talking about politics like 'men'. I am not even sure if women were talking about 'politics', they were talking about the prejudices of both groups, but is that 'politics' in and of itself? Nevertheless, Fatma clearly knows how to control the women. First, she compares them to each other, and if this does not work, she compares them with men and accuses them of being like 'men'.[21]

Fatma uses 'emphasized femininity' (Connell 1987) as a management tool. Through reminding women that the realm of politics does not belong to them, she indirectly accuses the women of not behaving according to the 'rules' of being a 'proper' woman. This accusation is sufficient to put an end to the women's argument. This form of management, however, is not enough to quell Mefaret's anger about being forced into precarious, intermittent work. Furthermore, it is not enough to prevent Mefaret from attacking her rivals on the land. She saw working on the land as a chance to attack to Kurdish women, who have stolen her job. As she says:

> When I come to land, I am trying to show the landowning family how these women [Kurdish] are not as good as us. Just think, if there were enough work in their hometown, they would not come here. They do not know how to work on the land [in saying this, she is implying that if the Kurdish women knew how to work on the land, they would not need to migrate in the first place]. They might know about taking care of animals, since they have them in their homes, but working on the lands is our job. And, look they are too young and so not strong enough. 'Our lot' [implying the landowning family] also know that we are better workers than the Kurds. But they do not want to pay us more. I am okay with working in planting since it is 8 hours of work and daily pay, but how I can keep picking all day? These Kurds came here, and they reduce the prices. They even accept less than the minimum wage just to steal our jobs.[22]

The tomato land is not only a battlefield for Mefaret to prove her superiority in terms of being a 'good' worker, but also for other local workers. After one of the days we worked together on the land, I saw some of the local workers at an evening community occasion – *akşam oturması*[23] – and the locals told me that I was very lucky to have seen the local 'Turkish' people working and that because of this, I had seen and understood what is meant by 'proper' work. I tried to release the tension in the atmosphere by saying that there were very few differences between the two groups. I also said that some Kurdish women and some landowning family claim that Kurdish workers plant even faster than local workers. The locals at the community meeting laughed nervously when I said this and replied that because I am educated I do not really understand agricultural work.

This attitude of local women makes controlling the workers a more difficult task for the women in the landowning family. Fatma complained to me about how she gets more tired when there are also local workers on the land. She told me that she knows that local women usually create the problem, but she could not interfere. This is because she knows many of the local workers personally and they need the local workers for when the Kurdish seasonal workers return to their hometowns.

> We need 'our lot' in the late autumn Kurdish workers will return their homes, and we will need to harvest olives and at that point, we will only have the local women. I have to make peace with both groups of women. I do not take either the Kurdish or the local women seriously; I respond to both groups with jokes.

But, you cannot imagine how I am exhausted I get when we have to deal with having both the Kurds and 'our lot' on the land.[24]

By referring to the local workers as 'our lot', Fatma implicitly shows why Mefaret shows little hesitation when she attempts to control the Kurdish workers. Fatma and other members of the landowning family rarely point out this form of discrimination. Their ethnicity as well as their shared locality leads them to see each other as being in the same group when they have Kurdish workers on the land. Despite this, the landowning family's desire to make more profit ignores their 'similarity' and leaves the local women behind when the summer comes.

## Chapter 5

## WITHOUT KURDISH FAMILIES THERE WILL BE NO TURKISH AGRICULTURE: FAMILIAL LABOUR RELATIONS IN THE TOMATO PICKING

This is a bloody job. Everyone knows this and calls it a 'bloody job.' Look, don't you think that this land seems blood stained? (Gangmaster, 5 September 2013)

This chapter reveals the social relations underpinning what workers call the 'bloody' story of tomato picking. Workers use this metaphor to link the colour of tomatoes to the difficulty of the job. In this sense, it is not surprising that the landowning family's wives and daughters as well as local workers have left the 'bloody land' in the picking season, whilst the Kurdish migrant workers have remained. Since the planting season Kurdish women continued to work on different products, such as watermelons, melons, onions or peppers, with women from the landowning family while the tomatoes were growing. None of those products are produced for the factory but rather for national market consumption and so these products are not planted to make a profit per se, but to not waste time whilst they wait for the tomatoes. The same Kurdish women who were working on the land in the planting season work in the picking season, except for Melek[1] and the young labourers, who rarely work during picking season. Some of the Kurdish women will have continued to work on the tomato land doing tasks like pinching out excess growth while waiting for the picking season. At picking time, Kurdish men who had been working on different tasks such as ploughing or hoeing for the same landowning family join the women on the land. Since tomato land offers more money in the picking season because of the group-based payment system, more men come to the land and some women are sent back home to do domestic tasks.

The absence on the land of any members of the landowning family managing the labour process during the harvest means that the analysis of the picking process provides a very vital insight into the nature of capitalist production; it illustrates the way in which capitalist production generates control, deskilling and creating new hierarchies of power among workers themselves. On this basis, the impact of the production process on workers' autonomy and consent, as well as on the intersections of this with workers' 'external' consciousness including gender, ethnicity and age becomes evident. In the following, before listening to the workers' voices, I will once again set the scene by beginning with my perceptions of the land. Then, we will look at workers' various experiences during the harvest and the four different tasks assigned to them depending on their gender, age and position in the familial hierarchy.

## To my eyes: 'We are all factory workers'

The working day on the tomato land mostly begins with complaining about the factory's purchasing decisions. The ones who complain could be either workers or members of the landowning family, as in the following case:

> If you consider me a boss, you are mistaken. I am only like a worker in the factory. They play with us. They decide everything; price, amount, quality. You do not know how we have to give bribes to the factory workers [workers in the quality control section] to say that our tomatoes are of good quality. You don't know how we have to give bribes to purchase managers to give us more tractors when prices are high [when they sell in the open market and not to contract farmers]. What do I do? I just do what the factory tells me to do. And, they say different things every day. I wait until midnight to give them the tomatoes that the workers pick during the day. The factory doesn't take tomatoes as soon as they are picked but only once they have started to shrink from the heat. Then their weight decreases, and they pay me less. When I tell workers the weight of the day, they get very excited because they think that they have picked more than the factory has asked them to. It is true they always pick more than the factory ask for. But, what can I do? I will show them the invoice, but they continue to blame me.[2]

What Recep, member of the landowning family, said draws a clear parallel with what Fatma said about the planting season. When talking about controlling the workers, Fatma argued that in reality, the necessity to control workers is not out of her own choice but out of the obligation that she owes to her husband for the quality of the planting: she is trapped between the workers and her husband. However, the workers do not believe either Fatma or Recep. They do not see the factory workers in the quality-control section or the commissioners, who decide when, at what time and what amount of tomatoes the factory should take on that day, based on their appraisal of production across the region. However, these commissioners only have contact with the landowning family, who call the *dayıbaşı* in the late morning and tell them how many tractors the workers should fill for that day. They are mostly not happy with the amount since they would like to pick as much as possible, because of their desire to work for another landowning family for a higher price at the end of the season. Towards the end of the season, there is sometimes work available with other smaller landowning families who mostly sell their tomatoes on the open market. Kurdish migrant workers are often able to work for them for higher wages as they are employed by the day (even if they remain on the group performance–based wage system).

There is an unceasing tension between the workers and landowning family over the number of tractors. Workers think that the landowning family has the power to increase the number of tractors available to them. There is also the tension caused by the employment of casual workers later in the season. The landowning family employs casual workers when prices on the open market are high. In doing so, the landowning family try to cheat the factory because the factory does not want to accept fixed-priced tomatoes from contract farms until late in the season when the tomatoes have begun to shrink. I will talk more about the disputes between the factory, landowning family and workers in the next section. Here, however, I want to focus on how the group performance–based payment system structures the labour process of tomato picking.

In the literature, a performance-based payment system, as in a factory, is referred to as a 'piece work payment system' (Burawoy 1979; Glucksmann 1982; Pollert 1981). Burawoy (1979) highlights that the piece-rate payment system is used as a generator of consent. On the land, workers are paid depending on the amount they pick, the only difference is that workers picking the tomatoes share what they earn as a group. For example, when workers pick fifteen tons of tomatoes in a day, they earn 4,500 TL (almost £1,000 pound at the time of the study), shared between around thirty people. However, rural workers do not see who they are cooperating with or who they think that they are cooperating with as did the factory workers Burawoy studied. Instead, they are proud of resisting the landowning family. In this case, it is difficult to identify the 'capitalist'. Even when we think of who makes the most profit, it is still vague. As every social actor of the tomato production and processing chain claims that the ones above them make the profit. Workers on the land identify the landowning family as the 'capitalists', whereas the landowning family point towards the factory and the factory points towards the Japanese company. Here, there is only one reality. The reality is that; everyone in each subsequent step of the chain claims greater profits than those who work beneath themselves. The only ones who lose out are the workers on the lands as they are at the very bottom of the chain. For the workers on the land, the farmers are definitely the representatives of capital. The landowning family own the land and employ the workers but they do not have control over the direction of their production process. Instead, they take orders from the factory and they also think that they work for the factory. The requirements of the factory manage the process, but these requirements are invisible to the workers. Here, I want to draw a parallel between the positions of farmers in tomato production and mothers-in-law in the reproduction of rural Kurdish family. The reproduction of a rural Kurdish family will be discussed in greater detail in Chapter 7. The way in which the workers are controlled is very similar to the ways in which daughters-in-law are controlled.

In rural extended patriarchal families, older men determine the rules of social reproduction in Kurdish households, but as the mother-in-law is the main implementer of decisions, disputes between the mother-in-law and the daughter-in-law are highly visible, whereas conflicts between the father-in-law and the daughter-in-law, for example, are rendered invisible. Here, the Kurdish workers do not have any chance to be promoted to the position of a member of the landowning family. For the Kurdish workers on the land, they neither own land nor have opportunity to own land. This is not only because of their financial circumstances but also, crucially, because of their ethnicity. Yahya, the eldest men of the workers' family and *dayıbaşı*'s brother, told me how they wanted to buy a very old house and move to the region as an extended family. However, Yahya's offer on a house was rejected because the local villagers would not let the homeowner sell to a Kurdish family. Unsurprisingly, Kurdish workers are not eager to cooperate with farmers in a way that differs to the way in which daughters-in-law cooperate with mothers-in-law in rural Kurdish households. Therefore, the tomato land becomes a scene for conflicts between workers and farmers. Here, the workers do not cooperate with the farmers but indirectly cooperate with the factory.

> Today, Recai (one of the landowning family) said to me 'I am happy that you came back. Now, you will understand how workers do no not have any dignity. You saw in the planting season how they tire easily, how they work slowly and how they took long breaks. Look now, they are working like bees. They are even arguing with each other because some of them are slow'. I couldn't say anything to prove that he is wrong because he was not. Workers work differently now; they do not stop, they do not eat or go to the toilet. I could only say that money that they have been paid on the land is the undignified one, not them. But, I am not sure how I can separate them from what they want to have. The only thing I am sure of is that they are not less dignified than the landowning family, or me or any other person who lives in an undignified world.[3]

I use the word 'undignified' in relation to the workings of capitalism. However, for both farmers and Kurdish workers, this is also used to refer to ethnicity. The landowning families are sure that Kurds work harder in the picking season – when they work under a piece rate system – than in the planting season, because they are 'Kurdish'. They believe that the migrant workers are 'undignified' because of their Kurdishness. Kurdish seasonal workers are also sure that the landowning family tries to reduce their earnings by employing extra Turkish workers in the picking season. Turkish workers, moreover, are ungrateful for the labour of Kurdish workers. The Turkish workers and they see it picking the tomatoes as their own right to pick the tomatoes, not only because they were the ones to plant them in the first place, but also because they see it as their 'right' on the basis of their 'Turkishness'. How both groups blame each other is very similar to how local women workers and Kurdish women workers attack each other when work-related arguments quickly descend into racism (this was seen in the previous chapter). Kurds blame Turks for being 'cruel' and Turks accuse Kurds of being 'terrorists'. When they cannot see the enemy, they create an enemy. The enemy emerges from their 'different ethnicity' since it is the most visible difference between them, so they do not hesitate to attack each other over their 'ethnicity'. Indeed, the factory prevents any possible collaboration between the landowning family and the workers by acting as the 'invisible hand' in the labour process. In this way, both the workers and the landowning family try to break each other's hands rather than breaking the invisible hand. On the other hand, when members of the landowning family are not present on the land, as they absent during the harvest, a new 'enemy' division appears among Kurdish workers and their solidarity shatters. At this point, divisions based on age and gender become more visible and these categories lead to the creation of new 'enemies'.

## 'The oldest couple on the land': Managing workers from your family

When I went to the land for the picking season, I felt as if I was attending a training programme entitled 'the most effective way to create a capitalist in a day' because of the piece rate payment system. The way we earn money determines who we are. Capitalist tomato production reduces both farmers' and workers' earnings in order to increase profits and consequently, both farmers and workers try to increase what they earn. Unsurprisingly, this sometimes means that they scramble to gain what they can from each other. In trying to get what they can from the 'opposing' camp, workers are powerless, as they do not hold the means of production. Workers pick more tomatoes than they are supposed to. They use tomatoes to make tomato paste for both household consumption and to sell within their community. Workers are comfortable with what they do when they claim the fruits of their labour, as they think that the amount the landowning family gives them is not fair or commensurate with the amount of tomatoes they have produced. In this way, they try to redress the unequal distribution of production outputs in their own way by taking tomatoes from the field when they pick and by feeding the demand for tomato paste in their own community. For the working class, buying pre-made tomato sauce from the supermarket shelves is far too expensive. The same applies to tomato paste made at home from fresh tomatoes bought at the local markets, as there are significant costs involved (in terms of gas and electricity) in cooking and processing the tomatoes. So, workers sell tomato sauce, paste and purée that they have made using the tomatoes they have gotten from the *köylü pazarı* – 'peasant market'[4] – in the town, the village they work in or when they go back to their hometown.

Selling tomato purée is not their only strategy to 'take their labour back'; workers also manoeuvre to eject casual workers – who the landowning family try to employ outside of the group in order to sell as many tomatoes as possible before they over-ripen and decrease in weight – by threatening to go on wildcat strikes. Apart from these attempts to protect or increase their earnings or to increase them, capitalist tomato production causes them to compete with each other. This limits intra-group solidarity and causes workers to turn against each other. Here, I will elaborate on the above arguments by examining the way in which the oldest couple on the land navigate the division of labour, divisions between workers and divisions between the different actors involved in the production process.

My anger and disappointment about the piece rate payment system are not reflected in the workers' response. In contrast, the piece rate payment system is a key innovation of capitalism as it causes workers themselves to become capitalists and thereby limits resistance and abjures solidarism. It is evident that the piece rate payment system 'alienates everyone from everyone, everyone from everything and everything from everyone'.[5] Workers state that they come for this bloody job because they are paid by the piece and that is how they can earn money. Although this payment system makes them happy, as they are earning money, it also makes them dissatisfied with each other, as it seems that they reduce each other's earning capacity. Workers working on Recep's tomato land are first alienated from each other; the *dayıbaşı*'s extended family is alienated from his distant relatives. Then, they are divided again between nuclear families. They continue to be separated from each other within the nuclear families: 'Your sister or father cannot work like you. But you all earn the same'.[6] When your earnings are dependent on your group's performance rather than yourself, solidarity becomes impossible. Here, the payment system itself manages the labour process; there is no need for a controller, because all workers drive each other to work harder and faster. As Kadriye told me: 'Of course the landowning family leaves us alone to work on the land, they know just how much we need the money'.[7]

However, everyone's 'needs' have different limits. For example, Memdullah (male worker, twenty-three) left the land because of the heavy workload. He explained that the work on the land prevented them from *living* so he resisted by walking out on the job. He explained that sometimes it is vitally important to stop and rest but that some of the workers on tomato land do not stop, not even for a second. Speaking of workers in the *dayıbaşı*'s family, he said: 'What we do to our bodies on these lands is a sin. God entrusts our bodies to us, we should not use them for money in this way. These people are just greedy' (16 August 2014). In stark contrast to this, other workers who want to work harder claim that slower workers who take regular breaks commit the sin of laziness. They claim that slower workers unfairly gain from the work of others, that they are scroungers and that God does not like lazy people. It appears that sin is ever present in the fields of tomato land. The presence of such 'sinful acts', however, does not stop the workers from fighting. Only Yahya seems able to put an end to fights. He is the oldest male worker (forty-eight) and the *dayıbaşı*'s eldest brother. The *dayıbaşı* is the one who makes arrangements with the landowning families – the public face of the family – however Yahya, as the oldest member of the family, is the one who makes arrangements during the work: inside the family. Apparently, he wholeheartedly embraces tomato work.

> Today, I was surprised when Yahya shouted at the landlord about the tomatoes. He said: 'We plant, we pick. What do you do? You have the lands and seeds[8], but we are the ones who do the job. If we don't work, there will be no children' – by children he refers to the tomatoes. This metaphor makes me laugh just like the other workers. It is very exciting to hear how he views the relations of production. In Turkish slang, people refer to having sex as 'doing the job' and conception is often referred to using the metaphor of women as the earth into which the male seed is planted. So, when Yahya said that without the workers there would be no children, it seems that he is very aware of the vitality of their work.[9]

Yahya is the effective leader of the group for three reasons: firstly, because of his knowledge of how work is conditioned by the relations of production; secondly, because he argues with the landowning family on the phone over the amount of tomatoes that they will pick for the day; thirdly, because he initiates and maintains the principles of a system of 'scientific management'. Here, I do not refer to the actual meaning of the concept of 'scientific management'; rather, I am using this analogy to highlight the irony of calling the very human process of management 'scientific' management.

The actual concept of 'scientific management', also known as 'Taylorism', has been defined as an attempt to separate mental and manual labour by increasing segmentation in the division of labour and thereby deskilling work (Thompson 1989). In large-scale tomato production, global agribusinesses accomplish the elimination of mental labour by removing farmers' responsibility for producing seeds. No one who works on the land thinks about the 'well-being' of the tomatoes anymore; they only focus on their own personal well-being. In this instance, Yahya's main concern is not the division between manual and mental labour, but how best to focus on output efficiency through the application of Taylorist principles. Braverman (1974) in his influential analysis of *Labour and Monopoly Capital* suggests that this segmentation allows for the increasing of the control of the employer over the labour process by the employer, which in turn leads to more reliable output expectations. Although Yahya or other workers are not the employers, because of the piecework payment system, they embrace the work as their own and are thereby transformed into 'capitalists'. They begin to see the world through employers' eyes; they are selling their labour. In this sense, the workers do not have any qualms about ceding their limited control over the labour process to Yahya who, as the eldest male, is assumed to know what is best or pretends to know what is best to guarantee more output. Yahya applies the same method as industrial scientists, sociologists or managers (Braverman 1974) to reach the efficient organization of labour process, and so he divides tasks and task allocation by matching skills to equipment. He makes assumptions about skills depending on gender and age. This creates a division of labour based on age and gender. By dividing labour, he, as is to be expected, increases his control over labour.

According to Braverman (1974), workers are deskilled as a result of the division of labour. His work focuses on the deskilling of labour in the transition from craft and cottage industries to large-scale Fordist and Taylorist manufacturing industries. This does not fully translate into the realm of agricultural production. In the case of tomato picking, because the work is already deskilled, the division of labour 'de-skills' on the basis of age and gender – by defining some tasks as women's tasks and others as the tasks of the young. Women do not carry sacks as this is seen as a man's job and older women do not carry empty sacks, as this is a young woman's job.

Even before Yahya implements a gendered and age-based division of labour using Taylorist principles, Yahya uses Taylorism to ensure that greatest efficiency is maintained by breaking each small task down into further smaller tasks. This leads to more reliable output, the further deskilling of labour and increased alienation. He then combines this with an age-based and gendered division of labour. This is evident in the way that the tomatoes are uprooted and shaken. The older men are responsible for this task. Men mostly uproot the tomatoes by hand and if women do this, they use a knife. They then shake the plants so the tomatoes fall to the ground. Then women – always only women – next to them pick up the tomatoes and place them in sacks. At first, the tomatoes are placed into sacks that lie flat on the ground and once the sacks are half full, they are placed in an upright position. Yahya finds that this is the most efficient way to fill the tomato sacks.

One day after work, he went to town after work and bought ten large plastic washing bowls. Then, next day, he came to the land with his big innovation. He distributed the bowls, and the men began to shake their tomatoes into the basins instead of shaking them onto the earth. This enabled the women to pick up the tomatoes much faster than before. This innovation however created a new problem, as the younger women struggled to lift the bowls and tip them into the empty sacks. The younger and weaker women were consequently assigned the task of collecting tomatoes that had been missed by the first pick.

Yahya is the founder of 'scientific' management and manager of the labour process on the land. Zarife, Yahya's wife, takes on the role of forewoman and Melek is the absent middle-woman (as during picking season she remains in the shacks doing domestic work). Zarife (forty-four), as the oldest female worker and as Yahya's wife, embraces the informal role of forewoman. Yahya and Zarife always work side by side. Yahya is mostly interested in male workers from outside the *dayıbaşı*'s family, whereas Zarife's focus falls squarely on young women from her extended family. As the oldest 'bride' and mother of the largest number of sons, Zarife does not hesitate to use her power. She comes just below the oldest man in the familial hierarchy. With this authority, she does not do other works, which women do on the land such as preparing meals or bringing water to other workers, whereas every other women do these tasks too. In this sense, she has a very similar role to the landowner's wife in the planting season. Like her husband, she takes on the dual role of worker and manager in the picking season. She continuously criticizes the younger women for not working fast enough, either by directly chastising them or by complaining about them to Yahya.

> She seeks out our faults and then complains to my brothers. Her job is to increase the tension. She always wants us to serve her. I swear to you that she has not carried water once in the many years we have worked together. She is the first bride of our family. So, when the other brides came, she began to act like their mother-in-law. Did you see her serving lunch or making tea? It is not possible. She does not leave her husband's side for a moment.[10]

Zarife's attempt to control others is not the only reason for Songül's anger towards her. The familial relations shape the relations of production: when I met Songül on the land, she had recently separated from her husband and joined the work group. Her husband was Zarife's brother and Songül's second cousin. She was separated from him because she did not get pregnant within six months of their marriage. Because of this, her husband contracted a religious marriage with another woman. However, according to Zarife, the story is entirely different: Songül and her mother wanted more gold bracelets than what Zarife's brother had already bought for Songül. He (Songül's ex-husband) promised that he would buy her more gold bracelets when she gave birth. However, they kept insisting, saying that he had married an 'unproblematic' girl who deserved more bracelets. Apart from the impossibility of knowing the true story, the concrete result is an unceasing battle on the land between these two women and their respective supporters. One of the two other brides in the *dayıbaşı*'s family, also working on the land, supports Zarife, and the other believes what Songül says. Kadriye (Songül's sister) also takes Songül's side. This polarization combined with Zarife's hierarchical power sometimes made the women's lives more difficult.

> Today, I witnessed the biggest fight between the women yet. It was horrifying. We were almost ready to stop for lunch. Kadriye left about ten minutes ahead of us so she could light the fire to make tea. Then, Zarife left after her. After almost five minutes, we heard a massive outcry but we did not take it seriously; shouting is a part of our daily routine on the land. However, the shouting did not stop, and we could not see them because of the truck, which was between us. Everyone started to run there. When I finally came to a position from which I could see them, I was shocked. They were fighting with each other. Fortunately, Ahmet and Osman interfered and stopped them. Kadriye was crying and continued to shout at Zarife in Kurdish. Pinar was next to me and interpreted for me. She told me that Kadriye claimed that Zarife put water over the fire intentionally to create trouble for her, and Zarife denied the accusation and told 'I went there and the water bottle accidently slipped from my hand. Kadriye is just an attention seeker, so she exaggerated'. On the other hand, Kadriye told me that Zarife knows that in the end, nobody will ever say anything against her out of respect for her age. Zarife always suggests that the younger women of the family are the guilty ones. As a result, she can get away with anything.[11]

Kadriye implies a distinction between family and work relations that is not falling borne out. Working relations are not only shaped by how you work; sometimes on tomato land it does not matter how fast you work, your work relations are shaped by your interactions with other members of your family. I am sure that there may be other reasons why Zarife and Songül do not like each other. The levels of dislike expressed towards family members, however, are not stable. When I went to their hometown in 2014 after the picking season, I saw that Songül and Zarife's relationship had completely changed. When Songül returned to her family home because of her divorce, she was able to take a share of the money earned by the entire group (as opposed to a joint share with her husband). Zarife opposed this because she saw Songül as taking more than what she deserves and in so doing, reducing others' share. When I visited their hometown, however, after Songül had married the richest man in the village and had moved away, Songül became Zarife's favourite family member.

### *Young women workers: 'Collecting the remnants under the eyes of men'*

As clearly seen from Songül's case, not all women have the same power in the familial hierarchy as Zarife. As is to be expected from a patriarchal extended family structure, young women are positioned on lower rungs of the ladder in the familial hierarchy. This positioning also affects their place in the labour hierarchy on tomato land. The reason Elif is positioned at the very bottom of the family hierarchy – with the exception of the children – is also linked to the relatively low status of her husband, Ahmet, who is the youngest brother in the *dayıbaşı's* family. Moreover, Elif only has one infant son who is nine months old. Moreover, she does not have a close relationship with her mother-in-law and nor does her husband have close ties with the older men in the family. As a result of this, he is able to make only very limited contributions with regard to decision making on tomato land and is at the periphery of the production process. What is notable is that Ahmet had actually repeatedly proposed Yahya's great innovation of using large plastic bowls to collect tomatoes. As explained in the previous section, when Yahya introduced the system of large plastic bowls in which to gather tomatoes and to then deposit tomatoes from the bowls into the tomato sacks, he was seen as a great innovator. Despite this, both Elif and the others were aware that this was in fact Ahmet's idea but Ahmet was unable to take ownership of his idea because of Yahya's authority in the family hierarchy.

Elif is not fond of the new method. The same goes for the other young women (women in their late teens). The women who are not strong enough to lift up heavy washing bowls full of tomatoes and tip them into upright sacks lose out because of the new system. Their inability to lift the heavy bowls means that they are relegated to less important tasks and deemed to be bad workers. Elif was unable to switch to the new method because she was heavily pregnant. Like most of the other women, Elif is also unable to uproot the tomatoes even with a knife, as this also requires considerable physical force. As a result, she is even more vulnerable than the other young women who can uproot the tomatoes with a knife – this is not desirable as it takes more time but when women do this men's task most of them use a knife – because the young male workers (usually in their mid-teens) have to uproot her tomatoes for her. She cannot follow a line with the other workers, as she is a lot slower than them and cannot fill her tomato sacks at the same rate as the others. This means that she leaves her full sacks in different places to the other workers. As a result, the male workers, who carry the full bags to the trailers, have to double back on themselves to collect Elif's sacks. This slows down the process of carrying the tomatoes to the trucks, so instead of following the line of workers, Elif picks tomatoes close to the trailers. This creates the impression that she is not working hard enough to deserve her share. Other young women who are also struggling to follow the line (especially women who are made to pick tomatoes with the male workers) are sent to pick with Elif – picking remnants and tomatoes missed by the other workers. Elif often over-exerts herself in order to show that she too deserves her share. By doing this, Elif puts her health and the health of her unborn child at risk.

> Today the weather was hot. By 11.30 however, the heat was unbearable. I was working with Elif, and she seemed unwell, her face was incredibly pale. So, I suggested that we took a break and sat for a little while in the shade next by the trailer. She told me that taking a break before the other workers was not possible because the group payment system meant that she would have to keep a pace with the other workers. When I understood that she wouldn't give up, I carried

water for her. When I did this the other workers also wanted me to give them water, and I just started to walk around the land distributing water. I don't know how long it took, it is not a quick task since there are around 30 workers, and I had to fill the bottles more than once. When I returned to Elif's side, she was worse than before. I again suggested that she stop working, but she once again insisted on continuing. She said that the other members of her family would shout at her husband and he would shout at her if she stopped working. We worked for around ten more minutes, but her movements became slower and she even stopped chewing her gum (chewing gum is very popular on the land as the workers say that it reduces thirst). I told her that if she didn't want to stop before others, then maybe all the workers could take a break together because everyone had been complaining about the heat. I said that we could have lunch and return to work when the heat had worn off a little (at this point, the time was around 12.45). She said that she was happy with the plan. Then, I went to talk with Yahya to explain the situation; while I was walking towards him, I heard one of the women screaming in Kurdish. I froze for a minute and then, following the other, I ran to Elif's side. They carried her to the trailers, and they put water on her face; she was barely conscious. I said that we have to call an ambulance, but no-one seems to agree with me. Everyone thought that she was just suffering from the heat and that she would be okay in a short time. I was shocked, worried and sad. As she lay under the trailer while the others had their lunch; I sat next to her under the trailer, since it was the only shaded area. Even when the others started to work, Elif and I didn't. I told gangmaster we should call someone to pick her up and take her back home, but he told me that there was no one to pick her up at the moment. I said I that I would call my uncle. He told me it was not proper for her to go in a stranger's car without her husband or any other male member of the family, and that her husband could not leave work because they still had three trailers of tomatoes to fill.[12]

This is not unsurprising given the working environment, in which being fast is the primary requirement for being a good worker and, hence, occupational health and safety is of little importance. What I found the most shocking was how Elif would not be allowed to travel in my uncle's car with me even though her health was in danger. This in large part explains why Kurdish women have begun to join seasonal rural migrations: because they are able to work with their extended families where they will not come into contact with strangers and, in particular, with any unfamiliar men. This is very similar to what Kabeer (2000) demonstrated for Bangladeshi women's factory work in London. As with the factories in London, there are 'stranger males' who must be avoided. Bangladeshi women's employment in those places was thus strained and, as a result, they tended to work in their own homes or in the homes of other women. Unsurprisingly, working from home is also very common for women in Turkey. In the case of Kurdish women, they can be employed during the planting time as there are no men around during the day and in picking time they work with their family and relatives. Here, there is an exact link showing us how the piece rate payment system of tomato picking and patriarchal family relations overlap. Men need the women so that they can earn more under the piece rate payment system, so they began migrating with the women to western Turkey. As they have very large extended families, they can then control women's labour in the workplace.

In this chapter and throughout this study, the effects of patriarchy are flexible and target a range of family members. Ahmet is also subject to patriarchy: he had to stay quiet about his stolen innovation. Patriarchy however is not flexible in the sense that a woman cannot ride in a strange man's car even if her health is at great risk. That is why I term the gender regime at play here 'patriarchal' and Elif also recognizes the role of patriarchy but expresses it in a different way. When I got upset because she was unable to go to the hospital, she said: 'Don't cry. Our life is … but a sip of water in their eyes'.[13] Here, in addition to agreeing with her, I will also add that it is not simply the lives of women that are seen as 'a sip of water' but the lives of men too. This is particularly the case when the men are not seen as being 'proper' men and thus threaten the ideal of being a proper man. In the following chapter, I will examine the effects of the undignified world of capitalism (to which I have referred in the previous section) on 'the people' – the *el âlem*[14] – how the *el âlem* is the material manifestation of patriarchy.

## *The youngest women: 'Responsible for empty sacks'*

As soon as I went to the land, I was directly assigned to collect empty sacks from beside the tractors and deliver them to the workers. It seemed like a very easy job, but it was not easy at all. Because these empty bags are used throughout the season, they become more smelly and dirty with tomato juice day by day. Also, you always have to move around during the day, you cannot sit. And, because this task does not require you to work continuously – even if you are required most of the time – you also have to assume responsibility for carrying water to the workers, which also means that you have to move around the land with at least 10 kg of water bottles. This job is not assigned to particular women; every day one of the younger ones is assigned to it, and none of them is happy to be given this task as it places them on the periphery. When I worked with one of them, Hacer (fourteen), she explained to me why she doesn't want to do this job:[15]

> 'When I pick tomatoes, I am with the others, so time passes quickly. But, when I do this, I get really bored. Everyone thinks that you are not really working but it is still very tiring work. This is an outsider's job' (Hacer)
> 'What do you mean by an outsider's job'? (me)
> 'I mean now we are outsiders [referring to me and her since we were working together], look [pointing to the workers] we are working far away from them, working outside' (Hacer)

>> 'Do you think they want me to do this task because I am an 'outsider'? (me)
>> 'No, it's because you are not fast enough to pick tomatoes' (Hacer)

When you are not fast enough, you become an outsider and become distant from the centre of production. Although collecting empty sacks supports the continuity and the speed of the work, it does not lead people to think of it as integral to tomato picking, since tomato picking is seen as *the job* – the most important job of all. However, to put it simply, when the circulation of empty bags stops, the work has to stop. Workers become aware of this when the landowning family brings casual workers to the land.

> Today is once again very stressful because every time another group of workers arrive, empty sacks become a serious issue. I was collecting them as always, and I went to carry water for half an hour. When I returned to collect the sacks, I thought that there were fewer than before. Clearly the sacks were disappearing and I understood that women from the other group were hoarding them. I was very surprised. First, I could not understand their intention of collecting all the empty bags; we needed empty bags because we had filled all of them, and there were no empty trucks on the land at that moment. So, we could not empty our filled bags onto the trailers, however if we had empty bags we could continue to fill them until the empty trucks arrived. But, the other group of workers told me they could not give me any sacks and when I said this to my group, they got really angry. They told me that it means that when new trucks arrive, they will collect the other group's produce since they had more full bags than we did. Now we do not have empty bags, and our trucks are full so we have to wait for new trucks and when they come, the other groups will take them. Unsurprisingly, they fought with the other group. They first sent young women to try to take empty bags from them and did not send the men over in order to prevent the fight from escalating. Nonetheless, the women attacked each other. Then the young men from each group had to come and separate them. My group phoned the landowning family and asked them to bring more empty sacks. Otherwise, they said that they would leave the land and not come back to work. Since my group works for less money than the other group [the farmers pay casual workers more than they do for the boarding Kurdish workers] the landowning family could not risk losing them so within fifteen minutes, new sacks arrived. This was the first concrete triumph of the workers I had seen during my fieldwork.[16]

This struggle over bags and the workers' triumph do not change the overwhelming evidence to suggest that the youngest women have the most vulnerable and risky task in the tomato-picking process. The task is seen as vulnerable not because it is not imperative for the continuation of work, but because anyone can do it. You do not need to be physically strong and you do not need to use your mind, as there is no possible way to increase efficiency and productivity. On the tomato land, the prestige of tasks decreases proportionally according to the number of people who are capable of doing the task. In this sense, young women's work is seen as the least valuable and the young women are seen as the most replaceable. On the other hand, there is just one task that everyone agrees that only young men can do: emptying the bags into the trailers.

## Young men: The final stage of tomato production on the land

Most of the men on the tomato land, including the *dayıbaşı*, believe that they are doing a woman's job because they are Kurdish. As in other countries, work that is low paid and unskilled is labelled as women's work (Cockburn 1985; Elson and Pearson 1981; Phillips and Taylor 1980). Most of the Kurdish men on the land believe that they are subjected to tomato work because of the day-to-day discrimination, marginalization and racism experienced by Kurds at both the micro- and macro-levels. Some see this combination of being 'low-caste' and powerless as leading to Kurdish men being forced to do 'women's work'. The intersection of their working class and ethnic identities compounds their marginalization.

On the other hand, some of the young Kurdish men on the tomato land assigned to carry full sacks to the trailers believe that they are doing this man's job because they are Kurdish and therefore stronger and hardier than Turkish men. The fluidity in the discourses surrounding the definition and meaning of Kurdish identity means that for some young Kurdish men, carrying 20 kg sacks of tomatoes to and from the trailers is seen as a prestigious job that weak Turkish men cannot do. In this way, the manipulation of discourse imbues the same work with divergent meanings: some Kurdish men conclude that they do a woman's job because they are Kurdish and oppressed, whereas others, in Mehmet's words, are empowered because they see themselves as doing work that only Kurdish men can do. This illustrates the way in which the interplay between gender, class and ethnicity can subtly impact upon the way in which individuals self-identify and how they 'place' themselves within society. We can see the way in which gender, class and ethnicity can affect the job opportunities and tasks allotted to particular groups and we can also see the way in which categorizations derived from class, ethnicity or gender are in and of themselves fluid and subject to change. The men doing the prestigious job of depositing sacks are seen as important and irreplaceable despite being seen by some as doing a woman's job. At the same time, the men depositing the sacks become more secure in their masculinity *because* they are doing a demanding job that only men can do. Mehmet is the strongest and quickest amongst this group of young men and is consequently seen as the most indispensable and prestigious worker on the land.

> I should have sent Mehmet (22) back because of his relationship with Emine [implying that they fell in love with each other]. But, even Emine's father [he is against this relationship] does not want to get rid of him because otherwise, who would 'do the trucks' (doing the trucks is used to refer to loading the sacks of tomatoes onto the 'truck trailers'.[17] (*Dayıbaşı*)

When Mehmet leads the group 'doing the trucks', there is a recognizable difference in the speed at which the tractors are filled. Mehmet is also aware of this and this has empowered him to open up about his 'forbidden' love for 'Emine'. Emine's father insisted that her younger brother (seventeen) could do the carrying instead of Mehmet so they could send Mehmet back to his hometown. He said that otherwise they would have to leave the land as a whole family. The *dayıbaşı* had to accept this because losing the whole family would be considerably worse than only losing Mehmet and his two siblings, and even if Mehmet left with his entire family, they are far fewer than Emine's family. But, their plan did not work because Hüseyin (seventeen) was too young to 'do the tractors'. He simply was not as strong as Mehmet is. As a result, Emine's family were forced to accept Mehmet's continued presence on the land until the end of the season. They were forced to accept this as their wages also depend on Mehmet's performance. This makes Mehmet and the other men 'doing the trucks' appear to be even more prestigious; their role is proven to be the one that simply cannot be done by anyone else. This is the only task on the land that is not seen as a woman's job: 'To do this job you have to be young but not too young', Levent (nineteen) told me. This is also the requirement of hegemonic masculinity in rural Turkey. So, it was unsurprising when I asked Emine what she liked the most about Mehmet? As expected, she replied that it is because Mehmet is '*a manly man*'.

## *Autumn: Time to 'fight' for your profits*

How can workers resist capital when they are not organized? Hints to the answer to this question have been embedded in this chapter so far: 'family'. Family is not only the tool for resistance but it is also a tool used to control workers. As the tomato-picking season comes to an end, the power of familial resistance begins to lose its effect on the landowning family. Workers often threatened the landowning family with wildcat strikes and work stoppages, but as the season comes to an end, this threat is no longer as powerful as before. When the farmers' fear of losing their workers ends, the real battle begins.

> Today was horrible. Everything was normal in the beginning: I was working with Elif and we were talking to each other about her son. In the meantime, we were hearing that Yahya was shouting at someone on the phone. I could not understand what was going on because the conversation was in Kurdish. Since I was accustomed to his shouting, I did not pay attention but it was in Kurdish so that I was sure it was not with the landowner. However, suddenly they all began to talk loudly in Kurdish. I understood that something had gone wrong. Elif told me that we were going to stop working because Osman and the landowning family had gotten into a big fight and Osman had called Yahya to say that we were to stop working. I was surprised but not able to ask about the reasons because Elif was talking with the others. And, it seemed that something was wrong among the workers too. It turned out that some of the workers, workers who are not members of dayıbaşı's extended family, did not stop working, and it seemed that Yahya had tried to stop them from working by shouting at them. I didn't understand what he was saying, and then suddenly Yahya and Pınar's father began physically fighting.

I panicked and shouted at Ahmet to stop them. Ahmet pulled Yayha and Mehmet pulled Huseyin, then 'Ramazan said that we are not working because Osman said so. Even if we work, the landowning family won't pay. Elif translated this for me and said that we should have lunch whilst waiting to hear back from Osman. While we were waiting for news, the jandarma (military police more commonly seen in rural areas) came to the land with Recai and Halil Ibrahim (both members of the landowning family) and asked to speak with Osman. The workers said that they did not know where Osman was. Yahya told them that they had not seen Osman since the previous night. This was clearly not true. Then, as I feared they would, the landowning family asked me whether I had seen Osman on the land. I said I hadn't seen him since the previous day, which is true. However, I did not tell them that Osman and Yahya had just spoken on the phone. I felt close to tears. Recai (a member of the landowning family) said that I should go back to the village with him and the police since it would be unsafe to stay on the land. Then Ahmet began to shout at him. Fortunately, the police prevented this from escalating. I replied that I would stay on the land to continue to look after the small children who accompany the adults to the land. This was again, not truthful. The small children who often accompany the adults to the land are never looked after. Either way, I could not think of a better excuse to justify me remaining on the land until the resolution of the dispute. I knew that if I had told the truth the landowning family would report back to my uncle and that this would worry my family. So I stayed and the jandarma and the landowning family went back to the village. Then, I asked Elif what was going on. She told me that Osman wanted to increase the 'fixed price' since tomato prices are so high on the open market and the landowning family sold them to the open market. She explained that Recep (a member of the landowning family) was strongly against this, so they fought violently. Now, Recep had lodged a complaint with the police and Osman had made himself scarce. I asked Elif why Osman had gone away because he had not actually done anything wrong. She told me that she did not know. Within half an hour we all returned to the village. I am relieved that the situation did not escalate.[18]

Unfortunately, it did escalate. That night the landowning family came to workers' shacks – where they live during the seasonal work – and tried to convince those of the workers who are distant relatives of the *dayıbaşı*'s family to work for them instead of for the *dayıbaşı*. This caused significant tension between the workers who are part of the *dayıbaşı*'s extended family and the *dayıbaşı*'s more distant relatives. Then the workers began to fight with each other. Mehmet threw a stone at Ahmet's head and he was seriously injured. After that day, the Kurdish workers stopped working together, and they left the tomato lands not as one big group, but as smaller groups.

### Tomatoes turn workers into 'capitalists'

The family is central to shape the capitalist tomato production process on the land. And as we see here, capitalism makes capitalists of us all. In this sense, our 'capitalist families' re-construct and are re-constructed by the familial workplace. Different payment systems – daily wage and piecework – lead to different forms of organization and management of labour. These differing modes of organizing labour consequently lead to differing intersecting identities, causing either harmony, disunity, or, as is often the case, some combination of the two. In this way, the divisions within the organization of capitalist production are sustained by the workers' different identities – gender, class, ethnicity, kinship and age – which also reinforce the creation of masculinities and femininities which are important for understanding intersectional patriarchy in the labour process.

Assembly line production or the principles of 'scientific management' are not only possible in the factories, but the nature of capitalist production causes farmers or rural workers themselves to create their own assembly line – as we saw with both the picking and the planting. This occurs even without the highly technological aspects of manufacturing and industry and that gender, class, ethnicity, kinship and age become ways of effectively dividing and deskilling labour in the absence of technology. The study of the history of the division of labour and the spontaneous worker-led imposition of the management styles of control and the regularity with it arises as an area of significant potential further research. I have also explored the impact of gender-, class-, ethnicity-, kinship- and age-based relations as tools that shape both control and resistance in the tomato production labour process. Hopefully, the snapshots from workers' ordinary working days contributed to some of the key concepts of the labour process such as control, deskilling, consent, resistance and the division of labour by integrating the intersection of the different identities of labour. Throughout the chapter, I have showed how 'tomatoes' are also main actors in determining which workers' identities come to the fore and how the material condition of the tomatoes – whether they are seedlings, or mature tomatoes, or rotten tomatoes – determine the conditions of work in terms of payment system or working hours.

## Chapter 6

### INSIDE THE 'KEMALIST' TOMATO-PROCESSING FACTORY

In Turkey, 'taking bread from the lion's mouth' is an old expression used to refer to working under difficult conditions. Owing to the neoliberal economic policies of the current (2020) Turkish government, the AKP, this figure of speech has become a reality to the point where it is becoming more common to hear someone say that they are 'taking bread from the lion's stomach'.[1] The permanent condition of earning bread from the lion's stomach evinces the precariousness of contemporary working conditions. For many factory workers in Turkey, a permanent contract is now an unattainable dream. Indeed, subcontracting employment firms – *taşeron* – have mushroomed and deaths in the 'lion's stomach' are no longer very rare.[2]

This chapter, however, does not talk about a lion. Instead, it discusses workers' struggles with a *mechanical monster*. Using the imaginative allegory of likening a factory to a *mechanical monster* is a tradition in Marxism.[3] The term was used by Marx himself (1990: 503) to refer to machine technology:

> Here (in the most developed form of production by machinery), we have in the place of the isolated machine, a mechanical monster whose body fills whole factories, and whose demonic power, at first hidden by the slowed and measured motions of its gigantic members, finally bursts forth in the fast and feverish whirl of its countless working organs.

Here, the metaphor of the *mechanical monster* is used to refer to the moving assembly line in the tomato-processing factory 'Red'. 'The moving conveyor, when used for an assembly line, though it is an exceedingly primitive piece of machinery, answers perfectly to the needs of capital in the organisation of work, which may not be otherwise mechanized' (Braverman 1974: 195). Therefore, the production line of the 'Red' tomato-processing factory is viewed as an embodiment of the *mechanical monster*, not in terms of being an example of modern technology, but in terms of serving as an agent of labour control. However, asking 'how capitalist control of the labour process is obtained', the combined forms of control and the fact that the control structures of 'the assembly line cannot be reduced to a technological dimension. It may have altered the role and pattern of supervision, but its successful operation always depends on human agency' (Thompson 1989: 150). As such, the control of the labour process is 'technical', but also 'humanised' and hence a 'varied' process that occurs inside the 'mechanical monster'.

While Marx did not state his reasons for using this metaphor (maybe, for Marx, what underlies the monster metaphor is self-evident), the reasons behind my adoption of this metaphor are elaborated in the following entry in my fieldwork diary:

> You cannot imagine how frightened I was when I first entered the plant. It was like stepping into somewhere out of this world. There was no fresh air, it was unbearably hot, loud and smelly. I saw exactly why people kept saying that they were earning money from the lion's stomach. Even the thought of a lion is more comforting; less alien and less forbidding than the actual work that takes place under these conditions. The work we do here is otherworldly; it is so mechanical that it cannot possibly be equated with the idealised images we have of proud lions roaming pristine savannahs. There can be no natural feelings or emotions in a place like this. Inside the plant, I feel like I lose all connection with reality. I think that if I were a surrealist painter, I would paint the production line as a constantly moving mechanical monster.[4]

In this chapter, underlying my surreal image is the 'reality' of this 'monster' as I witnessed it in the summer of 2014. To explore how gender ideologies of the Kemalist factory regime are used to control labour inside of the *mechanical monster*, I will provide snapshots of my observations during my time on the shop floor. By these snapshots, I will reveal how femininity is seen as an impediment to global production in Turkey and how political ideologies have the power to shape the organization of labour processes inside of the *mechanical monster*. The *monster* has neither a heart nor brain of its own, but it is the people inside of it, mainly women, who dedicate their hearts and minds to its operation. How and why they give their hearts, their minds, or both to this *monster* are the main questions that this chapter addresses. While answering these questions, I suggest that their minds and hearts shape and are shaped by a Kemalist factory regime. The concept of a factory regime (Burawoy 1985) refers to the informal rules and relations that workers outwardly and voluntarily accept to work. I suggest that this *mechanical monster* is a distinctly Kemalist because of the key social divisions mobilized by management and workers, including the hierarchy of masculinity above femininity and the typology of femininities deployed by Kemalist ideology, which structure the way the factory is governed.[5] As discussed in Chapter 2, Kemalist ideology entreats people to be faithful followers of Atatürk's principles and reforms (Bora 2003). Mustafa Kemal's reforms refer to a series of changes in the social, legal and political system of the country to create a 'modern' and 'western' Republic (Abadan-Unat 1978) and women were in the centre of this project. Here the chapter highlights the three contrasting images of women in Kemalist ideology to examine the gendered factory regime. The first image is educated 'Daughters of the Republic', the second one is wise 'Anatolian Women' and the third is 'Backward Religious Women'.

*Devaluation of femininity in global production in Turkey:*
*Three images of women in a Kemalist factory*

How should we understand the construction of gender on the factory floor? For most of us researching women's labour in global production, Elson and Pearson's article '"Nimble Fingers Make Cheap Workers": An Analysis of Women's Employment in Third World Export Manufacturing' (1981) was a turning point. 'Nimble Fingers' demonstrated that gendering the labour process had become crucial to global production and questioned whether this would increase gender equality. This is because factories were employing women as a source of cheap and compliant labour. Thus, the new international division of labour literature suggested that the construction of women as a cheaper and more docile labour force rested on women's position in society, especially in the household, where they were seen as dependents rather than breadwinners. Pioneering feminist factory studies (Glucksmann 1982; Pollert 1981; Westwood 1984) focused on the interweaving relationship between family and factory life as a way to demonstrate that women brought their low social status with them into the workplace. 'Women do not do unskilled jobs because they are the bearers of inferior labour [i.e. they are not less skilled than men]: rather, the jobs they do are unskilled because women enter them already determined as inferior bearers of labour', said Elson and Pearson (1981: 24). Similarly, Phillips and Taylor (1980: 79) argued that 'women workers carry into the workplace their status as subordinate individuals, and this status comes to define the value of the work they do', keeping them trapped in low status work. 'Multinationals want a workforce docile, easily manipulated and willing to do boring, repetitive assembly work. Women, they claim, are the perfect employees, with their "natural patience" and "manual" dexterity' (Fuentes and Enrenreich 1983: 12–13). This assumption of the management regarding the association of femininity and docility is called the 'trope of productive femininity' by Salzinger (2003, 2004). Although she (2003) agrees that women have been increasingly filling the world's assembly lines, Salzinger argues that scholars who assume that capital is dependent on women's prior construction as cheap labour and docile, compliant bodies have confused cause with consequence. This is not because women are already readymade docile bodies, as 'Nimble Fingers' suggested, but rather docile bodies are produced within the production relations of the workplace. The management, therefore, asks for femininity, not necessarily for female bodies.

The answer of the question on whether women are already docile bodies or they become so in the production process is related to how gender is perceived: a 'being' or a 'doing'. West and Zimmerman (1987, 2009) identify gender as an ongoing process: a 'doing' rather than a 'being'; gender lies in the social interactions, they say. In this sense, the concept of 'doing gender' enables researchers to explore multiple femininities and masculinities that are constructed through social interactions in organizations. '"Doing gender" means behaving so that whatever the situation, whoever the actors, one's behaviour is seen in context as gender appropriate' (West and Zimmerman 1987: 234). This means that both men and women can exhibit femininity and masculinity depending on the context. For instance, Pilgeram (2007) shows that female farm operators in the United States should manifest themselves as masculine because the recognition of their ability as farmers is tied with their ability to perform hegemonic masculinity. Very similarly, Ainsworth et al. (2013) demonstrate that women perform masculinity in voluntary firefighting to be seen as capable as a firefighter. All occupations are gendered (Acker 1990, 2006; Cockburn 1983, 1985); both livestock farming and firefighting are perceived as masculine occupations, as they both require physical strength and endurance. Women, therefore, feel that they need to perform masculinity in these occupations. Assembly line production, on the other hand, is perceived as feminine: it is a 'light' industry. Consequently, feminist factory studies are able to demonstrate multiple femininities constructed on the shop floor (Kondo 1990; Lee 1998; Ngai 2005; Salzinger 2003) because femininity is a desirable feature of the global factory production.

The studies on women's work in Turkey, however, indirectly challenge the argument that 'femininity was always imagined and linked to performance as a good worker' (Ngai 2005: 145) by exploring how women are seen as 'potential problem makers' (Beşpınar and Topal 2018: 300). Drawing on a textile factory in a small Anatolian town, Beşpınar and Topal (2018) demonstrate how managers assume that women's 'main responsibilities' as mother and wife would lead them to have internment employment patterns. This belief, consequently, causes women to be assigned to low-skill tasks and not being promoted. Many years before, Ecevit (1991) also noted that 'whenever I asked why women were not upgraded or given responsible positions, their being home-bound figured strongly in the answers. It has been argued that women, because of domestic responsibilities, are not as reliable as male workers' (67). Thus, the feminization of labour literature suggests that this low-skilled categorization of women's labour inevitably leads firms to select women as factory workers because they are cheaper, docile and dexterous and, therefore, enable higher profits to be made (Cravey 1998; Elson and Pearson 1981; Fernandez-Kelly 1983; Lee 1998; Pollert 1981; Westwood 1984; Wolf 1994). This, however, did not happen in Turkey, as femininity is not seen as productive but as an impediment.

In 1990, ten years after Turkey shifted from an import subsidized growth model, Çağatay and Berik suggest that in Turkey, export-oriented growth has been achieved without an accompanying or subsequent feminisation of labour. This is the first challenge arising from the Turkish context, to say that export-oriented industrialization does not always lead to an increase in women's work in manufacturing. Therefore, scholars working on women's labour in Turkey mostly focus on the reasons of not having such an association (Arat 2010; Buğra and Özkan 2012; İlkkaracan 2012), differences between married and single women on the effect of the export-oriented growth model (Başlevent and Onaran 2004; Gündüz-Hoşgör and Smith 2008), as well as the effect of unregistered work (Kümbetoğlu et al. 2010), homeworking (Çınar 1994; Eraydın and Erendil 1999; Sarıoğlu 2013; White 1994) or small family–based enterprises (Dedeoğlu 2010, 2012), which have been noted as reasons of that.

Despite their different focuses, these studies mainly apply two interrelated concepts: 'patriarchy' and 'family'. Women's familial commitments (Gündüz-Hoşgör and Smith 2008; Suğur and Suğur 2005), the necessity of the approval of their family to be able to work outside (Beşpınar and Topal 2018) and the need for the recognition of the workplace as 'honourable' and 'safe' by their social environment (Dedeoğlu 2012; Ecevit 1991; Nichols and Sugur 2004; White 2004) are mostly cited as the preventions of women working outside, which are seen as a result of the patriarchy. Their work is not recognized as a breadwinning work but as pocket money and, as such, this prevents women from being employed in skilled tasks or invested in to teach skills. The result is a vicious cycle, in which women are always at the bottom of the employment ladder. While these studies suggest that women's roles as mother and/or wife in their family also shape their employment trajectory in Turkey, they indirectly indicate that in Turkey, the presence of 'women' at work is seen as problematic and as something that has to be dealt with discursively through the organization of work. Working at home or in small family-based enterprises located in the basements of the buildings in the neighbourhoods is the most popular way of doing this. These global companies have incorporated subcontracting family firms mostly in the textile and garment sectors; however, for food manufacturing, this was not the case. Nevertheless, food factories also deploy the concept of family to manage women's labour (Erdogan 2016). Family – both as literal enterprises and as a discourse – has been used to desexualize and to domesticate the workplace (Beşpınar and Topal 2018; Ecevit 1991; Erdogan 2016). It converts 'dangerous and disapproved' working places to 'safe and honourable' places. To sustain this image, management's priority becomes creating a workplace to be suitable for 'honourable' women (Beşpınar and Topal 2018; Erdogan 2016), as discussed in Chapter 2.

Sarıoğlu's (2016) work, on the other hand, shows that the attempt to create a respectable factory for women has not been successful. Thus, national gender discourse on women's work continues to stigmatize particular forms of working-class femininities (such as factory girls), promotes middle-class femininities (such as professional women) and domestic femininities (such as housewives) (ibid.). While women's professional careers have always been encouraged, for working-class women, the same support has not been available. Sarıoğlu (2016) explains this polarized attitude by applying the hegemonic discourse of Turkish modernity that was mainly constructed by the early republican political elite – which I call here as Kemalists – along the axes of secularization and Westernization. In the Early Republican Era, the image of a modern woman unveiled and an active participant of public life has been promoted to demonstrate the break from the Islamic formation of the Ottoman Empire (ibid.). Women's work outside the home in high professions, apparently, has been constructed as being modern. However, this category does not apply to women working in low-skill jobs, such as factory work (ibid.).

Looking at the Red factory enables us to see how the national discourse of modernity has been applied on the shop floor when all women are 'factory girls'. Apparently, managers and women workers constitute the Kemalist factory regime by deploying the three categories of womanhood imaginatively constructed by Kemalist ideology, as discussed in Chapter 2. The assignment of different women to different parts of the production line mirrors the division between these categories: 'Backward Religious Women' are allocated roles at the beginning of the assembly line, where they are responsible for sorting the overripe tomatoes from the usable tomatoes; 'Educated Modernised Women of the Republic' are assigned to control the machines, while 'physically and emotionally strong rural but wise women of Anatolia' – 'Anatolian Women' – are permanently employed in the warehouse. The Kemalist factory regime does not 'accept' femininity on the shop floor and, thus, attempts to construct 'Anatolian Women' as more masculine and 'Educated Daughters of the Republic' as less feminine. Women working on the sorting lines, on the other hand, are seen as feminine and, as such, they deserve to be humiliated and strictly controlled, as femininity is seen as an obstacle to modern factory production by the management.

## *'Politically' situated visions of managers: The journey to the factory and reaching its 'Kemalist' manager*

> In every factory, gender has a distinctive architecture, structured and bounded by managers' ongoing, sometimes contradictory, efforts to constitute productive workers.[6]

Salzinger, in a similar vein with other feminist factory studies (Glucksmann 1982; Kondo 1990; Lee 1998; Ngai 2005; Ong 1987; Pollert 1981; Westwood 1984), identifies gender ideologies as a dimension of control on the shop floor but with an emphasis on the managers' role. 'Gender matters in global production – *she says*–; how it matters is determined by the situated visions of managers around the globe' (34). By 'situated visions', she means managers' 'location within structures of gender, nation, and corporation, and the perspectives that emerged from this placement' (163). Managers develop

> a new set of a new set of meanings for 'femininity' that freed from its connection to female bodies at all and reconstituted it as a set of transferable characteristics, including cheapness, natural docility, dexterity, and tolerance of boredom. In the process, their description became prescription, and the transnational trope of productive femininity became the new standard for maquila workers, women and men alike. (ibid.: 37)

She underlines that differences between gendered regimes of the factories lie in 'the way managers understand themselves, their jobs, and their workers' (ibid.: 160). However, how this understanding has been framed by wider structures needs more articulation in her work (Blair 2005; Williams 2013). Thus, this chapter attempts to locate the manager's views into the wider frame by focusing on how the general manager's views about femininity have been framed by the socio-political history of Turkey.

Red's factory manager's outlook is embedded within the wider social context and conflicting ideologies inherent in the legacy of Kemalism. Red's Kemalist factory regime, therefore, is very much a part of the received wisdom of how a modern factory ought to be run. The factory manager's statements regarding subcontracting will give us our first insights into the contradictions of the Kemalist factory regime:

> I am a leftist. Neo-liberal policies are being applied by this government to corrupt our country. I wrote lots of letters to the general board of managers about subcontracting but they did not reply even once. I am totally against subcontracting. I am trying to talk to the union to prevent this, but they are not interested in real problems, they are too busy encouraging the workers to stop working properly. They are saying to workers, 'do not miss a minute from your break', 'breaks are your rights', and so on. I hate the unions.[7]

The apparent contradiction in the general manager claiming to be a leftist but simultaneously hating trade unions sheds considerable light on the workings of the Kemalist factory regime. The factory manager's assertions, which arose in the context of talking about the women who work in the warehousing section, do not differ significantly from when the chief executive of Turkey's largest industrial company, Ali Koç, said: 'Capitalism should be abolished because it is the source of all inequality' at a G-20 Summit in Antalya, Turkey (14–16 November 2015). Apart from being ridiculed on social media as a result of its obvious contradictions, Koç effectively revealed the conflicting ideological position of the Turkish bourgeoisie. As Buğra and Savaşkan (2012) and others (Onis 2012; Tuğal 2009) highlight, the Turkish state is the midwife of capitalism in Turkey and the bourgeoisie often express that they owe their existence to the founding of the Turkish republic and promulgate the founding values and principles of the Turkish republic: Kemalism.

Here, attention should be drawn to the links between the history of the left in Turkey, Kemalism and unionization. Turkey's first political party, which was established by Mustafa Kemal Atatürk, the Republican People's Party (CHP), is seen on the left of the political spectrum by majority of citizens – evidently not by socialists and Kurds. The party, on the other hand, does not necessarily place itself on the left but closer to centre-left. It does this based on its own anti-imperialist legacy, stemming from the establishment of the republic and its commitment to creating a de jure welfare state. Although the CHP contradicts the universalism of 'left wing politics' by excluding minority groups, many (both supporters and others) still see it as a party of the left. This can be seen as stemming from the ideology that lies at the heart of the CHP and also because of its emphasis on secularism.[8] Furthermore, the CHP as *the party* of Atatürk nationalism embodies many of the nationalist tenets more commonly associated with right-wing politics. Kemalism, therefore, has become an internalized ideology on both the left and the right. This internalization, however, is deeply symbiotic. The conflation of left-wing anti-imperialism and social democracy with exclusivist nationalist politics embodies the contradictions implicit in the factory manager's position. Beyond these contradictions, however, the factory manager's self-identification as left wing and his disdain for trade unionism present a secondary contradiction that needs further unpacking. This is particularly necessary because the trade union active at Red is renowned for being a Kemalist union.

After the 1980 military coup, unions in Turkey, by cooperating with the state, effectively undermined worker's solidarity (Adaman et al. 2009). This is also valid for the union at Red. From the union's actions, the general manager is right to say that the union does not act either to prevent subcontracting or to defend the rights of warehouse workers. Thus, the union does nothing for them and warehouse workers are not even on their agendas. Furthermore, the warehouse workers told me that they could not join their union since it is forbidden by their subcontracted employment agency. However, this is not seen as a loss. Even if subcontracted agency workers were to join their union, nothing would change. The women view the union as ineffective, inefficient and not acting in their interests. Interestingly, all the women on the production lines are registered with the union because if they are union members, they are paid more. I asked them why this was the case and they told me that they did not know. Additionally, they did not even know the name of their union. When I asked the name, they told me that 'it is a union' and then they laughed at me. They were belittling me for not knowing that a union does not really need a name – that the union is just a union. Until I visited the union's offices, I did not know its name either. While there, I saw that 'the union' is allied with the Confederation of Turkish Trade Unions (Türk-İş),[9] which is the biggest union in Turkey and has a reputation for being both Kemalist and close to the state even now (Cemal 2012), when there is a real tension between Kemalist ideology and Turkey's current moderate Islamist government. However, it is not so surprising when we look at the history of unionization in Turkey after the 1980 military coup and the ways in which unions have become a means for the Turkish state to control workplaces. The union laws put into practice following the 1980 coup prevented effective and worker-oriented unions from forming (Adaman et al. 2009). In this way, the Kemalist unions of the post-1980 period can be seen to be a close bedfellow with the current politics of Islamist[10] capital.

Furthermore, the union's closeness to the state can be seen as one explanation for why the women saw the union as just 'the union'. Secondly, the union's proximity to the state can be seen as a possible factor explaining the general manager's categorization of the workers along Kemalist lines and how his letters to the union erased the women who he thinks are less amenable to the Kemalist conceptions of women. The manager's communications with the union regarded only the 'Anatolian Women'[11] who work in the warehouse. This illustrates the ways in which the manager seeks to 'save' only the 'Anatolian Women' who are worthy of being 'saved' by the state, as they are the women closest to the state's ideal of womanhood with their republican daughters – women working on the machines in the lower lines. However, as they are already saved by education, the manager does not need to do anything extra for them. On the other hand, he did not express any sympathy for the plight of the other workers, the 'backward religious' workers sorting the tomatoes.

The manager has worked in managerial positions in food factories in the region for eighteen years. Therefore, he thinks that he knows the region very well because he has witnessed the transformation of the region's rural population. Although his above statement implies that he is not fond of neoliberal policies, he does not think there is a relationship between these policies and farmers' migration to the towns looking for jobs. He is certain that small farmers leave their land because they are lazy. In addition to his anger towards farmers and workers as a whole, women are his specific targets. He asked me: 'Can you believe it? I have to run this factory with all these lazy women.' According to Hakan, women have inveigled their husbands into selling their lands and then forced them to move to the towns. Because of their laziness, they do not want to work on the land, to light the charcoal stove, to live with their mothers-in-law and so on. He is sure that they are lazy, because if they were not, they would work as hard as the warehouse workers. In this way, it is evident that he sees relatively older seasonal workers – not student seasonal workers – in a different way than warehouse workers despite both groups' common rural background. From his point of view, one group of women encapsulates the idealized rural woman of the republic, whereas the other group embodies the lazy, backward religious rural woman who blindly supports conservative and neoliberal policies. His dissatisfaction is evident in what he says about the women who work sorting tomatoes:

> I hate most of them, really. They are not working. You know that the warehouse workers work for 12 hours a day, they carry 30 kilogram crates, but they don't complain. But the others ... they only come here for 2 months but they complain continuously. They work for only 8 hours, but they seem tired all the time. How difficult can it be to sort tomatoes?[12]

Before answering his question about the difficulties of sorting tomatoes, let us first look at the women's journey into the factory. The journey begins in different neighbourhoods of the same town, but the piazza is the most crowded. During the months of August and September, when the tomatoes are being harvested, the shuttle buses leave at 23.10, 7.10 and 15.10, for shifts beginning at 00.00, 8.00 and 16.00, respectively. If you are near the piazza at those times, you will see lots of people, mainly women, waiting for shuttles going to different factories. You will also see how different sex couples – sister and brother, wife and husband, mother and son – walk together until they reach the piazza. Once there, they wait for the shuttles separately in two different corners. The men wait with the men and the women wait with the women. When a shuttle comes, you will also see that the men use the backdoor and the women use the front door to enter the bus. If one reads the reports of the Turkish Association of Trade, s/he could safely conclude that most of those shuttles are going to the tomato-processing factories. Indeed, tomato processing is the biggest industry in this town, with nine tomato-processing factories producing almost a quarter of the total processed tomatoes in Turkey. As the report suggests, at the time that this study was conducted, they produced this amount with a total workforce between the nine factories of 50 engineers,

8 technicians, 65 craftsmen, 67 administrative employees and just 249 workers (TOBB 2014). Nine factories with just 249 workers – may seem to contradict what is seen in the piazza, which is not the only pick-up point, as even in the piazza, at any one pick-up time, there are more than 249 workers. Apart from the crowds at pick-up points, there is much evidence indicating that there are more workers than the official reports suggest: the numbers of shuttle buses, the amount of meals the factory purchases to feed the workers, the number of uniforms as well as the number of boots. It is enough to look at the number of workers in just one shift to prove that the reports do not show the exact numbers.

Assuming this is a mistake would be naïve in the world of the *mechanical monster*; rather, it relates to the workers' contractual status. The official number of workers in the report comprises only the workers with permanent contracts. The factory manager confirmed, 'There is not even one permanent contract worker in one of the biggest tomato processing factories in Turkey.' Indeed, he added that as far as he is aware, none of the factories employ permanent workers. Then, I asked him, what number is this in the report? He replied, 'I guess this is the number of warehouse workers.' These workers are permanent, as they themselves have claimed to be and the factory manager confirmed that some of them had worked there for over ten years. However, working for ten years in the same factory has not enabled these workers to enjoy the social rights of permanent employment. This is because they are not officially permanent employees, but remain contract workers. Moreover, they work long years on three to four months contracts through their subcontracting firm.

However, the women on the shuttle, at least when they are on the shuttles, do not seem to worry about the type of their employment contract, as this is not an issue at any time on the shuttle buses. Although the conversations held on board the shuttle buses that take the women to the factory do not vary a great deal, it is worth noting that one prominent conversation topic and source of pride is that Red's shuttle buses are the newest and most comfortable. It is the only time of the shift that changes the content of the conversation. When women wait for the night-shift shuttle, the main topic of conversation is how much sleep the women have had. Workers waiting for the morning-shift shuttles tend to mostly talk about what they did the previous evening. When these discussions are not related to household labour, they tend to be about weddings, as most weddings happen during the summer months. Sometimes, women arrive at the piazza where the bus picks them up wearing full make-up and with salon hair-dos. This is a sign that they have attended a wedding the previous night and is usually an excellent way to strike up a conversation. Although it is acceptable for younger women to wear make-up to work, this is not the case for older, married women. However, if married women have attended a wedding the previous evening and come to work the following morning still wearing make-up and with their hair elaborately styled, then this is far less frowned upon. Here there is little room to discuss that for women weddings are important occasions to 'safely' display their bodies. However, we can at least quote from Westwood (1984: 102) and use her work to highlight that 'weddings' are a tool to cope with the boredom of work. 'If there was one area of excitement which never seemed to wane, it was the glamour of white weddings. Everyone was excited by the prospect of a wedding because it kept romance and sex alive through the boredom of sewing side-seams day after day.'

Returning to our journey to work: as soon as the shuttles arrive at the factory, the hustle begins. Firstly, the women rush to clock in with their fingerprints on the clocking-in machine. A queue always forms in front of these machines because most women struggle to use them. The women commonly fail to press their fingers to the reader firmly enough for their fingerprint to register. When it does not work, they panic that their attendance will not be registered, so they continue to try more than once. At the gates of the factory, one can observe the first division between these women, namely, by age. However, this age difference also correlates with a difference in educational levels, as young women are more likely to be educated. Indeed, workers are assigned to different tasks according to their age. This is because managers assume that the younger women are better educated and are consequently more likely to be modern 'Daughters of the Republic' who will be able to cope with 'complicated' machinery.

These divisions are reflected inside the plant; we begin our journey into the factory at the clocking-in machine, where the first division between the workers and how these divisions are utilized by the Kemalist regime becomes clear.

> Helping the women use the clocking-in machine takes me more time each morning than it does to change into my work clothes. They really worry about it. As soon as I get off the shuttle, some of them surround me. I take their fingers inside my hand and we press down together. They can do it themselves, but they panic very quickly. And when they panic, they press down continuously and the machine does not respond. I don't know why the factory has this system, because it basically doesn't work.[13]

Why does the factory use these machines that do not work properly? The human resources manager told the women that if they could not use the machine, it would not affect their official timesheets at all. This means that the clocking-in machines have no real function. When I asked the factory manager about this, he told me that using the clocking-in machines was far more modern than simply shouting out a register. I told him that they still call out a register of names even when people clock in with their fingerprints. The response I received closely mirrors the Kemalist ideology that cites modernization as one of its key tenets: 'The women will have to learn to use the clocking-in machines because we will not give them up, machines like this are best suited to a factory like ours'.

When I see women trying to press their fingers to these English-speaking, 'foreign' and, hence, 'modern' machines, I feel that the management uses this technology to intentionally make some of the older, uneducated women feel that they are incapable of coping with the 'new technology' because they are not modern and/or educated enough. Those women also panic when something goes wrong with the machines. Some women even do not want to work in the machines section because they think that sorting out overripe tomatoes is preferable to the responsibilities of working with machines. These are generally the same older women who are discomforted by the clocking-in machines at the factory gates. Putting these machines at the factory gates and insisting that the women use them seem to me to signal the presence of the modernist factory regime from the very beginning, which alienates and controls workers and, thus, ushers the workers at the gate.

Women, on the other hand, already have assumptions that Red is different from other factories in the region. They know that it is a Kemalist factory and they participate in the performance of the elitism that this entails. For example, they think that Red is very selective when it comes to recruitment. The factory manager, however, refuted these claims and explained that they take on everyone who applies because it is difficult to find seasonal workers, as they share the same labour pool with several other factories. Red also differs from the other factories in the region based on its reputation. It is accepted amongst workers that Red is the best in terms of canteen food, its regular payment of wages and its hygienic conditions. It is also renowned for legally employing workers. On the other hand, it is also known for being the strictest factory to work in. This feeds a dual dichotomy of love and hatred for the factory. This duality also maps onto the binaries created by Kemalist ideology: its inside/outside binary, combined with the binary between Kemalism's progressive core that underlines the equality of both sexes, national sovereignty and welfarist principles, *contra* its tendency towards totalitarianism and regular state intervention by the military.

## *Rivals in Kemalism: Working together in the assembly line*

Once the women clock on and change into their work clothes, they assemble for roll call just outside the Human Resources building which is located just inside the factory gates (see Figure 6.1 for the outside of the plant). When all the names have been called, the *çavuşlar* – forewomen in Turkish (directly translated as corporals) – gather their groups and begin to walk through the doors of the plant. As they do so, they pass through the male workers working amongst fully laden trailers of tomatoes. I call this outside place 'limbo'; I feel that in every step I am moving away from 'heaven' and going to 'hell'. I feel uneasy when I walk. It is somehow better to be inside the plant as soon as possible rather than walking towards it. After passing through limbo, women entered inside the factory: dark, hot and loud and run to their lines.

I thought of the line as the 'tongue' and 'throat' of a *monster*, as this tomato-eating *mechanical monster* first chews tomatoes in the upper lines – tomato sorting lines – and then swallows them in the lower lines – in the machines. Tomatoes are processed differently depending on whether they are being chewed or swallowed by the *monster*. In line with this, the women's work changes depending on whether they are on the tongue or in the throat of the *monster*. While the 'Backward Religious Women' mostly work on where the sorting process takes

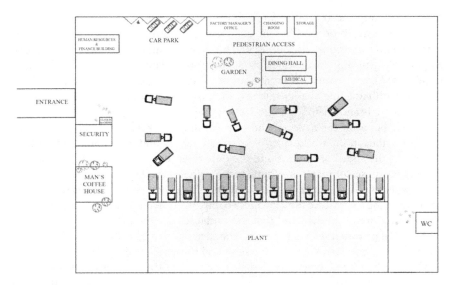

**Figure 6.1** External environs of plant.[14]

place, 'the Educated Daughters of the Republic' are in where women control the machines. These are two of the categories of women identified by Kemalist ideology. Republican women who are emancipated by the state do not see rural women – apart from Anatolian women celebrated as the Republic's mothers – as sisters but as the 'backward' other. Red divides them on the shop floor with the same assumption; the machines are more privileged and 'modern' than the tomato sorting lines, which are a bit 'backward and traditional'. In the following, first I will picture the 'backward' tomato sorting lines then fill this in with women workers and the *çavuş*. Then, I will do the same for the 'modern' machines.

## Picturing the tomato sorting lines

The tomato sorting lines are around five metres above floor level. On these lines, tomatoes are selected in several phases: first the whole tomatoes are sorted, the women checking to see if they are green or overripe; then the machine peels them and women again check whether they are green or overripe, this time when the tomatoes are hot; after the second selection, some tomatoes go directly into the huge boilers to become tomato sauce. The rest become 'diced' tomatoes inspected for a third time after the machine dices them.

There are twelve lines for tomato sauces and two lines for diced tomatoes. The factory does not just produce tomato sauces and chopped tomatoes for its own brand, but it also produces for other national and international companies. Thus, these lines process different-quality tomatoes depending on their buyers. Consequently, working on some of the lines is more difficult than others. Apparently, working on the lines producing for the Japanese shareholder's brand is relatively easy because the tomatoes are less overripe or green. Workers call the most difficult line the 'disgusting' line, as it produces for a cheap national supermarket brand. Although the factory manager told me there is no quality difference between the national and international markets, the quality difference is very obvious in the workplace. Women can understand for whom they work by looking at the speed of the line and the quality of tomatoes. There is no 'specific' line for Japanese company or others; technically, all the lines are the same. But, if a line works with the worst-quality tomatoes for a long time, it is cleaned deeply before starting to produce for a Japanese company. When managers say that we will do cleaning, we all understand that the tomatoes destined for Japan have finally arrived. 'Their tomatoes are different', the factory manager told me. 'Their seeds are different, their fertilizers are different, and these are totally different tomatoes.'

On the other hand, given the Kemalist leanings of the company, it is ironic that the factory also produces tomato sauce for companies that have close ties with the current government. Öniş (2012) suggests that the AKP government tried to create its 'own' alternative bourgeois, especially after 2011, following its third major electoral success and the completion of its debt repayment to the IMF. The country's internal social and political divisions are even mirrored in consumers' supermarket trolleys and at the checkout. Those who oppose the government tend to buy produce from 'opposition companies'. As can be expected, the relations of production in Red are also as politicized as consumption relations. Knowing that some people buy Red's products *because* they do not support the government's policies, I wonder what the public's reaction would be if they knew that Red also sold to companies with close government ties. I imagine that they would be disappointed. When I asked the general manager (who is very critical of the government) about this conflict of interests, he said that 'if our consumers knew about this, we would lose our reputation. But, you know, we have to do it to survive' (16 September 2014). As I am not well versed in business, I do not know if this is strictly true. On the other hand, although I am no business person, I know from an old Turkish expression that 'money does not have any religion or faith'. It is based on this that I think that a Kemalist factory has no hesitations about cooperating with supporters of its rival ideology. However, the management does not like to talk about this situation as if there is no connection. Instead, they prefer to emphasize how they have Japanese shareholders. The emphasis on Japanese shareholders feeds into the modern and, hence, prestigious image that the factory tries to sustain. Both managers and workers are proud of the factory's modern outlook. Women workers are even grateful that the factory has foreign shareholders.

> If Red was not there, what would we have done? Conditions in the other factories are really terrible. Our factory is really big. Atatürk – the founder of Turkish Republic – himself established it. We are so lucky to have the Japanese. When

the Japanese come, they check everywhere; they even eat in the same canteen with us. So, our food is good, and our factory is clean most of the time, especially when the Japanese visit.[15]

Red is the oldest tomato-processing factory in the area, but Atatürk did not in fact establish it. This is a very common myth among workers that no one attempts to correct. On the contrary, everyone including management and some of the workers enjoy this myth because it makes identifying with the Kemalist factory regime easier.

Returning to the lines, whilst the conditions between the lines vary, as discussed above, the conditions along the line are also very different. In some ways the beginning of the line, where the tomatoes are selected, is more comfortable to work in: it is cleaner, because the tomatoes are cold and recently washed, and cooler, since it lies towards the outside edge of the plant. But, the difficulty is that the tomatoes bring lots of rubbish and dead animals with them to the line, because they are not picked one by one on the land; rather, they are first shaken onto the ground and then are dragged to the bags. This means that rural workers do not see what goes inside the bags and sometimes if there is rubbish or dead animals on the soil, these also go inside the bag. So, in the factory you have to act quickly to dispose of bits of chewing gum and dead animal. Some women are willing to work here since it is cooler; some of them, however, prefer working on other parts of the 'line' since they say that, at the very least, it is a 'clean' job even if it is a 'hotter' one.

In the second part of the line, peeled tomatoes come to the lines and women again sort them depending on whether they are overripe or green. Since they are selected a second time, redder and fewer overripe tomatoes come to this line. But, these tomatoes are hot and since they have been peeled, the acidic, juicy surface causes your hands to swell. There is fresh water on the lines to clean your hands but this water is both shared and limited, so the water gets tomato-saucy very quickly. Moreover, the more you wet your hands, the quicker they swell. Although everyone knows that wetting your hands causes more trouble in the long term, it is often worth it in the short term as the water provides a temporary relief from the burning sensation.

In the third part of the line, tomatoes come to the line to be diced. They just look like red meat cubes. Here, the difficulty is that they are very small, so when you follow and pick out some green amongst lots of red cubes for eight hours, you feel dizzy and when you look away from the line, all you can see is red and green.

In all parts of the selecting lines, there is another belt, which moves in the opposite direction from the main line, onto which women place the discarded tomatoes. In the first and second parts of the line this belt runs over the main line, as shown Figure 6.2, and in the third part it runs under the line. When this additional line is under the main line (Figure 6.3), onto which the women throw the 'green ones', the women do not complain about pain in their arms. But the first and the second parts of the line, where women have to lift the rotten or green tomatoes onto the 'over' additional line, cause lot of arm and shoulder pain.

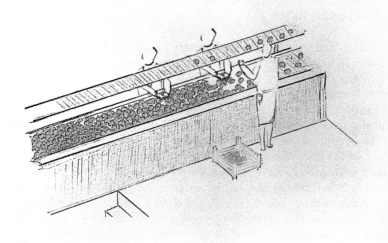

**Figure 6.2** The first and second parts of the sorting lines.

**Figure 6.3** The third part of the sorting lines.

All women on the tomato sorting lines stand all day; there is no place to sit. When trailers are being changed in the 'tank' outside the plant, sometimes lines stop for one to two minutes. These moments are life-saving: women fill the water cups with clean water and sit just on the floor. The factory manager told me that before he came to the factory there were seats on the lines, but as soon as he began his job, the first thing he did was remove the seats. Since, he told me, no one could earn money while sitting and talking with each other for eight hours: this is not the (women's) 'kitchen'.[16] As seen here, the factory manager does not see the women working on the selecting lines as workers but as lazy women. His prejudices are also shared by the warehouse workers, who are constructed as 'Anatolian Women'. The warehouse workers think that the other women could also work permanently – as the warehouse workers do – but that they choose not to because they are lazy. In reality, women selecting tomatoes work almost the whole year round but in different seasonal jobs around the region. They do not want to be employed permanently – although finding a permanent job is also very difficult – in the same factory because of both their familial commitments and their social environment, which does not approve of women becoming full-time factory workers. This is because, out of season, the number of women factory workers decreases dramatically and factories become male-dominated workplaces. Therefore, women prefer working in the factories when women dominate them. So yes, those women are 'more conservative'.

### Çavuş – sergeant – feeds the line

From the *çavuş*'s perspective, selecting tomatoes on the line is an unskilled task. For this reason, the forewoman selects the *işe yaramaz* for the lines. The *işe yaramaz* are what the *çavuş* calls useless. These women overwhelmingly tend to be older. If I showed you a photo of the whole production line, you would see that middle-aged women are on the upper lines where they select tomatoes, whereas the relatively younger women are in the lower lines, working at the machine (see Figure 6.4 for the position of the upper and lower lines). In that sense, 'age' seems to be the

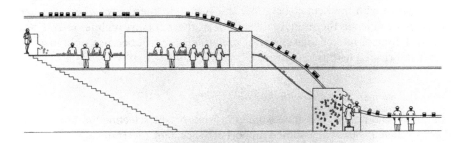

**Figure 6.4** The upper and lower production lines.

main criterion for task allocation. However, if you spend time in the plant or you talk with the forewoman or any managers, you eventually understand that youth is not just a physical criterion; they see younger women as being more 'energetic', more 'capable' and more 'confident'. For the managers and the forewomen, these characteristics stem from their education.

Lots of university students work in the factory as seasonal workers. Based on this, the forewoman assumes that younger women are students or at least she assumes that younger women are more educated. As far as the continuously increasing education level in Turkey is concerned, it can be assumed that younger women have more chance of being more educated. I discuss younger women's work – 'Daughters of the Red Republic' – in the machines in another section. Turning back to older women and their selection, it is possible to say that the forewoman deems older women to be 'useless', 'uneducated' and 'needing close management'. As discussed above, these characteristics map onto the characteristics imposed upon more religious women. By older I mean older than university students but these women are mostly in their late forties, and more religious women are directly labelled by the Kemalist factory regime as supporters of the AKP, the current government. Kemalists find their legitimization for assuming that AKP supporters are 'uneducated' and 'conservative' in statistics. Reports suggest that as education level increases, the likelihood of voting for the AKP and self-identification as conservative decreases (KONDA 2018).

Religious groups cope with the labels such as 'uneducated' or 'backward' by trying to develop their own elite consisting of educated, liberal democratic, moderate Muslims. This was also the image that the AKP sought to create and was a key factor in securing the support of more 'marginalized' religious people who did not conform to the Kemalist ideal. However, the AKP and connected religious groupings' self-construction and widely promoted image as being moderate, liberal Muslims have not been able to save the uneducated, older women working seasonally at Red from being labelled 'useless'. These women's position on the peripheries of Kemalist ideology leads to the perpetuation of their perceived role as useless, as fit only to work selecting tomatoes on the lower lines. In contrast, the younger educated women represent the modern, Western ideal of a woman, so they are trusted to work with the machines. These latter women are assumed to be compliant with the Kemalist regime. This raises the question of whether either group can challenge the militaristic control of the Kemalist regime. Here I use Kemalist control interchangeably with militaristic control because militarism is deeply imbricated within Kemalism.[17]

### 'Religious' women's struggles with 'Kemalist control'

The *çavuş* does not choose some women to work on the selecting lines to punish them for their apparent or assumed support of the current government. She chooses them because they are older and hence more likely to be uneducated. But the management assumes that the majority of these women are more likely to support conservative ideologies and therefore support the AKP as the main representatives of this group in the current political arena. There is no indication which political party these women actually support. But, their rural backgrounds, the neighbourhoods they live in and their irregular employment history lead the management to assume that they are government supporters. However, the management does not overtly use 'supporting the AKP' as a reason to legitimize its 'Kemalist' control. In fact, the surveillance of the women on all parts of the sorting lines resembles Bentham's panopticon (Foucault 1991). Women are more closely supervised on the upper lines, and harsh attitudes, including shouting and arguing, are more prevalent on the selection lines. Here, the perception of religious, conservative women is used to justify harsh control. The women chosen for the sorting lines are seen as 'traditional', 'backward', 'lazy' and 'incapable' 'followers'.[18] The treatment the women receive on the selection lines is much harsher than elsewhere in the plant.

This does not differ greatly to the way in which Kemalist ideology constructs the image of conservative women (İlyasoğlu 1998). Indeed, the *çavuş* believes that strict control of these women is necessary. She justifies her attitude by saying that 'these women are used to doing what they're told. They only understand harsh words and do not understand what you're trying to do if you treat them humanely' (23 August 2014). The general manager shares the same ideas as the forewoman and claims that these women prefer to be commanded rather than governed democratically: 'Those women do not know how to think as they are lazy. Following is easier for them. So, they don't care if someone commands them, they like it and they prefer being bossed around to being treated fairly [by this he implies the prime minister (in that day) Recep Tayyip Erdoğan's "authoritarian" attitudes]. We see this everyday'.[19]

He then went on to explain that the reason why the AKP are still in power is because of passive, mindless people like the women in the factory. He further argued that this is similar to how these women are dominated by their husbands and that these women deserve to be treated the way they are because they do not think for themselves; they are completely passive and mindlessly obey.[20]

Poor treatment of the women working on the lines is seen as what the women deserve as they are neither trustworthy nor hardworking. In this sense, it is not surprising that the 'forewoman' is called *çavuş* – corporal. The *çavuş* herself claimed that if she did not behave authoritatively enough, the women working in the lines would not do their jobs properly. The women working on the selection lines, on the other hand, seem to expect this strict control and find it 'normal'.

'Of course, they need to control, otherwise how will they earn money? This is needed for both them and us. We need this factory', says Hatice.[21] Women workers at Red 'accept' and 'tolerate' the control as being just the way things are. This, however, does not mean that they are satisfied with the status quo. These are the thankful women of Turkey, people created by socio-political history of the country. However, these women still find ways in which to resist the norm; some women are waiting to be rewarded by God, and all of them are trying to have greater autonomy over break times as well as have longer breaks than permitted. The following demonstrates how religious women workers construct their means of resistance and how 'Red' blocks them.

*'God sees everything except break times'*

> Our working place is like a 'Survivor' island. I think they should do this programme[22] in the factory rather than a remote island. When work becomes harsher, women become more selfish and, as on the programme, as time passes, people start to fight. Since everyone begins to focus on saving their own strength, everyone is looking for ways to ease their work. I think that there is no exception about it. Just that some women make me think about the second time; they seem to be fine with their burden and are not trying to ease their work. I don't know about 'masochistic' behaviours and I am worried about claiming something wrong 'scientifically'. As I observed, these women think that the more they suffer, the more virtuous they become. Better than others; different to the others, more respectful than others. It is actually what the religion suggests and patriarchy also leads to what women feel about themselves. When I asked one of these women, Fahriye (39), why she accepts everything from the forewoman and also other women, she told me that 'Since God sees. I don't need to do anything. When they behave unfairly to me, I become happier since it means that I will be rewarded'. I didn't know what to say to this.[23]

If the *çavuş* heard Fahriye, she would probably tell her, 'god sees everything except you taking longer breaks, doesn't (s)/he?' – just as she had told one of the women previously. By saying this, the *çavuş* implied that women are committing a sin by not returning from their breaks on time. This is because they are effectively stealing money from the factory by taking longer breaks. According to most of the workers, however, they are working hard enough to deserve their wages. Apparently, for the management this is not the case. It seems that for the *çavuş*, managing the women selecting tomatoes mostly involves deciding their break times. Breaks are at the centre of the women's relations with the *çavuş* and also with each other. This is similar to what we saw on the land, but this time the control of management over them is much stricter. For example, our line manager (on the diced tomato line) was always waiting in front of the ladies' toilets in order to make sure that everyone returned from their break on time. He shouted constantly, 'Women from the lines it's time to go back inside' (they called the upside of the lines, 'lines' and the lower sides, the 'machines'). He asked us whether we were on the machines or on the lines. He was really frightening when he was shouting; he also violently hit the tin shacks in which the toilets are housed which made it all the more frightening. He did not ask the younger women working on the machines when they started their breaks, but constantly kept track of the women working on the tomato selection lines. He usually sends women from the line back from their breaks fifteen minutes early because of the time it takes to walk back to the line from the toilets. He uses his anger as a means of control and it works. I heard from lots of women saying, 'Let's go, before this madman starts shouting.' He makes people feel uncomfortable while they are on their breaks, so they feel like it is better to go back to work as soon as possible. This reflects how the factory regime causes women to internalize control through creating fear by being as authoritarian and aggressive as possible.

Since all women cannot go for a break at the same time – the lines never stop over the twenty-four-hour day except for changing trailers or maintenance – sometimes the *çavuş* chooses who goes first and who waits for later, and when she chooses, it is always either as a reward or as a punishment. Break times for the day shift (8.00 am to 4.00 pm) are normally at 10.00 (fifteen minutes' toilet break), at 12.00 (lunch, half an hour) and at 14.00 (fifteen minutes' toilet break), but they usually do not apply all the time.

> Contrary to my expectations, we could not go out on our break until 13.30. I began to feel dizzy, like the surface of the floor was slipping from beneath my feet. When I looked in front of me at Yeliz and Mehtap, I couldn't see them as stable; it was like they were moving with the line. I already had chocolate in my pocket but it wasn't enough. At 13.00 I told Yeliz, I don't feel good; she told the forewoman, who came and told me that we would not be allowed to break until 13.30. It was almost unbelievable that all the women were complaining before she came, but none of them said anything to her. I asked her why we were waiting and she replied that it was because the cafeteria gets very crowded and there was not enough space for all the workers. Half an hour later, she returned and said everyone could go to lunch except Necla and me. We had to do cleaning. It was apparent that she punished me for my previous comments. If I said nothing to her, I wouldn't have had to stay behind.[24]

Although in the above example waiting for the second round was a punishment, taking the breaks first is not always desirable, especially on night shifts. Break times on night shifts are normally at 2.00 am, 4.00 am and 6.00 am. While on day shifts the forewoman usually starts break time later than normal, on night shifts she always sends women on breaks earlier than this. I thought many times about why she came earlier on night shifts but I couldn't find a reasonable answer. On night shifts, productivity decreases as time goes on and most women say that the most difficult hours are between 3.00 am and 5.00 am. You begin to feel that your eyes are closing after around 2.00 am and standing on the line becomes harder. Thus, it is not reasonable to send women to breakfast earlier, but the *çavuş* does. When I asked the women what they thought about this, most of them just said because the *çavuş* did not like us, so she intentionally chose the worst break time for our line. I did not think that this could be the reason behind her choice and I asked her why she sent us out for our breaks later on the day shift and earlier on the night shift. She just told me that: 'It must be like this'.[25]

*It must be like this* is an expected answer under 'militaristic' control, that there is no reasonable answer for every question. I could not claim that I was getting on well with the *çavuş* or that I had adapted to control. The *çavuş* always accused me of questioning everything and complaining. I do not think that she was wrong. I was really wondering about everything and complaining more than most women. She was also uncomfortable with my role as a researcher, as she told me more than once: 'I don't know what you will write about me. But, next time just do research about being a forewoman. It is really difficult when you are responsible for everything. Managers continuously shout at you and women continuously gossip about you. Ask any of these women, who wants to become a *çavuş*. I tell you none of them'.[26]

She was right; on many occasions, I saw the managers shout at her. According to the forewoman this is because the managers do not want to address the workers directly. The general manager confirmed this when he said: 'I don't want to see close relationships between the managers and the women; they don't need to know each other otherwise the women won't work properly. They should refrain from speaking to the managers. You know that the *çavuşlar* (plural of *çavuş*) are also workers so they speak the workers' language'.[27]

The *çavuş*'s position is very similar to the 'middle woman' on the land; they are stuck between workers and managers, and neither group thinks that the *çavuş* is on their side. However, this is to be expected from the position of a *çavuş*, the sergeant, as sergeant both commands and is commanded. This position makes it almost impossible for her to satisfy anyone's demands, as she is literally on both sides and hence on neither. But, there is one group of women who like the *çavuş*, the protector of the regime; this is the 'Daughters of the Republic': educated women working with alongside the machines.

## *Picturing the machines*

The machines refer to the lower parts of the line, to which the assembly line brings tomatoes after they are selected. Here women basically prepare the tins to be sealed. Women are still standing on the moving assembly line, but now they have full tins rather than tomatoes. Managers and women called these parts of the line 'machines'. It is because women also have to engage with the machines, which fill, weigh and seal the tins. Women's involvement with machines is limited. They are just responsible for informing technicians when they realize that something has gone wrong, such as slowing down or making a different noise.

The first part of the 'machines' is 'filling'. Two women stand at this station. The assembly line sends tomatoes down from the upper lines into a huge container and in the meantime a moving line brings cans to this container. Women push tomatoes into the cans, while this big machine stirs the tomatoes in the container. This task has a reputation for being the most difficult task of all the lines. When the tomatoes fall into the container, they are boiled and women have to push tomatoes inside the very hot water with gloves on, standing all day.

At the second set of machines, two women weigh the filled tins. They check whether they are heavier or lighter than their intended weight. In the diced tomato line, the cans are 5 kg, so the weight should be between 4,800 and 4,900 g. This is an especially tiring task when women have to lift 5 kg tins constantly while remaining standing.

In the third part, which is called 'cover', where I mostly worked, two women pour tomato sauce into the tins on top of the tomatoes, to make up their weight, and then put the covers into a machine to cover the tins. It is one of the hottest places to work, since basically, there is a boiled tomato sauce tap and women take the sauce from there continuously. The tap is usually open so the place is usually hot. After this part of the line, the tomato tins go into a cooling section and they wait there for three hours. Although they wait there, the lines do not stop because the factory runs twenty-four hours a day seven days a week except for maintenance and cleaning, which only ever occurs in the run-up to a visit from one of the representatives of the Japanese shareholders. Once the tomato cans are sealed, they are out of the production part of the line; they wait for women to scan their barcodes.

## 'We have the power to stop the line': 'The Daughters of Red Republic'

Today was a disaster. I caused the production line to stop for a whole three hours. Can you believe it? I still feel very anxious. Everything started when Ayfer went for break. I was alone and pouring the tomato sauces into cans, as always. While leaving, Ayfer told me that she had already fed the machine with the covers. I didn't need to put extra covers for five minutes. So, I only focused on the cans. In the meantime, Süheyla (working after me, controlling the covers) came and started to talk with me about her boyfriend. How he doesn't give her 'permission' to swim in a bikini, how he is jealous and so on. Since I was so angry with him, I become too engaged with her talking and I totally forgot about the covers. I could keep pouring the tomato sauce automatically, but the covers are behind me so I wasn't seeing them. I didn't realise that there were no covers inside the machine and cans were going to the cooler without covers. Also, because Süheyla was with me, there was no one to control the covers. Everything happened in 3–4 minutes. Suddenly, tins stacked in front of me, and when I looked behind me; I saw an endless queue of cans, all stacked. I just pushed the emergency button to stop all the line. I felt like I was going to faint. But, as I learned in the factory, fortunately I am not that weak. I can keep going on even if disaster happens.

Anyway, after I stopped the line, Süheyla and I ran to the end of line and started to take down the cans from line to the floor. We tried to take down as many as we could before technicians and managers arrived. If they would see how many they are, they would have understood how long it took for us to realise that there was a problem. We managed to take down half of them and the floor was covered in cans. When the technicians came, they directly thought that the settings of the cover machine had broken down, so they started to change the settings. It made everything worse since the machine actually didn't break down. Solving the problem took them an hour. But when the lines started to work again, we just realised that the cooler had also broken down, since lots of cans went there without covers. It took another two hours to repair that too and they had to change some parts of it. I was really stressed, because of Süheyla and me production in the whole factory had stopped for three hours, we didn't work. Süheyla told everyone it happened because of me (I think, it was also because of her, but she just acted like it was only my fault). Some of the women came and told me 'please do it again'. On the other hand, some of them threatened me, saying 'don't be afraid we won't tell anyone' and laughing at me. But, clearly they were just trying to tell me that they could tell anyone that I was to blame.[28]

Women are not observed or controlled strictly in the machines. The *çavuş* does not manage these women, since she trusts them. They are her 'smart daughters', as they are educated and 'modern' enough to observe and monitor the machine. It is another question whether she trusts us as a management strategy or she actually trusts the machines and not us. In the machines section, the assembly line continues to move and the machines do the work; women just help the machines. So, even if no one were there, the process would not stop. The task itself is enough to control us. But, *çavuş* always emphasizes that only educated woman can work on this part of the line because there are a lot of responsibilities here. Older women (implying women working on the selecting lines) could push the wrong buttons on the machines. As a consequence of this trust, we decide our break times; we stay on break for more than fifteen minutes or half an hour for lunch; it all depends on your agreement with your colleagues. Since in every position two women are working, when actually one woman is enough, they can arrange their break times with each other. When managers or forewoman see you are alone, they assume that your friend is on their break and they do not ask you when she went or will come back. When I was selecting tomatoes, *çavuş* and managers shouted at me to be quick, as they did to everyone, but on the down side of the line, *çavuş* gets on well with all women. No shouting, no controlling, no problems. *Çavuş* and managers imply to us that we are 'smart' enough to put covers inside the machine. But, apparently, I am not as smart as they thought I was. In the above example, the technicians immediately thought that it was machine's fault, not mine, since I am the most educated woman on the line. How would it be possible to forget to put covers into the machine? Indeed, they trust their machines and they think that they try to guarantee their machines' well-being while putting 'the Educated Daughters of the Republic' there, who are hardworking, trusted as well as sexually modest.

### *Are the 'Daughters of the Red Republic' suitable for the managers?*

Flirtation in the factory usually takes the forms of gazing, talking, smiling and subtle insinuation; it is not conducted openly. This mirrors the image of modesty portrayed by Kemalism. Machines could be the boring and exploitative part of the line, since workers do not have any control over the production and are controlled by the machines. However, by adding romance or the promise thereof, the workers transform this part of the line into the most enjoyable part of work. The management also encourages this by allocating all the young workers to the machines and not controlling them strictly. This is apparently what Burawoy (1979) implies when he outlines the cooperation of workers with capital to create their own consent in the hegemonic factory regime. On other parts of the line, however, where work is more hands on, the management aims to prevent flirtation as the quality as well as the amount of the production depends on workers' efficiency: coercion comes easily to the management. As bound up with the material conditions of the work, flirtation is only tolerated between 'educated' couples that are 'suitable' for each other and where there is a possibility of marriage.

Although, like the managers, the 'Daughters of Red' are educated to degree level, they believe that the managers are above them because they come from 'different worlds'. Here, the expression 'different worlds' addresses different socio-economic backgrounds. This is clearly a reflection of how women from rural and conservative families who have entered tertiary education have increasingly begun to challenge the terms of an older 'category' of secular, urban educated women. But, this is not apparent from the point of the management, as they only see 'young educated' women, and because everyone inside the factory wears a cap, they cannot see which of the women wear headscarves. Although the general manager continues to 'trust' educated women, he views flirtation in the workplace differently from his colleagues: 'I know that some women and men who come to the factory come here to find a partner. But, that is good, isn't it? At the end of the day, it doesn't matter why people come to work here, it just matters that they come. Otherwise, you would not have these young people here'.[29]

Begüm (twenty-one) points out her reason for not attempting to flirt with managers as 'they cannot attempt to flirt with us because they cannot be sure if we are suitable for them. You know, anyone can work there. We are not like the women in quality control'.[30] Although management continues to assume that these women are like the 'Daughters of the Red Republic', because it is difficult to see social differences among them, managers prefer not to risk flirting with these workers and flirt with women working in quality control instead. The women who work in quality control are employed by interview and this means that managers can guarantee that these women are from the same world as they are.

Therefore, it is mainly the male workers, who are young seasonal workers and usually students just as women are, whom the women working at the machines see as the recipients of 'proper' flirtation. There are no male workers with permanent contracts in the factory. Someone may say that 'love' cannot be reduced to the statement of being appropriate for one another due to similar backgrounds. To these people, I would say that love (at least in this factory) is also a matter of convenience. There is a very popular Turkish expression that is used to refer to the vitality of being together with someone like you in terms of your social background: '*davul bile dengi dengine çalar*', which has a similar meaning to 'birds of a feather flock together'. However, while the English idiom is more about common interests and values, in the Turkish the emphasis is on similar backgrounds and, specifically, class. I know it seems very depressing, at least for me. I wish I could have written that convenience is not the condition of love, but it seems that our logic decides who is loveable and then our heart loves. Picking someone from outside of 'loveable' pools for the women in the factory leads to their fate being determined by sheer chance and, for them, chance is always much far too risky. Rather, they believe in 'destiny'. From their point of view, flirting with male workers is much more their destiny, whereas flirting with managers would be playing a dangerous game of chance. At least inside the factory, as Filiz who is twenty-one, told me, 'If we would encounter with Halit (one of managers), I would like him. He is very nice, but here we are in different positions. It is not appropriate'.[31] We call the managers *Bey*, which equates to 'Sir' in English. This is another obstacle to flirtation and this is how Kemalist ideology makes the public domain suitable for women to work in: by professionalizing all relations.

### 'Anatolian Women' in the warehouse

And the women,
> our women
> with their awesome, sacred hands,
> pointed little chins, and big eyes,
> our mothers, lovers, wives,
> who die without ever having lived,
> who get fed at our tables after the oxen,
> who we abduct and carry off to the hills
> and go to prison for,
> who harvest grain, cut tobacco, chop wood, and barter in the markets,
> who we harness to our plows
> and who with their bells and undulant heavy hips surrender to us in sheepfolds
> in the gleam of knives stuck in the ground-
>         the women, our women.
>                 Nazım Hikmet Ran

The above poem is extensively cited to highlight the ambiguous image of the 'Anatolian Women'. On the one hand, she is powerful, capable and sacred; on the other hand, she is undervalued (Durakbaşa, 1998). Although I do not personally like some parts of Nazım's poem, because I feel that it underestimates the women's agency, one can readily see how rural Anatolian Women are perceived contradictorily. This portrayal of 'the toilworn village woman' in terms of their heavy workload in rural life fills the gap between the 'sophisticated urban women' and the 'backward village women' in the eyes of Kemalists (Durakbaşa 1998). The emphasis on their devalued work in both Durakbaşa's conceptualization and Nazım's poet is also reflected in how the women warehouse workers are perceived by management.

The warehouse is the only section of Red factory in operation year-round. Thus, its workers are not seasonal workers, but, as mentioned at the very beginning of the chapter, they still do not have permanent contracts. They are employed via a subcontracting firm, and their contracts are renewed every few months. These are mainly women workers; there is just one male worker here, who works permanently – again via a subcontracting firm, but he does not work under a permanent contract officially – and he is the foreman of the section. In the warehouse, the main task is to put products into boxes. For each product, the way of doing it varies and it mainly depends on the weight of the product. There is a machine, in the shape of a line – everyone calls it a 'machine' – which can pack the products when they are above a certain weight. However, for 5 kg products, the women have to do it themselves. This is the main work in the warehouse.

Firstly, you have to set up the box and put six tins inside it. This is the easy part, at the end; they have to align their 30 kg boxes as a tower. They call these towers 'pallets'. Then, a male worker comes and takes them by using a lift truck. This is exhausting physical work. In my case, since I couldn't manage to pick up 30 kg boxes alone, so I made pallets with one of my friends, who also struggled to stack hers alone. It was still hard. All women working there complain that they have to do a man's job; however, they do not give up. Although they complain, doing men's work brings them admiration from factory managers including the general manager but not from the women working on the sorting lines. The women doing the seasonal work sorting the tomatoes disrespect the warehouse women, who they see as not like 'women'. They are seen, so warehouse women can do the men's job, and the women on the sorting line would not like to do this.

The Kemalist factory regime tries to make women working on the warehouse more masculine by emphasizing their physical power. Red achieves this by assigning those women to 'men's' tasks and then appreciates the 'Powerful Anatolian Women'. As the factory manager told me: 'While these women try to do men's work with all their power, how can others complain about selecting tomatoes while standing?'.[32] This is all to explain why he wrote a letter to the company's general board to complain about the use of a subcontracting firm employ the warehouse workers on temporary contracts when, as he sees it, they work harder than anyone else – harder than men. The manager also complained that the men are lazy and do not want to work in the warehouse: 'They are not even as good as women'. Unfortunately, there is not an alternative 'hero' image of rural men in the Kemalist ideology, so men have to stay in the category of 'backward rural people'.

Although the general manager does not trust or like rural men, he wants to employ male workers in the warehouse, since he knows that it is a man's job, but the conditions of work do not attract men as subcontracting work is too insecure. As I wrote in my diary:

> The factory manager said that men prefer being security guards with the same wage. Since they are sitting all day. They are lazy'. What about seasonal male workers, I asked him, could you employ them in the warehouse at least in the season? He answered me in the following way: 'don't mention them. They are show-offs. They come here to flirt with girls. They do their hair, they wear their jeans and they hang around the plant, they are no different from the women. Even if we had one of them here, we would not be able to have a single woman in the warehouse.[33]

In this very contradictory statement, the manager seems to like having women working in the warehouse, basically because they are doing a difficult man's job, and he does not like male workers since they are doing 'women's work', and not doing it properly as men, but like women who care more for their appearance and flirting than doing a good job. He has a very rigid division between men's and women's work in his mind and he is very upset about not being able to apply it in the factory properly. He is even ashamed of this since he told me he was really sorry that I had to work in the warehouse. On the other hand, although women working in the warehouse complain about it, they are also proud of doing man's job. Zeliha told me that 'Emine, are you also writing about the warehouse ... Then, write about how we are even more powerful than men. Write that men do not want to work there, but we do it easily'.[34]

Unfortunately, they actually do not do this work 'very easily'. They work for twelve hours a day for the whole year with one day off a week. In peak season, they work twelve-hour shifts and start work four hours earlier than the other workers. They also cannot enjoy the benefits of a permanent contract, even if they work for the factory for long period of time. These women also earn less than women who work on the production line seasonally. But, they say, 'they always have a job and others work just seasonally. That is why they earn less. There is a price for everything'. They also say that 'we appreciate having this permanent job[35] since it is very difficult to have a job permanently in this town where there are mainly food factories and they always employ workers with temporary contracts'. These women are just how the factory manager desires them to be: they work more than everyone else in the factory but they do not complain even though their conditions are precarious: they are sufficiently toilworn to be respected and thought of as sacred. At the same time, this means that they are undervalued as women.

The contradictory assessment of the warehouse women workers, who I have argued are constructed in a similar way to the 'Anatolian Women' of Kemalist ideology, shows us that employing women in a 'man's job' does not necessarily lead to the undervaluation of that work, contrary to what previous literature suggests (Chant and McIlwaine 1995; Phillips and Taylor 1980). Rather, in the Red factory it increases the 'reputation' of those women by masculinizing them because of the men's work they do. Phillips and Taylor (1980: 79) state that 'women workers carry into the workplace their status as subordinate individuals, and this status comes to define the value of their work they do'. When women are employed in skilled work, usually men's work, they downgrade the value of that work because they are 'inferior bearers of labour' (Phillips and Taylor 1980). Skills and the definition of their value are saturated by 'sex' (Chant and McIlwaine 1995; Phillips and Taylor 1980); men do skilled work, but when women do the same work it becomes seen as less skilled or unskilled work. The masculinizing of 'Anatolian Women', on the other hand, and respect for their work demonstrate that in this factory the prestige of a job is more about it appearing to call for masculine or feminine traits, and this then affects how the workers are seen: the task itself is already masculine or feminine before people are employed. Regardless of their sex, workers are masculinized and feminized on the shop floor but with reference to politics of the manager and his understanding of feminine and masculine.

## The shop floor: Subcontracting and intersectional patriarchy

The *mechanical monster* of Red finds a guiding heart and brain in the labyrinth of Kemalist ideology. It is in this way that Kemalism forms the ideological bedrock categories of labour control that allows the beast to continue to 'live'. The Kemalist factory regime organizes labour in Red through reconstituting the three categories of women in Kemalist ideology on the shop floor, and women give their heart and brain to the hands of the ideology, as they believe that this is the best option for them to survive. Red convinces women of the factory's preciousness, thanks to the modern core of the Kemalist ideology. Women regardless of their category in the Kemalist ideology are happy to receive their wages regularly and according to the amount of employment law requires, be given good and enough food, safe transportation, and fixed working hours. Although they cannot press their fingers properly on the English-speaking clock-in machines at the gates of the factory, and they always complain about having to clean when the Japanese come to visit the factory, those complaints do not prevent them from showing off at the pick-up points where they wait with all other women working in the different tomato-processing or food factories around their town. This is not different to what women think about Kemalism outside the factory. Many feminists also continuously criticized the authoritarianism, elitism and homogeneity of Kemalism, but are nonetheless positive about it when and if they see potential dividends from it (Arat 1998a). However, recognizing the advantages of the Kemalist ideology does not mean that women cannot also resist Kemalism.

One might argue that Kemalism is feminist because of its progressive core that underlines the equality of both sexes. However, very little of this so-called emancipation is self-directed, and women, having had no agency in the so-called feminist revolution in the early Turkish republic, perpetuate the patriarchal norms that it seemed to challenge. This is very similar to the way that Red offers women far better conditions than other factories across the region in terms of transportation, lunch as well as in wages, but it still sustains the patriarchal forms of control over women of all 'three categories' of women in Kemalist factory regime.

Red's Kemalist factory regime is patriarchal as it sees femininity as an impediment to modern production. The adaptation of global production to local conditions takes place through the deployment of Kemalism and its contradictory views of women's strengths and weaknesses which it allocates to different types of women. It constructs women working on the machines as gender neutral and defeminizes them whereas warehouse women are seen as masculine. Women on the production line are seen as feminine and that is why they are humiliated. It is evident that only masculinity gets respect. Thus, if women are to be treated with respect, they have to be seen as 'men'; they can't be respected as women. Similarly, men doing women's jobs are feminized, as in the way the manager depicts men workers in the factory. Masculinity governs femininity in different forms – educated women and/or Anatolian Women – in Red. This shows us the operation of intersectional patriarchy on the shop floor.

'Egalitarian' Kemalist ideology has not tried to destroy patriarchy, it has just tried to change the image of ideal women, and the Kemalist 'leftist' bourgeois management of Red has not tried to destroy capitalism, it has just (re)constructed capitalism. The 'emancipation' of Turkish women, which is in the hands of the state and mainly men, only includes secular, educated urban women and hence exacerbates the class divisions, which are impossible to separate from religion and ethnicity. This also draws parallels with what we see in Red in terms of the management's assumptions about women working in the sorting lines – 'Backward Religious Women' – and women working at the machines – 'Daughters of the Republic'. However, this distinction does not exacerbate the differences among women as expected by a Kemalist regime, since these two categories now overlap. As Kemalist ideology began to lose its hegemony outside the factory gate after the early 2000s, educated women no longer include only secular 'Daughters of the Republic'. This is a challenge to the Kemalist factory regime. In order for Red to continue organizing labour as it does, it will need to respond to the shifts in Turkish society and, in particular, to the shifting tectonics of religious and secular movements.[36]

## Chapter 7

## *EL ÂLEM* SPEAKS: THE CONSTRUCTION AND PERSISTENCE OF RURAL PATRIARCHY

Drawing on observations made at the landowning family's home and at the seasonal agricultural workers' homes, both the shacks the latter live in while working on the land and at their own homes in their hometowns, I identify different forms of rural patriarchy, which occur in parallel with the actors' different relations with tomatoes. I apply the term 'intersectional patriarchy' to reveal how patriarchy has taken different forms in the landowning family's household and in Kurdish migrant workers' households. I, then, will examine household relations in the families of the Red factory manager and workers.

*El âlem* in Turkish refers to a group of unidentified 'real' and at the same time 'imaginary' people who are outside the family. Speakers refer to these people when explaining why it is necessary for them to do this or that. *El âlem* is both an abstract concept and a concrete term, which refers to a particular form of social control serving to contribute the persistence of patriarchy. In the following passages, I first discuss the definitions of household and family with reference to the usage of the terms by people in the study. Then, I reveal the varieties of patriarchy at the household level through conceptualizing *el âlem* and discussing its relation to honour. In the third section, I examine how *el âlem* 'decides' which kinds of household structure women and men should have and how this depends on their position within the process of tomato production. Firstly, I focus on the households of women from the landowning family who are involved in planting tomatoes on the land, and then I look at Kurdish seasonal migrant workers' homes, both the shacks they stay in during seasonal work and their 'real' homes in their hometowns.

### *Conceptualizing households and family*

The difficulties in agreeing a universal definition of the household and the pitfalls of using the terms 'households' and 'family' as equivalents of each other are widely discussed in the literature (Chant 1997; Chant and McIlwanie 2009; Dunaway 2014; Kabeer 1994; Kandiyoti 1985; Walby 1990). Also in this particular context, they are not always necessarily coterminous. I have two main reasons to explain this situation. Firstly, the existence of kin marriages and their function as a means of organizing production and reproduction relations causes an overlapping of families and households, especially for Kurds. When households consist of kin, they become vehicles for familial ideology (Chant 1991) and this is valid for rural Turkey (Kandiyoti 1985). Secondly, I have linguistic reasons to use to refer Kurdish workers' households. In the Turkish language, family is called *aile* and household is called *hane* (*or hane halkı*). *Hane* is the direct translation of household, but it also carries the meaning associated with economic and social cooperation and not always inside the same dwelling. *Hane* (household) is different from *aile* (family) as the former is seen as an economic unit rather than a social one. For example, when a woman gets married and moves to her husband's parents' house, it means that she leaves her *hane* (*haneden ayrılmak*) and becomes a member of her husband's *hane*, but she does not leave her family (*aile*). Family is here associated with kinship relations. It is different among Kurds. In the Kurdish language, there is no particular word for households, as Chant and McIlwanie (2009) also observe for Tanzania (or for southern Mexico, for instance). Rather, Kurds use the word *mal* interchangeably to refer to both 'household' and 'family' (Yalçın-Heckmann 2012). *Mal* refers to a social and economic unit in which members depend on the same labour force for consumption; even when they are not living in the same dwelling. As explained by participants in the study, *mal* is the direct translation of an 'extended family'. But differently, the word also includes the lands, properties and/or animals of those who share a common budget even when they do not live in the same space. The size of *mal* can be large, over 100 people, and it is the smallest section of an *aşiret* (ibid.)

As the *mal* cannot be used only to refer to households but also refers to family, I use the word 'family' when it is necessary to underline the kinship relations. I also use the word 'family' to refer it as a site of conflict and cooperation. On the other hand, for the purposes of understanding the households mostly Turkish households, involved in my study, I deploy the definition, which sees a household as a unit 'in which members inequitably pool and redistribute labour, resources, and survival strategies that are grounded in both unpaid and paid (non-waged and waged) income sources' (Dunaway 2014: 57), because it offers a better chance to show the interdependency of household relations and production relations. I use this definition as the majority of women do not live in the same dwelling as members of the same household but lived in the same apartment building, neighbouring buildings or even in different places (e.g. a town and a village). However, they still referred to each other as belonging to the same household because of their joint budget and/or dependence on each other's productive or reproductive labour. This demonstrates that household members do not necessarily live under the same roof and that definitions of household vary. This runs contrary to one of the most widely deployed definitions; 'households as spatial units where members live in the same dwelling and share basic domestic and/or reproductive activities such as cooking and eating' (Chant 1997: 5).

## *Pluralities of* el âlem: *Pluralities of patriarchy*

It is well known that the degree and forms of patriarchy are various and depend on social contexts (Bozzoli 1983; Kandiyoti 1988; Walby 1986, 1990). In this book, the key differentiator of forms of patriarchy experienced by women is the different positions in the tomato production. Revealing these different positions of women through the intersectionality of gender, class, ethnicity and age allows us to see that these intersections shape and are in turn shaped by patriarchal household structures. However, exploring the ways in which patriarchy is (re)constructed still may not tell us why patriarchy persists. Drawing on my informants' own explanations of their reasons for contributing to the re-construction of patriarchal relations, I conceptualize (the) *el âlem*[1] as a particular form of social order – in this particular context – serving as an agential aspect of intersectional patriarchy.

## *Islam, social order and the 'eye' of Turkish society*

Mernissi (1985: 37) states that in the Muslim order it is not necessary for an individual to eradicate their instincts or to control them for the sake of doing so, but they must use them according to the demands of religious law. In the Muslim world, an individual cannot live without a social order. In the Turkish context, on the other hand, Mardin (1991) suggests that since the late Ottoman period Islamic law has been gradually displaced by the implementation of European laws and reforms. The Islamic order has been replaced by an all-seeing 'eye', which controls and governs Turkish society (Çakır 2008). For Mardin, neighbourhoods, the smallest administrative sections of urban areas, are the main agents of establishing and sustaining this 'eye'. His 1991 publication states that marriages, deaths, births, education, religion are all organized in and by *mahalle* – neighbourhood – under the eye of *mahalle sakinleri* – neighbours. He conceptualizes the social control of this all-seeing 'eye' as *mahalle baskısı* – 'neighbourhood pressure'. He first introduced the term in 2007 in an interview about his book *Religion, Society and Modernity in Turkey* (2006). In the early years of Republic, Kemalist reforms attempted to demolish the 'eye' through his modernist reforms (Mardin 1991). However, these reforms led to the creation of another social order called Kemalism. Therefore, it is not surprising that once the concept of neighbourhood pressure had been suggested, the Turkish media interpreted the term to refer to the demonizing of non-conservative groups by conservatives.[2]

Mardin does not directly say that 'neighbourhood' and 'neighbourhood pressure' refer to *el âlem*, a term people use in everyday life, but he sees neighbourhood pressure as a means to control both action and speech by forcing the social actor to reflect on how others perceive them.[3] I am not suggesting here that the concept of neighbourhood pressure is identical to that of *el âlem*, but that it is at least a close conceptual fit for how 'people' who are subject to *el âlem* as a form of social control define it.

Mardin's conception of *mahalle baskısı* has been criticized for not taking the relative isolation of nuclear households into account and not recognizing that urbanization leads to the diminishment of the 'neighbourhood' as an agent of social control (Subaşı 2008). Furthermore, despite the fact that there are strictly speaking no 'neighbourhoods' in rural areas, people living in such areas may in fact experience social control to a greater extent than people in the 'neighbourhoods' of cities or towns. The word *mahalle* – 'neighbourhood' – already bears too many urban connotations to capture the forms of social control in rural areas. So, the concept of *el âlem* might be a better way of understanding the changing nature of social control in Turkey, one which can be applied to urban or rural settings, especially since (the) *el âlem* is conceptually ubiquitous – referring, as it does, to every stranger (as well as everyone) in society.

*El âlem* can be understood as referring to the normative order and can either be abstract or personified depending on context. For instance, *el âlem* occurs in the abstract when a mother tells her 'educated' daughter that she cannot marry an uneducated groom. What will *el âlem* say about it? In contrast, *el âlem* occurs in a personified form if, for example, I ask my mother why she is exerting herself so hard over domestic chores, and she responds that the *el âlem* are coming for *gün* (gathering) tomorrow. In this instance, a significant aspect of the personified *el âlem* in the latter example is that it includes her relatives as well as neighbours, even her sisters. This distinction goes some way towards explaining why the Turkish Official Dictionary (TDK) defines *el âlem* as referring to both 'strangers' and 'everyone'.

## El âlem *and family honour*

Although the concept of *el âlem* has not been previously explored or adopted in the academic literature, the literature has already addressed the different forms of 'gendered' social order (Chant 1997; Chant and McIlwaine 2016; Fenster 1999; Lessinger 1990; Mernissi 1985; Moghadam 2003; Vera-Sanso 1995), particularly in relation to the concept of honour. These studies (Chant 1997; Chant and McIlwaine, 2016; Lessinger 1990; Mernissi 1985; Moghadam 2003; Vera-Sanso 1995) indicate how the social order serves to monitor or to control women's sexuality 'for the sake of family honour'. In Madras, for instance, a woman's participation in retail trading of fresh fruit and vegetables could only be possible when a male member of the family joins her in order to prevent possible sexual assault (Lessinger 1990). Fenster's (1999) study looks at how the policing of women's sexuality has been intensified by the modern planning project in Israel that has replaced traditional Bedouin living spaces. New tents have been designed to prevent women encountering 'stranger' men and hence they serve to protect 'family honour'. Chant's study (1991) underlines the pressure on women-headed households to protect the reputation of their family by acting in a 'sexually modest' way. Mernissi (1985) states: 'The concept of patriarchal honour is built around the idea of virginity, which reduces woman's role to its sexual dimension: reproduction with an early marriage' (cited in Moghadam 2003: 138). Moghadam (2003) argues that when women become excluded from productive activities, the control of women's fertility, sexuality and mobility becomes a subject of male honour. The honour/shame complex in Peshawar, for example, was thus not only a legacy of traditional patriarchal structure, but also a characteristic of extreme privatization of domestic sphere. These examples of mechanisms of social control over women's sexuality in the interest of men's or families' honour demonstrate how widespread these practices are (Kabeer 2000; Mernissi, 1985; Moghadam, 2003; White 1994; Wolf 1994). Here, however, *el âlem* does not only refer to the policing of women's sexuality. Below I discuss the different conceptualizations of honour in the Turkish language in order to expand this argument.

In the Turkish language family honour is referred to by two different words, *namus* and *şeref*. While the former is most strongly associated with women's bodies and sexuality, the latter broadly refers to acting in accordance with the moral norms of society. When a woman is disloyal to her husband, she is called *namussuz* (dishonourable), but not *şerefsiz* (dishonourable). For many, the control of women's bodies and sexualities is the only way in which one can be *namuslu* (honourable). Honour killings are called *namus cinayeti* not *şeref cinayeti*. *Şeref* is more associated with good reputation, and this reputation depends on the extent to which your acts are approved by *el âlem*: the extent to which you follow the demands of *el âlem*. For instance, when *el âlem* concludes that a worker deserves his/her wage thanks to their performance, this adds to their family *şeref*. If s/he does not deserve the wage, then *el âlem* talks about them and their family, how they do not have *şeref* and so on.

In this sense, deploying the concept of *el âlem* as a material manifestation of patriarchy offers a chance to understand why people are eager to sustain it. In other words, a woman can explain why she 'accepts' being 'governed' in the household by her mother-in-law in terms of organization of her unpaid labour or a man can explain why he 'needs' to go against his sister's wishes by pointing to *el âlem*. In this way, we can see how *el âlem* is exercised over both kinds of honour. In the former one following mother-in-law's demands by a bride increases the reputation of the family. *El âlem* will admire the harmony in the household and praise the family's honour – associated with good reputation. In the latter example, *el âlem* will praise a brother's control over his sister's sexuality. In this sense, we can also see how patriarchy is sustained and modified.

## El âlem *and the persistence of intersectional patriarchy*

> I know that you are on the women's side. But Emine [speaking directly to me as the researcher], do you really think that I don't like Hazal and I don't want what is good for her? But, if she runs away with someone, you know that we [implying her brothers] have to do something. Otherwise, we cannot continue to live in our village. How would we look others in the eye? This is why we have to prevent this from happening. That's why I cannot give her a phone.[4]

Above is a quotation from Mehmet (a young male worker), the twenty-two-year-old brother of fifteen-year-old Hazal, who demonstrates the role of *el âlem* in sustaining patriarchy. Hazal also works on the land. And, Mehmet fell deeply in love with one of the women working on the land, but his beloved's father strongly disapproved of their relationship. On that occasion, Mehmet seemed to me to have a soft, romantic heart, arranging the tomatoes in a heart shape on the ground to send a signal to his lover. He related the above to me when I asked him why he wouldn't permit Hazal to have a mobile phone. His reply really surprised me. As he implied, they (Hazal's brothers) have to do 'something' if their sister decides to run away with a boyfriend. Here, 'something' might even imply physical harm; we have all heard about 'honour killings' in Turkey – *namus cinayeti*. However, Mehmet himself was in the same situation, insofar as he too was planning to run away with his lover. When I posed this contradiction to him, he told me 'but what can I do? I hope if she (Hazal) elopes, she will do so once I elope with Emine (the girl he loves), then I would not see and hence not need to do anything'. Mehmet is expected to control Hazal's behaviour,[5] Mehmet's father is expected to control him, Mehmet's older uncle is expected to control Mehmet's father, and some other people from their extended family are expected to control their older uncle, other people from the village also are expected to control their extended family and so on. They all justify their reasons for their responsibility for the behaviour of others by referencing a group of unidentified and at the same time identified people – the *el âlem*. The members of *el âlem* do not have a particular age or sex, and do not belong to a particular religion or ethnicity. They cannot be seen, but 'they' can see all your actions, feelings and even thoughts. If someone asks you to point to *el âlem* you cannot do so directly, but you know who they are when they begin to speak about the appropriateness[6] of your behaviours. Your father is a member of *el âlem*, your mother, your older or younger brother, your sister, your neighbour and even you. When you want to do something, you must therefore first ask yourself: 'What will "*el âlem*" say about it?' '*El âlem ne der*' is a very commonly used expression in Turkish and refers to others' perceived approval of your acts. Its equivalent in Kurdish is '*Werr xalke be ci?*', with the Turkish and Kurdish statements being direct translations of each other.

*El âlem* is the 'one' who governs people in Turkey, but it also manifests itself in different forms. While Hazal's running away with her boyfriend can be given as a reason for her to be killed, Fatma's father (Fatma is a member of the landowning family) wanted her to run away with her lover as he did not have enough money to pay for her *çeyiz* (dowry). Apparently, in Fatma's father's context, not having enough money to pay for his daughter's *çeyiz* would have attracted the disapproval of *el âlem* – as a man must provide money for his daughter's *çeyiz* – as it would mean she would not have a father who could marry her off 'properly' and this is not good for a family's *şeref*. In this case, according to *el âlem*, his daughter's running away would be preferable to the inability to provide a *çeyiz*. In this way, *el âlem* determines the 'appropriateness' of acts performed by everyone depending on their gender, ethnicity, class, age, education and so on.

The specific way a person is governed by *el âlem* depends on their position within the intersections of gender, class, ethnicity and age and, relatedly, masculinities and femininities. *El âlem* is an agential aspect of intersectional patriarchy. You cannot just feel patriarchy, but you can see it, almost hold it – practise it yourself – by looking at *el âlem*'s demands or judgements. Table 7.1 illustrates how the type of

Table 7.1 Types of patriarchy and associated masculinities and femininities within the household.

| Types of patriarchy | Degree of patriarchy = Intensity of the *el alem*'s voice inside the household/family | Forms of (hegemonic) masculinity | Forms of (devalued) femininity |
|---|---|---|---|
| **Rural** | High | **Turkish, landowning family** Authoritarian, knowing how to govern (with harmony), affinity with machines, belonging to public sphere. | **Turkish, landowning family** Obsessive about consumption (not aware of the value of money, not able to control money, unreceptive), lazy, competent at domestic work. |
|  | Very high | **Kurdish, migrant workers; families** Physical strength, aggressive, uneducated (or educated in certain areas such as law), arranging 'public relations' and/or 'working' relations. | **Kurdish, migrant workers' families** Belonging to private sphere, passive, seductive, prefer to be governed. |
| **Transitional** | Medium | Breadwinner, independent, regularly employed, having regular wage, taking care of a nuclear family. | Earning extra, eager to work (probably seasonally), taking care of an extended family, entering the public if it is necessary. |
| **Kemalist** | Low | Educated (or wise), physically durable (not need to be strong), hardworking, determined, affinity with machines, sexually modest. | Femininity is derided as irrational, uneducated, backward, lazy, religious, liking to be governed, always thinking about sex. |

patriarchy depends on the intensity of the *el âlem*'s voice in the household as well as on the types of masculinity and femininity that are constructed, in accordance with which *el âlem* decides the appropriateness of your behaviour.

Intersectional patriarchy also refers to the fluidity of the different positions of individuals in relation to kin as well as non-kin. The fluidity of these positions means that everyone ends up having a stake in the patriarchy. Power is consequently available to all individuals to different extents, as everyone is a member of *el âlem* writ large in their respective social positions. For instance, while Mehmet can exercise some power over his sister by controlling her sexuality as her brother, even Hazal can have the right to 'have a say' over Pınar, her fourteen-year-old niece. Someone thus monitors everyone's behaviour, and each in turn can monitor someone else's behaviour. Everyone has a chance to exercise power over someone else, as long as *el âlem* exists. The only way of having power over someone is to act in accordance with the dictates of *el âlem* and this, at the same time, sustains it. To be a member of *el âlem*, it is sufficient to be able to pass judgements on others' actions. Despite this, the concept is not particularly concrete, since it is impossible to label any specific person as being a part of *el âlem*, and few 'members' of *el âlem* choose to be part of it. Most of the women and men who took part in this study think that they are *living for el âlem*. *El âlem için yaşamak* is a common expression in Turkey and refers to the way in which people think they live their lives simply to satisfy the demands of 'others'. Some of them even believe that one *ought to* live for *el âlem* and that this is the way of the world, but there are others who say that they hate it and do not want to live for it.

I refer to the exercise of power which *el âlem* offers to everyone to a greater or lesser extent as 'masculine governing' for two reasons. The first is that it is more available to 'masculine' social actors, and the second is that it operates to protect the reputation and honour of these masculine actors. In the hierarchy of masculinity in rural households of tomato production (see Table 7.2) in Turkey, however, older women come near the top of the hierarchy.

Older women's place might come as a surprise to some but it is widely accepted by my informants. This is because when a woman reaches her menopause, she loses her femininity. For instance, when the women working on the land discussed the menopause, they spoke of it as the period in which women cease to be women. Mernissi (1985) states a very similar argument for Moroccan women. Her findings suggest that in a traditional family (to be found amongst rural

**Table 7.2** Hierarchy in masculinities in rural households.

| Hierarchy of masculinities in rural households | |
|---|---|
| **Turkish landowning family** | **Kurdish migrant worker family** |
| The oldest son (husband) (second generation) | The oldest man of the extended family (father in law) (first generation) |
| The oldest man of the extended family (father-in-law) (first generation) | The oldest woman of first generation (mother-in-law) (first generation) |
| The oldest woman (mother-in-law) (first generation) | Oldest son of first generation (second generation) |
| Wife of eldest son (second generation) (*elti*) | Sons (of second generation) – both married and unmarried) (third generation) |
| Other male members of the second generation (husband's brothers) | Wives of older male members (second generation) (*elti*) |
| Younger daughters-in-law (bride) (second generation) | Youngest daughters-in-law (second generation) |
| Third-generation males (sons of the second generation) | Daughters (of second generation, third generation) |
| Third-generation females (daughters of second generation) | |

and low-income women) mothers-in-law have control over the operation of households and they are perceived as totally asexual. Not surprisingly, daughters-in-law in her study stated that the most important person in their family was their mother-in-law. Although Mernissi (1985) explains this situation by referring to the close relation between mother and son (see also White (1994) for Turkish mothers and their sons), here I mostly explore this phenomenon by focusing on the organization of production and reproduction and their interaction, following Kandiyoti (1985, 1988), with cultural discourses around women's sexuality.

Turning back to mothers-in-law, 'there is no reason to protect her', said Nezahat when she explained to me why her mother-in-law went to the market instead of her or any younger members of the family. Here, 'protection' specifically implies the need to protect a woman who is capable of getting pregnant. If you have already had your menopause, then there is no need to worry about being impregnated by a stranger, and it is also more difficult to determine whether someone is having extra-marital sex. However, this does not bring women sexual freedom. Infertility defeminizes menopausal women in the eyes of rural people, since being a woman among women is intimately tied to fertility. It is therefore unsurprising that when women are no longer fertile, they have more freedom in the contact they can have with men. For both the Turks and the Kurds in this study, post-menopausal women are seen as becoming more like men. It is for this reason that they can exercise greater control over the younger men, as they are effectively older 'masculine' actors. This puts them further up the ladder in the 'hierarchy of masculinity'. In the following, therefore, you will see how mothers-in-law are the main enemies of both Kurdish and Turkish women.

## *Two common enemies of rural women:* Elti *and* Kaynana, *in two different forms of patriarchy*

> All women have two troubles in their lives; not a husband but a kaynana [a mother-in-law; your husband's mother] and a elti [a woman's husband's brother's wife], if you find someone [to marry] without a mother and a brother, this will the best thing, which you can have for your whole life.[7]

Fatma's above statement could seem harsh to those of us who have lived most of our lives in a nuclear family with a husband and children and are not subject to a mother-in-law's authority, and not obliged to compete with an *elti* for a greater share of the common budget or more authority in household decision making. However, for most women who live in a 'patrilocal family structure' where women marry into their husband's family, Fatma's statement is fair. They themselves have sons, so they may themselves become mothers-in-law in the future, and they may well already be someone's *elti*. A young *gelin*[8] (bride) in a rural household has not one, but two 'enemies': *elti* – the other brides of the family – and *kaynana* – her mother-in-law. While *elti* could become a bride's allies by virtue of having a similar position in the familial hierarchy, having a joint budget and problems that arise with regard to sharing money immediately destroy any possibility for solidarity between the brides in a family. This section mostly talks about women's struggles with their *eltileri* (plural form of *elti*), *kaynanaları* (plural form of *kaynana*) and the male members of their families over the distribution of resources, the control of labour and money, and the gender division of labour, which are all shaped by the interweaving of kinship and production relations.

### 'There is no family like us anymore': The triumph of the 'four generational', patriarchal family in the village

Describing her household, Nurhan, a bride in the landowning family, says:

> We are the richest people of this village. Everyone envies our money; however, I bet none of them prefer our life. We are the only family in the village who has three mothers-in-law at home. There is no family like us anymore in the whole village, maybe even in the surrounding villages. All of these families are separated and young couples move to the town. Who does not want to live alone with her husband and children? Honestly, I do not want money but peace. But, in a crowded family like ours there is no peace.[9]

Unfortunately, however, in order to grow tomatoes on their large portion of land, they have to live in a four-generational patrilocal household structure. When 'the material bases of classical patriarchy' were undermined by 'new market forces, capital penetration in rural areas or processes of chronic immiseration' (Kandiyoti 1988: 279), younger men and their nuclear families separated from the paternal household and the three generational patrilocal family structures began to fracture. This is the case for the factory women's families in the same region, which will be explored in the next chapter. However, new market conditions do not always drive the division of extended families into nuclear units; rather, they can also cause the reinforcement of the 'extended patriarchal family' as in the case of Nurhan's family and/or the intensification of patriarchal family structures like Kurdish workers' families.

In the case of the landowners' family, in order to make money from tomato production, they need to live as a crowded single household. There are two main reasons for this. The first is related to regulations governing land size, which put restrictions on having land of less than around four acres (Land Law 2007). Most of the land belonging to landowners is inherited from their fathers and these plots are too small to be divided further. Although the landowning family collectively possess around three hundred acres of land, the size of the largest plot is only around eight acres. Therefore, under the law, if they cannot divide their land into three. The second reason is that factories prefer working with bigger farmers as contracting farms, which is very common in tomato production. The general manager of the factory in which I worked explained his reason for choosing bigger farmers for contract farming by stating: 'We cannot spend time contacting every farmer. We have to watch the quality of our products while they are growing; we have to intervene if something extra is needed such as fertilisers. So, we prefer to work with a small number of farmers if it is contract farming' (18 September 2014).

Apparently, in order to obtain their raw material by working with a small number of farmers, they prefer to work with bigger farmers. Not being able to divide their land indirectly causes families to live in the same building because everybody wants to observe and thus to control each other's spending habits. Thus, nobody can move out of the building, nobody will let each other go and nobody is 'free' because they have too much money.

*'A man like a man' controls the budget*

To illustrate the structure of the landowners' extended family, imagine that you are one of the children in the youngest generation: your elementary family lives in the same building as your great-grandfather and great-grandmother, your grandfather and grandmother, your father's paternal uncle and his wife, your father's paternal cousins' nuclear families and your paternal uncle's family (for instance, imagine that you are Gamzenur, eighteen; see Diagram 7.1). When Gamzenur enters the building where her home is, she encounters three flats. She lives in one of them with her parents, siblings and paternal grandmother, and her uncles' families live next door. Those I worked with on the land (the third and fourth generations) are not in a literal sense the owners of the land, since their fathers (the second generation) – and indeed their fathers' father – are still alive, and the land is in their names. However, their fathers no longer work or supervise the work, so in this text, I refer to the third-generation male members of the family who are managing the work as the landowning family – two of them are brothers and the other is their paternal cousin. Their properties, work and hence their budget are shared. Nine people are working and nineteen people are dependent on the money generated by the profits of the farm on which those nine people work, including four women. Six of the nine are in the third generation of the family (between the ages of thirty and forty) and three of them are in the fourth generation (aged sixteen to eighteen). Unsurprisingly, distribution of resources as well as control over and access to money always create tension within the family, particularly among the women. Their direct access to money is limited, since the oldest man of the third generation, Recep, controls the majority of the money. The women complain about not being able to take decisions over how to spend what they see as their own earnings. All of the brides agree that being part of the richest family in the village does not benefit them as individuals since they are not able to do what they desire.

> I cannot buy a carpet for my house due to our joint budget. Everything in these houses is purchased as three. If I need a carpet, then I should wait until they also need one, or even if they do not need one, we also have to buy one for each other. I remember when I first married Recai; one day when he went to the town, he bought me some pantolon (trousers) as a gift. Then, my mother-in-law saw them and she did not give permission for me to wear them because of the risk of being seen by the other brides with my new trousers. Can you believe it? Recai also cannot buy himself even 'rubbish' that is different from the others, but at least he can go out, and he can spend money. We want money to buy some clothes or home stuff, but we cannot use it even for this. So, why do we have money?[10]

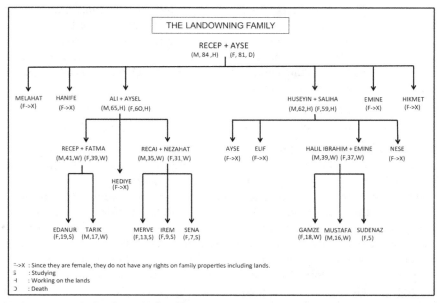

**Diagram 7.1** The landowning family.

These problems are more serious for the women than the men. This is because the men have more access to pocket money and more freedom to spend it. That being the case, in the household in question, Recep (the oldest male of the third generation) controls the budget and decides how much money he will give to others. Recai, the youngest of the three male brothers in the third generation, explains the reason for Recep's financial control as follows:

> Of course, I would prefer to have my own money in my hand. I still have to ask for money from my brother, it sounds, strange doesn't it? I have three children but I am still asking for pocket money. But, Emine [me, the researcher], it must be like this. We need someone to manage all of us. Otherwise, we cannot live together. Recep abim (my elder brother) was born to manage. He knows when he should be harsh or soft. It is difficult to have this balance. I am not that kind of person; I am a softie. But, you should not be, especially towards women and children, as they begin to exploit your softness.[11]

Recai (see Diagram 7.1) is the youngest male of the third generation of the landowning family, and he had a disability. 'His disability makes him very emotional', says Fatma (Recep's wife). According to her, after the motorcycle accident that disabled him, he became more reserved and emotional, making him incapable of governing. 'Also', she added, 'they [implying Nezahat and Recai] do not have any sons but three girls. This also makes them unwilling to work harder or to be more active in the family. They don't have anybody to give their wealth to'.[12] Fatma enjoys being the boss's wife. She is the oldest bride; her husband controls all the money and properties and her sons are older than Nurhan's son. Hence, unsurprisingly, she exerts control over her *eltiler* (Nurhan and Nezahat), as well as their husbands (Recai and Halil Ibrahim). She says, 'fortunately, my man [implying her husband, Recep] is a *man like a man'– 'adam gibi adam'* – which is a very common expression used to refer a man who meets the requirements of masculine strength in society. In this case, she used it to say that he is not diffident in his oversight of the budget and the other family members, this being seen as a sign of masculinity.

> I cannot stand a diffident man. I was the most beautiful girl in our village. I had many kısmet ['kısmet' refers to suitors wishing to marry a woman. This man is her 'kısmet']. My mother was a very smart woman. When my kaynana came to our house to ask for me to marry Recep, my mother asked her whether Recep went out for men's coffee, which age he began driving a tractor, does he know how to spend money, and could he elope with me. As my father did not have enough money to pay my 'çeyiz' (dowry), so my parents asked me to elope with him. They seemed to be offended for a time. Since el âlem could condemn them if they hadn't acted as if they were cross with me. Sometimes, I remembered and got angry with my family when Recep told me that my family got rid of me. But I know that they didn't have any other choice; we were 6 siblings and brothers, they needed money for my brothers' weddings. I frequently get angry with Recep, but I always tell him that he is my man. Others [in the family] also married by eloping [implying other couples – Nurhan-Halil Ibrahim, Nezahat- Recai], but Recep and me organised everything. If we wouldn't have been, they could not manage to do it.[13]

Fatma's above statement about the elopement shows us the flexibility of patriarchy as well as of *el âlem*. Her family had to pretend to disapprove of her elopement so as not to be shamed by *el âlem*, but in reality, this was what they wanted, in order to save themselves from a bigger shame – the inability to make a proper wedding for their sons. This shows us how people have the chance to negotiate with *el âlem* as well as patriarchy.

### *The extra man of the family: A man-like elti*

Not only did Fatma think that Recep was the 'man' of family, but so did her *eltileri* (Nezahat and Nurhan). They called him *abi* (elder brother). The following comment of Nurhan indirectly answers the question about whether an individual who contributes more money to the household also has more power when it comes to making household decisions (Pahl 1989; 1995):

> I got angry with him [Recep] too many times as he is spending more on his family, but God knows that Halil Ibrahim [her husband] can't do what he is doing. He makes agreements with buyers, he finds the lands to rent or buy, and he follows the new seeds or machines. Ours [implying her husband and

Nezahat's] can't talk too much. That is why Fatma speaks so much [implying her authority over other family members]. I tell Halil Ibrahim [her husband] to talk a bit more as I can speak as much as he speaks.[14]

As Recep is the one who brings the money-making opportunities to the household table, he and his wife can talk a lot. Besides her talkativeness, Fatma even drives a car sometimes. Although driving a tractor is common among local women in the village when the work requires it, driving a car is seen as exceptional. The village's *el âlem* would have it that 'men drive a car but rural women cannot drive since this carries a danger of being labelled as a "socialite"'. *Sosyete*[15] is a commonly used term in rural Turkey which pokes fun at someone who acts like an 'urban' person, and the term is often especially applied to women. Examples of behaviours that might attract the label *sosyete* include driving and wearing sunglasses or a large summer hat. However, Fatma was permitted to drive the car until she reached the edge of the village. Sometimes she had to bring women back from the land when they had travelled a long distance to the fields, and on those days she drove the car to near the edge of the village, and a man from the family or among the workers would come to pick us up from there. She explained to me that 'she couldn't pass by the men's *kahve* – coffeehouse – driving a car since this would be going against *el âlem*'.

Although she can't enter the village driving a car, this does not prevent her from being labelled a 'woman who is like a man' by workers. Fatma enjoys these kinds of comments. When they say that Fatma is a 'woman like a man', they always add *Maşallah* at the end of their sentences. *Maşallah* is used to invoke protection from the 'evil eye'. The idiom of 'woman like a man' can be both something to be appreciated, as in this case, and a term of opprobrium, when it is used for instance by Fatma's *eltileri* and *kaynanana*. This demonstrates the contradictions of patriarchy very clearly. In contradistinction to outsiders, other female members of the family are clearly not happy with having a 'man-like' *elti* or 'daughter-in-law'. Nurhan explained her reason to me by saying that they already have enough men and so do not need more; 'a woman must know her womanhood' ('*kadın kadınlığını bilmeli*', which means that a woman should act like a woman).

There is constant tension between Nurhan and Fatma, and it is not only because Fatma sometimes can be a 'man-like' woman. It is also because Nurhan is seen as the luckiest by her sisters-in-law since her husband has no brothers, so in the end her elementary family will have half of the landowning family's properties while the other two brides' elementary families will have to share the other half, since their husbands are brothers. Indeed, Recep and Recai were brothers, and Halil Ibrahim is their *amcaoğlu* – uncle's son. However, because of the young age of the senior men – Halil Ibrahim's father and the father of Recep and Recai (see Diagram 7.1) – the prospect of sharing the inheritance in the future is still a source of problems inside the home. As Nurhan told me, 'They (the other two brides) do not like her since Halil Ibrahim (her husband) will have more land than them.' On the land, it is possible to see that the advantageous position of Nurhan has already created polarization between her and *her eltileri*. While they are working, one can see that Fatma and

Nezahat always work side by side and at the same speed so they can continue to talk to each other, although they criticize each other's attitudes towards the workers. Fatma and Nezahat become one group when Nurhan is also on the land. Although Nurhan is Fatma's cousin (her mother's sister's daughter) – Fatma married Recep and she introduced Nurhan to Halil Ibrahim (Recep's *amcaoğlu*) – this does not seem to be enough to prevent Nurhan's loneliness on the land, so she finds her own solution: she forges a coalition with her daughter, who also works on the land.

The fact that Gamze (eighteen), the daughter of Nurhan and Halil Ibrahim, works on the land highlights the current money-sharing problems inside the extended family. Gamze and her brother, Mustafa (sixteen), both work on the land. Mustafa is responsible for driving tractors, collecting workers, bringing water and so on. This means that from Nurhan's family, four people are working. Three of Fatma's family and two of Nezahat's are also working. Since they divide all the profits by three, the unbalanced number of people working from each family creates tension. Nurhan says,

> Edanur [Fatma's 19-year-old daughter] is studying and mine is working on the land like a worker. We are paying for Edanur's education. Does it make sense to you? We are four, and Nezahat's are just two, but we have the same amount of money to spend. When the children were small, it was easy. But, now it is really difficult. Edanur (19) is going to do a university course. Who pays? We are paying. Now, the children have begun arguing with each other because of the unfairness. *Tarık* [Fatma's son] spends money like crazy. He smokes; he spends too much money buying phone credits. Who is earning money for his phone credits? They are earning less than us, but spending more than us. Do you think it is fair?[16]

Nurhan is not the only one who thinks that the other elementary families spend more than hers. Nezahat also complains that the others' children are grown up so their expenses are higher than those of her own three small children. Fatma, on the other hand, believes that they are more hardworking as a family, so even though there are three of them, they work more than the others. 'You can see how Gamze works, but she still counts as working. She hates working; she is always talking on her phone. She is always sick because of the heat. Sometimes, it is better not having her since when the workers see her laziness they also slow down their work. But they still continue to complain about Eda's education expenses'.[17] While the *eltiler* do not get on well with each other, when money sharing comes to the table, thinking about their mothers-in-law can lead them to share the same feelings very easily.

### 'Mothers-in-law as cooks and fashion designer'

All three wives of the third-generational men in the landowning family have a mother-in-law in their section of the house, and none of them are happy with the situation. As such, while they can gossip about each other and how they spend money in secret, when the subject of the difficulty of living with their mothers-in-law arises, they band together. The main responsibility of their mothers-in-law (two of them since the older one cannot cook because of her age) is cooking while their daughters-in-law work on the land. Although the landowning family have enough money to pay for domestic servants, there is no tradition of having domestic servants in the region. This does not even enter into people's minds as *el âlem* cannot countenance that a proper rural woman needs a servant. For this reason, female family members, including those of the fourth generation, are responsible for carrying out the domestic work. While cleaning is the task of brides, cooking is the mothers-in-law's task. Daughters are responsible for helping both their mothers and grandmothers, and are not assigned an exact task. Although the brides are mostly dissatisfied with the cooking of their mothers-in-law, the main reason for arguing with them is, of course, again related to money. The mothers-in-law are in a position to spend money more freely than their daughters-in-law, since they can go to the market every week on Tuesdays to shop for the home and for themselves. This shopping is the most popular topic of conversation on the land on Wednesdays for the women from the landowning families.

> She makes me crazy [referring to her mother-in-law]. Yesterday, she bought a bracelet as a present for my sister's daughter's wedding. You should see it. It is not 'heavy' [the value of a gold bracelet depends on its weight] but she bought a 20 gr. bracelet for her sister's son's wedding. She also bought a dress for herself for the wedding. You should see it; it is like a girl's dress. It is almost a vivid blue. How old is she? She competes with me. I have the same colour dress for this wedding. I argued with Recep all night. I do not want this bracelet for my niece; he has to buy a new one! [she wants to buy a more valuable bracelet for her niece as a wedding gift].[18]

The weight of gold bracelets, which are given as gifts at weddings or worn by women themselves to the weddings or *Eid*s, is a sign of their status in the eyes of *el âlem*. More gold jewellery makes them more prestigious in the village or even in the region. Fatma and her other *eltileri* are very proud of the fame they garner for their gold jewellery. Nezahat told me this indirectly as an explanation for my own supposed distaste for attending wedding ceremonies; she told me that as I (me, the researcher) don't have any gold jewellery; it cannot be enjoyable for me to attend a wedding ceremony. Women dress up for weddings or *Eid*s, and this involves putting on gold jewellery in addition to heavy make-up and fancy hairstyles. Nezahat told me that she began to enjoy wedding ceremonies and *Eid*s after she married Recai, as now she can dress up, whereas before, she told me, without money, how could she?

All the brides of the family therefore love putting on gold jewellery for another reason: it is also what their mothers-in-law want. In this way, they are able to make *el âlem* both 'jealous' and 'approving' (the latter in virtue of *el âlem*'s strict ordinances on the role of brides' heavily adorned bodies as a source of familial pride through the conspicuous display of wealth). When Aysel (Fatma's and Nezahat's *kaynana*) spoke to me after my engagement, she despaired at my lack of gold jewellery. She told me, 'I am so sorry for your mother-in-law, how can she feel that she has a bride if you don't put any gold on you? I will stop complaining about my brides. They will wear whatever I want' (2 September 2013). She is quite right when she states that all brides and their daughters in the family wear what their mothers-in-law (also as grandmothers) approve of, taking into consideration what is permitted by *el âlem*. Putting on gold jewellery and avoiding trousers or mini-skirts are the main dress codes for brides; their daughters need only avoid mini-skirts.

Although brides are agree with their mothers-in-law in the practice of putting on of gold jewellery as a way of showing off the wealth of their family, their struggles with them come to the fore when control over money arises. While sometimes the reason for arguments can be over something as valuable as gold, sometimes it could just be over coffee. However, the gravity of such disputes is similar.

> How old am I? I am almost a mother-in-law, but still my mother-in-law buys coffee for me. I told her to buy Nescafe to make a dessert for my guest. I found a new recipe and I wanted to try it, but no. She didn't buy it. Why? Since it is expensive she said. We are the richest family in the village but I cannot make a dessert with Nescafé. But, my mother-in-law continuously gives money to her daughters. I am working and her daughters eat desserts with Nescafé. I told Halil, I am not making desserts at home anymore.[19]

Nurhan's resistance to making desserts did not last long since Halil Ibrahim (her husband) bought the Nescafé and appeased her, but the brides' resistance to their mothers-in-law seems to persist as long as they live together. This might be because, as Nezahat says:

> I don't know anyone who likes her daughter-in-law or vice versa. It can't be a coincidence. I even hate my mother-in-law's clothes; can you believe it? Sometimes, when I think about it, I feel guilty. Since it is 'sin' to hate someone older than you. Maybe, if we could live separately, I could like her. But, now we are always on opposite sides. We always have different ideas for everything. She is old and the world is not like it was in her time anymore. But she still wants us to behave like them. We have one house and it is my house. But she thinks that it is her house. So, problems are inevitable and we always have tension. Recai says that we cannot live separately from each other since we are powerful when we are together. This is the rule of nature. Look at animals, he says to me, they are not separated from each other; otherwise they die. God creates all people to live with their extended family, he says to me, to survive. I don't know, I am looking at others who are separate and they seem to me happier than us. Even Kurds do not work and live with their amcaoğlu (paternal cousins), just with their brothers. Even they seem to me more modern than us.[20]

Nezahat is right that the extended family structure of Kurdish seasonal migrants is smaller than hers since it consists of only three generations, but she is wrong to say that they do not work and live with their cousins, since they are already married to them. And, as I discuss below, Kurdish women's resistance is more constrained by the authority of men and mothers-in-law than is the case for the women in landowning families.

### Patriarchy as we all know it! The 'patriarchal homes' of Kurdish seasonal migrants

The 'classical form' of patriarchy is defined by Kandiyoti (1988) as a senior man's authority over women and younger men. However, 'senior man' is too 'sacred' and 'respectful' figure to comment on the operation of 'daily life' in the household. Therefore, the 'senior man' – who could be a father-in-law, father or husband – is 'invisible' in the daily life conversations and discussions of the extended family; he is the 'God' of the family; his rules are known by everyone so he doesn't need to repeat them. Repeating the rules may be seen as a sign of weakness in his authority as it would indicate that his words are not valuable enough to follow on first utterance. Hence, senior women (mothers-in-law or mothers) and the sons of the family (husbands/brothers) enforce the rules on daughters-in-law or daughters. Therefore, in the following analysis of how masculine control is practised over women, the reader will barely see 'senior men', but more often 'mothers-in-law', husbands or brothers. Here, the difference between classic patriarchy and village patriarchy is that in the former the assumed wishes of the 'senior man' is the family members' reference point, rather than the more generalized *el âlem* that determines their ideas about proper behaviour.

The following section consists of two parts. In the first part, I introduce the shanties that Kurdish migrant workers live in during tomato planting and harvest, and in the

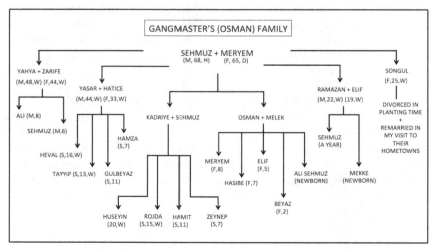

**Diagram 7.2** *Dayıbaşı's* family.

second part I explore their permanent homes located around 1,500 km away. While the first part shows how kin marriage organizes the division of labour, in the second part, I reveal the operation of 'extended patriarchal households' and reproduction of labour power. We will see that through kin marriage, women's productive and reproductive labour is controlled very strictly in Kurdish workers' families.

*'Making tandır[21] for your elti: Kurdish seasonal migrants' shacks in the gardens of landowners' families*

The seasonal rural tomato work lasts for around six months. Some of migrant workers do not return to their 'homes', but instead continue to travel around the western parts of Turkey for other seasonal rural work. Elif is relatively lucky, since at least she can imagine returning to her home when the tomato-growing season finishes after six months of heavy work. She arrives at the workplace with her extended family, which consists of her husband, his five siblings and their spouses and children (see Diagram 7.2). They travel together from their hometown by coach for almost two days. When they arrive at the workplace, some shacks are offered to them by the landowners – a shack is the best option for Kurdish seasonal workers.[22] Fortunately, Elif's family was allocated a shack, but most seasonal migrant workers are only offered tents. Usually they do not have proper toilet and bathroom facilities; there are no white goods in the accommodation, and not enough rooms for each elementary family. These living conditions and photographs of Kurdish migrants are very popular subjects in the summer issues of leftist Turkish newspapers;[23] there is an awareness that they are 'living' in those horrible conditions but the public do not have a clue about 'how' they 'live' in those conditions.

Unsurprisingly when we enter the shacks, we encounter a 'crowd', again like in the landowning families' homes. These crowded Kurdish family premises are needed in order for the tomatoes to be picked. When we think about the difficult working conditions, the long working hours and the group performance–based payment system during tomato picking time, it becomes clear that landowners require a large workforce that can work collectively and share the money they earn depending on the number of unblemished tomatoes they pick during the day. The landowners also need workers who can work very long hours since the tomatoes should be picked as soon as possible so that they do not become rotten as a result of the heat or possibly rain later in the season. The Kurdish migrants can supply this labour, thanks to their extended families. Thus, in Turkey, rural landowners draw most of their employees from Kurdish seasonal migrant workers and capitalize on the features of their extended patriarchal families.

Kurdish seasonal workers come to the workplace as large extended families. They are three-generation patrilineal families that also include daughters-in-law as part of the family (all couples are first cousins). Fortunately – in the women's words – their mothers-in-law and fathers-in-law stay in their hometowns. Apparently, the mothers-in-law of Kurdish women workers are in a more privileged position than their daughters-in-law, so the mother-in-law does not stay in the shacks, but in her 'proper home', waiting for 'money' to go on a pilgrimage. As such, not surprisingly, every woman is waiting to become a mother-in-law so that she does not need to do any work either on the land or at home. 'To send them on a pilgrimage, we will give them almost 80% of our earnings from this year. I told Osman (her husband), we are poor; going on a pilgrimage is not an obligation for us. But he called me "profane". Do you think I am wrong?'.[24]

Unfortunately, my agreement with Melek will not help her; she has to continue to cook for thirteen people during picking time, wash their clothes by hand and take care of the children while her *eltileri* are working on the land with the male members of the family. In the case of Kurdish extended families, since all of the money goes directly to the grandparents, not to the brides' husbands, the brides do not argue with each other over money sharing. Their fights are more about who works the most. This discussion, unsurprisingly, centres on the division between those working in the shacks and those working on the land.

> Every morning, I make tea before everyone wakes up. The men want to drink tea before going to the land. In the meantime, I also get their lunch bags ready. Since it is too early, they do not eat breakfast here. I also put their breakfast into bags. When the men also work on the land with women in the picking season, it is more difficult: they want better food. It takes me longer to prepare. They want more than one course. In planting time, our job is easier because they eat their lunch with the landowners. Now, they continuously complain about the quality of the food. After the workers have left for the land, I prepare breakfast again [this time] for the children. When breakfast time finishes, I begin to wash clothes. There are always clothes to wash, so I do not try to finish them. I just wash until lunchtime and then I feed the children, wash the dishes and begin to cook for the night. I cook a lot, so we can take the next day's lunch from it. I also cook some extra food like kısır – bulgur salad – because sometimes the work on the land can be longer. So, they need extra. Then, if we do not have tomatoes to make a purée, I make tandır – a special kind of bread. Making tandır is the most difficult part of my work. Tandır is very important; it is like 'water' for us'. If it is not good, everyone has the right to complain about my cooking.[25]

The above is a typical day for Melek and her *eltileri*. She is the luckiest among them since she is not working on the land. Why it is she who stays at home is unclear. It is very difficult to answer this exactly because of the women's perplexing answers. According to Melek, she is at home because it is more prestigious than working on the land and she is the wife of a *dayıbaşı*. However, she has to keep complaining about the difficulty of staying at home and doing domestic tasks since it is not given as much value as working outside. On the other hand, according to the other brides, Melek has to stay at home because she has problems with her husband's sister so they create tension on the land together and Osman (*dayıbaşı*) thinks that the squabbles between these women will cause their work, and that of the other workers, to slow down.

Aside from the ambiguous reasons given for Melek staying at home, it makes it possible for the others to work very long hours, and she insists on emphasizing this. However, her intentions of making a contribution to the family are not sufficient for her *eltileri* to see her domestic work as work, and that's why their arguments are inevitable.

> We are not talking with Elif for a week. She is crazy; she wants me to bath Şehmuz [Elif's nine- month old baby] everyday. Do you think it is reasonable? You can see our shacks. How can I bath all of the children everyday? I know that she is doing it when she is at home, but then she does not have enough time to cook tomorrow's lunch properly. She told me that I am escaping from work. You see how I am working all day and doing their work. Do you think that it is easy to do housework here? We don't have a kitchen for cooking [they cook on the garden stove], we don't have a bathroom. I am bathing the children in the garden in the basin, but she is still not satisfied with my work. What can I do?.[26]

It is difficult not to agree with her about the problems of doing housework in the shacks. One day I helped her:

> Today, I [me, researcher] stayed at home because of my eye infection. Before and after I went to hospital in the town, I went to help Melek wash the clothes; since their washing machine has broken down again she called me for help. We washed endless clothes in the heat in the garden. My hands got creased because of the water. But I continued since she has too much work to do. For example, she is taking care of the children. Others bring some of the children with them to the land. Every day the number of children at home is changing, Melek says to me. They are all ages and I think they are in danger. All of them are playing with whatever they find around, including a knife as I saw today, or the small ones are eating whatever they find. The sewage pipes, which are behind the shacks, have just broken down and they were playing around them. Melek cannot take care of them alone; it is not possible. When the others come, they do not ask about the child-care, she told me, but food. So, she has to pay more attention to cooking than watching the children, she says to me. What she has done at home is crazy but still the others do not recognise it and she is continuously arguing with her eltileri. It is strange when I also think about the fact that they are also relatives of each other. Melek told me that if they were not relatives, they could not live together in those conditions even for a minute. She told me that 'I can even bear my 'sister' only with difficulty, [they are not literally sister but cousins], how could I stand a 'foreigner'.[27]

What Melek says about kinship relations between her and her *eltileri* is very similar to what the male members of the families say regarding the legitimization of kin marriage. In this extended family, there is no 'bride' that is not connected with a husband through kinship relations before marriage. They mainly give two reasons for this kind of marriage: the first one is to protect your family's power over other families in the region, and the second one is that other members of the family, who are already connected through kinship, can isolate a 'stranger bride'.

Hüseyin is the father of Emine who loves Mehmet, who does not have any kinship relation with Emine. The answer Hüseyin gave below was to explain why he is against Emine and Mehmet's marriage and why he insists on forcing Emine to marry his brother's son (Emine's *amcaoğlu*).

> I am not saying that you do it 'wrong' [implying people who do not make kin-marriages] but we do the 'right' thing. I don't know how you can trust a 'foreigner'. When you already have people around you, why look for someone who you have not known for your whole life? You don't know anything about his life, his parents, his siblings. I don't give my daughter to a stranger and I don't want a daughter-in-law whose parents I don't know. How we can live with a 'stranger'? Then, our grandchildren cannot be totally from our blood[28]. Then, our family will break down; it will be separated. God knows the right thing for us and he does not punish kin-marriage. So, how can ordinary people claim that they know better than God? Don't be offended but I saw you when you hugged your amcaoğlu[29] [my paternal uncle's son]. I could not believe how that is possible on the earth. You are entitled to marry even in our religion. But, I think it is not your fault, but your parents'. They should warn you about that. They should inform you about the rules of Islam. Don't worry; it's not you but your parents who will be punished for this, in the other world [implying after death].[30]

While Huseyin is a fervent advocate of the necessity of kin marriage because of the rules of Islam, not all men are so rigid about this.

> I fell in love once when I was in the military. She was working in the hospital and while on duty I had serious stomach problems and stayed in the hospital for a week. We met there and continued to meet for a year during my military service. I told her I would marry her. Of course, I had known that I could not because it was not possible for us to marry a 'strangers'. But, I could not say that directly to her face, and I also tried my chance with my parents but of course they did not accept it. My mother told me, 'if you marry her, that will be the worst thing in her life. How can she get on well with your family? How will she adapt to your life? No-one will talk to her, and she will always be 'strangers'. If you move to town with her, then it will be a disaster for you. How can you work and live among the 'strangers' 'alone'. She was right. I gave up, called her and said that we could not marry. She told me, 'I hope you cannot love your wife'. This is one of the worst curses to place on someone, isn't it?[31]

It is difficult to say whether Osman loves his current wife, Melek. She is his paternal cousin, but apparently for Osman, not marrying a 'stranger' is a matter of 'staying in his comfort zone'. He concluded by saying,

I did the right thing. These women do not even get on well even though they are relatives. I could not imagine them with a 'stranger bride' in the same house. I know from my distant cousin who married a 'stranger' that he had to move to another town since he could not continue to work with his brothers. Because other 'brides' united and discriminated against his 'stranger wife'. They didn't help her.[32]

It became obvious what Osman was referring to when he said, 'they did not help her' – Elif's words when I asked her about her possible feelings towards being an *elti* with a 'stranger':

Melek is my 'abla' (elder sister), so I try to help her as much as I can. She has more children than me, so she has more work than me. So, in our homes [implying their hometowns] mostly I make tandır. I mostly look after our elders [their mother and father-in law] we arrange the division of our work mostly in favour of Melek and Zarife [her other elti] since they are older than me. I am like their sister. I have known them since I knew myself. We grew up together. Although we have disputes sometimes, you know 'you cannot spare your nail from your finger' [Common idiom: 'et ile tırnak birbirinden ayrılmaz']. But, I don't know about some 'stranger'. I could not do most of the things that I should do for my own people [implying her related eltileri]. Also, I think they would not behave towards me as they behave towards their people.[33]

Apparently, the Kurdish seasonal migrant workers who pick Recep's tomatoes see their extended patriarchal family based on kin marriages as the only way to sustain their lifestyle and family solidarity. So, it is possible to say that tomatoes can only be picked when a Kurdish woman makes a *tandır* in the shack of a Turkish landowner, in order for her *elti* to send their parents-in-law on a pilgrimage or to do another thing that is 'possibly' one of the biggest desires of their life.

*Sending 'kaynana'*[34] *on a pilgrimage or building new homes to be separate from an extended family: The 'real home' of Kurdish seasonal workers*

If we only look at women's shacks in order to get to know Kurdish women and hence their motivations to sustain these working and living conditions, we would fail to see their picture fully. In order to understand the social actors of tomato production, we need to know their homes, so this study followed Kurdish families to their hometowns to see their 'actual' homes.

When I first saw the village from a distance, I was quite surprised by its appearance; it included lots of new houses, extensions and houses under construction, which was contrary to my expectations. The construction is also continuing in Yassır abi's current house's roof to add an additional floor of the house for a new apartment. This new extension dominates all of our conversations. How it should be, how it will be. We went to the construction site twice today with

Hatice abla (elder sister), she talked to me about her plans in detail and asked me about my opinions about the shapes and sizes of the rooms. Now they have just two rooms in the home, one for her four children and one for Hatice and Yaşsr. In the new plan, they will have four rooms and a kitchen and a bathroom, which is now outside the house and also has the toilet facilities. The kitchen is also very small now, but it will be huge, she told me. Hatice kept saying that they will also buy sofas and bed frames like in our homes and next time, when we come, we will have comfort, she told me. I told her that sitting on mats is also fine; I like it. But she insisted on saying that every proper home should have sofas like 'our' houses [implying the houses in the village where they work].[35]

During my time in the village, I came to understand that building a new house and having a sofa is the goal of almost all of the women. Building a new house has two phases: in the first phase, a young couple with small children build a small house for themselves so as to live separately from their extended family; then, when their children get older and are close to marriage (sons), they build another bigger flat, mostly on top of their current house, which is also the case for Yaşar and Hatice, and they create their own three-generational extended household through their sons' marriages. Construction is continuous in the village, mostly with the money from the seasonal work they do during the summer in the western part of Turkey.

However, for recently married younger couples, building a separate home away from the groom's parents is still only a dream, at least for daughters-in-law. While they are saving their money to build a separate house for themselves, they also have to give most of their money to their mother- and father-in-law. Consequently, separating from the elders takes ages and until they leave the 'extended family house', not surprisingly, daughters-in-law are responsible for all of the housework, including cooking, cleaning, taking care of the elderly and children. Moreover, they grow plants in the garden of their homes for household consumption and rear animals to sell. In the case of the group that I worked with, Elif and Melek live with their husbands' parents and wait for the time when they will be free from work. So, every penny they give to send their mother- and father-in-law on a pilgrimage takes them further from their dream. Thus, the possibility of a good relationship between daughters-in-law and mothers-in-law is erased as the labour of the daughter-in-law pays for the mother-in-law's dream.

As I heard so many daughters-in-law's stories about their heartless mothers-in-law during my fieldwork on the land, I became more anxious about meeting with the mothers-in-law in their hometown. However, during my time in their hometowns, I understood that these people strike a temporal balance regarding who is paying for whose dream. In other words, daughters-in-law know that first they should pay for their mother-in-law's dreams as their mother-in-law has already paid for her mother-in-law's dream. Paying for your mother-in-law's dreams is the only way to become a mother-in-law and consequently find someone to pay for your own dreams. When I met their mother-in-law, she saw me and kissed me on my forehead, which implies a blessing from her. This surprised me because of the stories I had heard about her from her daughters-in-law on the land, which had given me a colder impression of her. During my time at their home, I spent a lot of time with her since she is responsible for entertaining guests because of her old age. Apparently, it is not proper to spend time with youngsters when elders are at home. She continuously gives orders to Elif and Melek (since they are the youngest brides and live in the same household as their mothers-in-law). This made me very uncomfortable because she literally did not do anything.

As Kandiyoti (1988) points out, in the extended patriarchal family, since all daughters-in-law know that they will become a mother-in-law in the future, the power relations between a mother-in-law and a daughter-in-law can persist. However, the reason that this relationship reminds me of that between landowners and workers could be related to the understanding of power. Neither brides nor workers take issue against the authority itself, but they are against its usage over them. They do not have problems with the existence of 'authority' but they only do not wish to be the 'subject' of it; rather, they want to be an 'agent' of it. 'Power' is embedded in the situations in which people are positioned as workers or landowners or as mothers-in-law or daughters-in-law. As people shift their positions, power shifts and this shifting makes it durable as everyone has an interest in maintaining the system because they all benefit at some point. In the case of the relationship between mother-in-law and daughter-in-law, tension does not prevent them from building 'closer' relationships than that of workers and landowners, as 'brides' are sure to have power in the future and giving birth to a male child is vital to strengthen their hand in their struggle.

From the time, I spent in the homes of Kurdish seasonal women workers, I came to understand that 'freedom' is a contentious and delicate 'thing', and it is quite difficult to pin down in 'reality'. These women told me that only having many 'sons' and living in a separate home could bring them freedom. When being a *kaynana* is the only way of being 'free', 'sons' become the most important figures for women. They see 'sons' as the guarantee of their future well-being. Although 'sons' are also important for men – as a son brings his father recognition and prestige in the family – the relationship between a mother and her son is closer. White (2004), in her study of urban women's employment in Turkey, highlighted that 'sons' in the patriarchal family feel themselves to be 'kings' due to their mothers' attitudes towards and care of them. Sons in Elif's extended family continue to be spoiled by their mothers. They do not worry about anything related to daily life; their mothers do and think of everything for them or they tell their daughters to do what needs to be done and to think only of their elder or younger brothers. Mothers create these 'kings' so that they can become 'queens' in the future. Therefore, they cannot stand hearing that their sons are not masculine 'enough'.

> I was surprised seeing how all the women think that their sons are aggressive, naughty, and strong. Today when we talked about Şehmuz [Elif's nine-month-old son], I told her he was very calm. And, unbelievably, she became offended. She told me he was not calm but very aggressive most of the time. I should have seen him in the mornings. He even woke up angry. Not only Elif, but also other

women try to compete by stating how aggressive their sons are. During the last days, when I told Kadriye that her younger son is calmer than her elder one, she also became offended and proudly told me that both of her boys are the most mischievous and strongest ones in the whole family. Her children beat all the other children, even those older than them. They are like a 'the part of a flame', she told me.[36]

Having a son is not only a fulfilment of women's desires, but they must have a 'proper son' who is a 'go-getter', 'fighter', 'aggressive' like a 'part of a flame'. Kurdish men are not different in those desires and most of them see education as dampening those features that make 'real men'. Yasşr told me that education makes the boys henpecked; there are only two occupations that his sons can be solicitors or politicians. It is not surprising to see that they want their children to be solicitors or politicians as they also see these occupations as helping their 'freedom war'. 'We need solicitors or politicians. We don't need engineers, we should first save ourselves then we can make buildings', says Cumali when I asked what he thought about the future of his children. They view their political struggle with the Turkish state as a 'battle', using the same words to refer to their sons' characteristics and those of Kurdish actors in Turkish politics. As Ahmet told me, 'Ours [implying the Kurdish politicians] are like part of a flame, Turks are henpecked except Erdoğan [current president of Turkey], that is why Kurds also vote for him. Even our women [implying Kurdish women politicians] are more men than Kılıçdaroğlu [the leader of the main opposition party (2014) in Turkey]'.[37]

While men can only accept an educated son if he goes into a specific set of occupations due to the danger of losing his status as a 'proper man', women also do not desire their sons to pursue education in certain directions due to the 'danger' of acquiring a strange bride. Zeynep explained her fear to me after her son went to boarding school: 'I am happy that my son is studying. I want him to save himself. But, you know, sometimes I have to think that if he meets an educated girl in the city, what can we do. If my daughter meets a "stranger," it is not a problem for me. But, I don't want to lose my sons'.[38] Although women have different concerns than men about having an educated son, they share the main concern that 'educated sons' can change the structure of the family. Zeynep put this concern into words, saying: 'How can an educated bride live with us and work on the land? Then, I will lose my son!'

## The power of el âlem

Identifying two forms of rural patriarchy has hopefully demonstrated the intersecting relationship between kinship relations and production relations in agricultural tomato production. Here I conceptualized the term *el âlem* as an empirical example of how intersectional patriarchy works. I examined two forms of rural patriarchy within the households of women who are involved in growing tomatoes on the land: the wives of landowners and Kurdish seasonal migrant workers. The conflicts in patriarchal households and the different ways in which women generate consent depend on the intersections of gender, class, ethnicity and age, some of which are generated in the labour process. This shows that patriarchy is variable and fluid, as well as sustains and is sustained by *el âlem*.

People can negotiate with *el âlem* to get what they want. For instance, Fatma's family had forced her to elope with her husband to save themselves from her wedding expenses. They pretended to be offended, as they had to be according to *el âlem*. Or in the other example, we saw how Fatma's driving has been approved, as it is required for work. Those examples do not simply tell us about the flexibility of patriarchy but they also tell us why people re-constitute it. It is negotiable and the extent of negotiation is the main reason why two different patriarchal forms could be identified. Apparently, in the Kurdish families' households' women have less chance to negotiate. There are two ways they exercise power – as wives and mothers of men and as postmenopausal 'women' – and women are located in the hierarchy of masculinities also depending on these positions.

# Chapter 8

## 'KEMALIST' AND 'TRANSITIONAL' PATRIARCHIES

Household structures that are neither extended (portrayed as traditional and rural) nor nuclear (portrayed as modern and urban) are assumed to be transitional (Kandiyoti 1995). By conceptualizing this as 'transitional patriarchy', here I discuss two further forms of patriarchal household structure which characterize the factory manager's and the women factory workers' homes, and which I identify as 'Kemalist' and 'transitional' patriarchies.

Here I will again focus on the interrelationship of production and reproduction relations as the kernel of the construction of patriarchies, but in contradistinction to previous chapter, we visit the town in which tomatoes are processed. We see that in the town, *el âlem* do not talk as much as they do in the villages, but patriarchy is still alive and continues to 'govern' femininity. Kemalist and transitional patriarchies are different in terms of both their degree and kind (see Table 7.1). While in transitional patriarchy what *el âlem* says is still important in shaping people's behaviour, in Kemalist patriarchy, living according to *el âlem* is a sign of being 'backwards'. However, this does not mean that in Kemalist households there is no *el âlem*. *El âlem* can still talk but about different issues, such as the necessity of being educated, and its volume is not as loud as in transitional households. There is not or will not be a linear historical shift from transitional patriarchy to Kemalist patriarchy but that these patriarchies coexist in the same period of time in different households and are related to the organization of tomato production.

The following is divided into two sections. In the first section, we see the factory manager's 'Kemalist' household, the operation of which is recognizable based on the materials presented in Chapter 6. Then, we look at factory women workers' 'transitional' households. I call these households transitional as they include both a mother- and father-in-law in the village and a nuclear (most of the time) family in the town. Factory women have mostly migrated from the surrounding villages in the last ten years as a consequence of the capitalization of Turkish agriculture. These women's husbands are emancipated from their extended patriarchal family and their familial structure is in transition from an extended to a nuclear one. Husbands' families' control over the newly separated nuclear families of the factory women is still visible, but more tenuous, so I term this form of patriarchy 'transitional patriarchy'. Besides, women are living in an actual 'transition' process during the factory work, as they have to go to their mothers-in-law's homes in the villages to see their children, who are looked after by the grandmothers. Here, I should note that I do not have any intention of saying that when the transition is completed, patriarchy will necessarily be diminished. Rather I would like to emphasize the blurring of boundaries between two households, one of them being the home of the father- and mother-in-law in the village and the other the factory women's 'nuclear' home in the town.

## A Kemalist factory manager of a Kemalist factory and his Kemalist patriarchy

Before talking about the factory manager of 'Red' tomato-processing factory, I should remind the reader briefly about Kemalism and Kemalist patriarchy. The founders of the factory, which is the biggest and oldest family business in Turkey, are 'Kemalists'. It is little surprise that the factory manager is a member of this 'imagined community', which is considered to be a replacement for kinship relations in the 'modern' world. Kemalists have a strong belief that 'education' will enable them to fulfil their aim of matching Western societies in terms of economy, science and political power. Therefore, uneducated and religious populations are seen as obstacles to the dream of becoming a modern, model Westernized country. Kemalist ideology views women as an active participant in the process of development.

Although the ideology attempts to create 'masculine women', the gender division of labour does not vanish, and women continue doing their 'womanly' jobs in a more 'manly' fashion. Here I explore how the factory manager sees factory women as being physically weak, lazy, uneducated, prone to gossiping, fond of vanity, when comparing them with his 'Kemalist' wife. I do not argue that all factory women are educated or hate gossiping, but rather I assert that the factory manager dislikes the women as he thinks that they are not sufficiently like men. Although his family also has a rural background and migrated to the city when he was of primary school age, he is willing to state without any hesitation that 'peasants are lazy, ignorant (*cahil*), uneducated and religious'. Kemalist patriarchal attitude of the factory manager relates to seeing 'femininity' as an enemy of 'modernism', as discussed in Chapter 6.

## 'No-one puts me in an apartment with a swimming pool': Factory manager's 'Kemalist/opponent' patriarchal home

'They are all working in this factory since they want to live in apartments without their in-laws', the general factory manager says of the women workers in Red factory. According to him, all of the women workers are obsessed with an urban lifestyle and the most important element of this is an apartment.

I begin with a quotation from him about women's homes, since he described and told me about his own home and familial relations while comparing them with those of the women workers. This strange and – as one might easily argue – meaningless comparison seems to arise in his mind in order to justify his offensive attitudes towards women workers in the factory, especially those who work in the tomato sorting lines. When I asked about workers, it was these women he immediately began to talk about, not the educated young women who also work seasonally or the warehouse workers. Apparently, in his mind the other two groups of workers do not belong to the category of 'workers'; they are 'students' and 'ours', which is what he calls them. He sees the (sorting) workers as a group of 'lazy, uneducated, ignorant, selfish, conservative and religious women' and in his 'Kemalist' mind they are representatives of the current conservative Turkish government and represent a corrupting influence on his 'western modernised country'. According to him, as for many opponents of the current government in Turkey, the construction of 'their disgusting buildings' is one of the main elements of this corruption. So, he said,

> They can't put me in these apartments with swimming pools[1] ... they cannot find people that know how to swim for their big 'swimming pools'. They [implying here, the current Turkish government and their supporters] can just find women who continuously eat sunflower seeds on their swimming pool view balconies. Sorry, but my wife does not have that much spare time; she has more important things to do than gossiping about neighbours, her mother-in-law or görümce [her husband's sister]. We don't need to have a house with a big balcony or a swimming pool. We are working most of the time. Recently, our old friends from university came to visit us after a long time from another city and they were shocked to see that we were still living in the same house after so many years. They noticed that it does not have security guards at the entrance and they said, aren't you afraid? I asked them, what would we be afraid of? Can you believe how people are going crazy? Why do you think they need security? Who are they? Everyone thinks that they and their children are the most precious people in the world. So, anyone can attack them at any time. I just laughed. What has this government done to these people? They build lots of houses to make money for themselves and they bring a 'mortgage' here, so it puts lots of debt on those people but nobody complains; they love them. They are crazy, this country all goes crazy.[2]

The factory manager continues to contrast 'those uneducated and lazy' women workers of Red factory with his 'educated and hardworking' wife whom he met at university. He also underlines how his wife is different from the women workers by being 'educated', 'independent', 'powerful', not partaking in 'womanly' daily life activities or concerns, such as taking care of the home, 'gossiping', worrying about their mothers-in-law and eating sunflower seeds on the balcony while gazing at the neighbours. His wife is like 'him': working all day and not caring about the 'simple things' of social life, such as buying household goods.

When he mentions women's insistence on living in apartments or buying new sofas, he actually implies that they are showing off, which is seen as a sign of being 'backward' by Kemalists. This could be linked with Kemalists' attempt to draw rigid lines between the new Turkish Republic and the Ottoman Empire, which can be described with pride. Showing off is a habit of Easterners and is associated with being 'traditional', thereby close to Islamic than secular Turkish identity. Those who show off are living for *el âlem*, to enjoy *el âlem*, to get approval from *el âlem*, to be liked by *el âlem*.

On the other hand, the factory manager and his wife 'do not live for the approval of *el âlem*' (as he implies) so they do not need to move to a luxury apartment. Moreover, his words also imply that insisting on living in his old-style apartment is a part of his resistance to the new political actors of Turkey.

> We are working all the time; we are not children of high-class people. We did everything by ourselves together. I cannot believe these women who expect everything from their husbands. My wife can manage everything on her own; she is even more powerful than me. I am also a village boy. So, some of my childhood friends have married uneducated women from villages even though they are educated. They claim that an urban wife would not get on well with their family, but now they are listening to complaints from their wives about their mothers and fathers, since those women do not have any other work. My wife has a very respectful relationship with my family. They do not interfere with each other. You shouldn't be afraid of an educated woman but of an uneducated one. I wish you could meet her. I am sure you would like each other. I understand that you are a bit feminist; she is too. So, she can tell you better than me about the danger of being sympathetic towards those women. Believe me, they are not like you [including me and his wife] they are only thinking about moving to a town and decorating their house as they wish. I haven't seen my wife buying something for our house for a long time. It is not her kind of thing. In our spare time, we ride our bikes; we walk in the limited 'empty space' that we can find. We don't stick ourselves to shopping centres as they want us to do [implying politicians].[3]

It should be pointed out here that he told me all of the above when I asked him, 'You said that you are a leftist so what do you think about the working conditions of the women workers in this factory?' At first glance, his words seem irrelevant to my question. However, as we go deeper, his justification of the 'bad' working conditions can be seen. Those women deserve those conditions since they are not hardworking like him and his wife, and they support the current Turkish government, which is mainly responsible for all of the corruption. They act without thinking and follow what their politicians want; this means that those women want to move to the town and buy a fancy house with credit from a bank. But is he right?

### *Lazy women's 'luxury apartments': Factory women workers trying to have nuclear transitional patriarchal homes*

Almost all of the women workers I spoke to at Red factory lived in villages before moving to the town, where they were the unpaid family workers of small farmers for most of their lives. When survival as a small farmer in rural Turkey became almost impossible due to neoliberal economic policies, they moved to the towns of the region to find a job in the factories. However, their low income does not enable them to live totally independently from their extended families. So, although the husbands' parents mostly stay in the village, they continue to give economic 'help' to those couples who are 'trying to be a nuclear family'.[4] Their help takes two forms: the first is that they sell their small piece of land and give the money to their sons to help them buy a house in town. Although men have more permanent jobs than women in the factories (this is an assumption from asking about their husbands' working conditions), the low earnings of those couples make their lives more difficult as they also pay rent for their accommodation. Thus, selling their parents' small piece of land in order to have the money they need to buy a house in town and to get a mortgage becomes the most reasonable solution to improving their living conditions. From this perspective, 'desiring to have a house' does not appear to be an absurd 'obsession' of the women workers, as the factory manager claims, but a necessity in order to adapt to their new economic conditions. However, obtaining money for a new home from the husband's parents means that the elders are still in a position where they have a right to direct the couple's life. The second possible way in which these older couples, especially mothers-in-law, help their sons and daughters-in-law is to take care of the children and cook when they are both away working in the factory. At that point, 'transitional patriarchy' enables to look at the (re)distribution of the resources of the extended family and the newly structured division of labour.

### *'Son-like daughters' or 'still troubling mothers-in-law': The new but still gendered division of labour*

The women workers of Red factory mostly send their small children to the villages while they work in the factory and visit them whenever possible. Women do not like this solution, since sometimes they cannot see their children for two weeks at a time. Some villages are far away and they have to wait until they can have a day off. None of the women trust their husbands to take care of small children, so their mother-in-law is their only option. Moreover, most of their husbands also work in the factories and they also work on the shift system. It is not rare for a wife and husband to work the night shift at the same time. So, sending children to the villages becomes the most reasonable option. This option is also what makes women's factory work possible. The seasonality of factory work apparently fits with children's schooling and makes it possible for them to go to the villages.

However, this option does not solve the problem according to the women. They always complain about this relationship, sometimes because of their mother-in-law's attitude towards the children and sometimes because of their attitude towards the women themselves.

> Whenever I go to my mother-in-law's house, I always buy lots of food and I always clean her house. Since she is looking after the children, she cooks for them. So, this is my obligation. I am not complaining about it. But she always complains about me and my work in the factory. But this is a good option for us; we are paying our children's education fees, I am buying some stuff for the house. This is good.[5]

According to the women, the common problem with women working and mothers-in-law helping is that mothers-in-law do not give enough support to daughters-in-law while they do factory work. Mothers-in-law expect their daughters-in-law to do some domestic tasks such as cleaning on their days off.

> Yesterday, I didn't come to work since my mother-in-law called me last night and told me that if I did not come the next day and help her with cleaning and stuff, she would not look after the children any more. I told her, there is no day off this week, but she insisted. So, I didn't come to work, although I didn't have permission, and I went to the village. She even asked me to clean the windows. What do my children do to the windows? Thank God, she likes my children and looks after them. But God knows she hates my factory work. I am as tired as on a factory day.[6]

The women's stories were similar; when a woman with children did not come to work without asking, going to the village to help her mother-in-law or staying at home to help were considered the reasons why. In these conditions, a 'helpful' daughter of their own comes on the scene as a heroine for women workers. She can do all the work that a mother-in-law can do and she is not interfering or 'trying to dominate' the household'; she also enables their 'nuclear family structure' to be sustained during her mother's seasonal work. Thus, it is not surprising for factory women that having a daughter becomes a desire just as having a boy is desirable for women in Kurdish extended families. So although it is not typical in Turkish society and, more specifically, in the region where I did my fieldwork, there are expressions about the luck of women who have daughters and women verbalize these frequently, especially when they talk about the work done at home when they are in the factory. As one of the women told me,

> I have two daughters since I am loved by God. Do you know an expression that says if a woman has two daughters, it is like a celebration of 29th October [the day the Turkish Republic was established]? If she has a daughter and a

son, it is like a celebration of 23rd April [the day of the establishment of the Turkish parliament]. If she has only boys, it is like 10th November [the date on which Mustafa Kemal Atatürk, the founder of the Turkish Republic, died]. I am always celebrating the 'republic'. When I go home, there is always food for dinner; they also take care of their brother. What more could I want from God?[7]

The expression she used and other similar expressions that highlight the 'importance of having girls' are very common among women in the factory. In their new conditions, under which women are trying to create and sustain their own independent nuclear families through working in the factories seasonally, 'helpful daughters' become more attractive than 'useless boys'. She takes care of her brothers and can do housework. She is "my hand and my foot"' (*'elim ayağım'*).[8] Those daughters are mostly under the official working age. That is why they work at home rather than in the factories. When they reach seventeen, they can begin to come to the factories with their mothers. Most of them also continue with their education. 'A woman cannot want more than an educated daughter', says Feride. Lots of women in the factory seemed to agree with this statement, since they believe that when their daughters work in white-collar jobs, they will earn regular money and a daughter's regular money means support for them.

> Everything is changing. Women are like men now. They have money. They put their mothers in their cars and go everywhere together. A bride's mother is like a 'camping gas'; it is always in the car [implying you will always go out with your daughter's nuclear family]. But if you are a groom's mother, you are like a 'house gas'. You always have to stay at home [implying your bride does not want you to go out with them]. Now having a girl is even better than having a boy.[9]

Women are aware of the fact that mothers-in-law are losing their power over other members of the family, especially their sons and younger brides and, due to economic changes and the impact of these changes on the household, they prefer to have 'helpful, sensitive, hardworking daughters' to support them rather than 'useless, thoughtless, henpecked sons'.

### *Now is the time to be enemies with the* Görümce: *The new structure of distribution of resources within extended family*

It is no coincidence that in this section we do not discuss factory women's *eltis* – their husbands' brother's wives. Even though they no longer live together, they are still 'potential enemies' when the issue of sharing the resources of their husbands' parents arises. However, this relationship does not play such a disruptive role as when they lived in a rural setting within an extended family structure. They now have their *görümce* (husband's sister) to contend with instead. When the 'daughter' of an 'extended family' begins to work in paid employment, she also becomes a more powerful figure in the familial hierarchy and is in a better position to fight for an equal claim on her parents' property.

As we have seen, the main objective of young couples who have just migrated to town is to buy a house. This is because paying rent and education expenses for their children on a husband's official minimum wage and a wife's seasonal wage is impossible. As they mostly arrive from rural areas, and their families have survived the first wave of rural transformation driven by mechanisation in the 1950s, they are likely to possess a small plot of land. In this sense the region in which I conducted this study has become the region which has one of the highest rates of buying and selling properties in Turkey (TÜİK 2014c). Under these circumstances, it is mainly the husband's parents who still live in the village or want to move to towns with the young couple, who sell their land in the village and divide the money between their sons, but not their daughters. They legitimize this difference by saying that 'if everyone gives money to their sons, then their daughter will also have money from her parents-in-law'. Moreover, everyone still thinks that 'a son has to take care of his mother and father when they get older and not a daughter', so they are trying to guarantee their future. In those conditions, the enemies of the extended family – *eltiler* – make a peace agreement through sharing the money and becoming allies against their new shared enemy: *görümce*.[10]

*Görümce* is the sister of husband and is the one who is most subject to discrimination in the sharing of the properties of the extended family. Passing the lands on to 'sons' is not a new phenomenon in rural Turkey; however, *görümceler* have also migrated to towns and hence need money to buy a house there. In this scenario, if their parents-in-law do not have anything to give them and their natal family gives all the inheritance money to their brothers, they become offended. Zile, factory worker, explains her situation with her *görümce* as follows:

> She [implying her görümce] is the devil. She envies us [implying her nuclear family]. My mother-in-law has to take care of me, not her. I will clean their shit! [Implying taking care of her mother and father-in-law, when they get older]. I can't take care of them in el âlem's house, at least I deserve it. I don't adore her crumply parents, I wish they could stay with their beloved daughter, however, they would not go there, but will come to me. She wants to have the house and make me look after her parents. See, how smart she is. No one gives you five köfte with three lira [üç kuruşa beş köfte, a commonly used expression, its meaning is similar to 'there is no such thing as a free lunch'].[11]

Zile believes that she deserves money for a house from her husband's parents because she will have to take care of them in the future. And this is what *el âlem* requires women to do:

I wish my mother-in-law could go to my görümce. I don't want anything from her. I don't want her money, without peace what is money? She gives us money and continuously says that she is feeding us. She interferes with everything we buy, wear, everywhere we go. My children learn to tell lies because of her. As we have to hide everything from her. I told my görümce, if she wants she can have her mother and money. But, you know, Ali [her husband] told me that we have to accept that if we send her to my görümce, el âlem will cause trouble for us. They will speak about us. Everything we have done until that time will be forgotten. And they will just talk about how ungrateful we are. Ali can't stand hearing such things. He is very proud.[12]

While some women achieve their 'dream home' in exchange for their unpaid labour they take on caring for their elders in the future, for other women whose parents-in-law do not yet require care and/or still live in the village separately from them, women's obligations mostly take the form of cleaning their husband's family home.

I don't know where my home is. I am always between two houses. They [her husband's family] do not accept that we are not living with them anymore; they are always calling us for everything. My mother-in-law is obsessed with cleaning and I am her favourite bride. Don't think that it is a good thing. Don't be the favourite bride of your mother-in-law! This is abla's [elder sister] recommendation. My mother-in-law thinks that I am the best at cleaning, so I am always there. And, of course, if you go to clean, you can't just escape with cleaning, I always cook when I go there. I'm complaining to mine [implying her husband], but he always tells me what more I want? They are [implying both mother and father-in-law] giving us everything. He of course is happy, because I am doing everything, but he just gets the money.[13]

## Changes on gender relations

This chapter has introduced two different forms of household-based patriarchy and demonstrated how they shape and are shaped by the intersectionality of gender, class and age, which also constructs masculinities and femininities. In the first section of the chapter, we looked at the factory manager's household and explored how Kemalism erases femininities due to its belief that 'femininity' is the anti-look of modernity. The factory manager compared 'feminine' workers with his 'masculine' wife and concluded that she is far better than women workers, thanks to her 'masculinity'. Her masculinity is, in turn, constructed through education and particular forms of white-collar employment and is superior to 'femininity', which is backward and is displayed by uneducated women factory workers who are employed seasonally. A second form of patriarchy was identified as 'transitional patriarchy' and it also includes the appreciation of a masculine character – 'son-like daughters' – who are emerging as educated young women who can help their mothers with domestic work and who will gain white-collar, 'masculine' jobs when they seek employment. These women might be the future 'masculine wives' of Kemalist husbands. They are preferred to sons by factory women because they not only earn and control their money as men do, but also they still help their mothers with domestic tasks. In this way, different types of masculinity are shaped by the intersectionality of age, education and gender and affect the form taken by patriarchy within these different households.

# Chapter 9

## CONCLUSIONS

### *Where 'our' tomatoes end up*

In May 2015, from one rainy day in London, I went to another rainy day in Tokyo via İstanbul to see the fate of the tomatoes that I had been following for the two years. When I arrived there, I was only thinking of how tired I was and of how it could not possibly be profitable to purchase tomatoes from such a long way away.

> The reason for our tomatoes' lengthy journey to Japan results from the difficult working conditions on the tomato lands and in the factory; making such profits in spite of such distances is possible because of low pay and long working hours. All this travelling has made me feel like a squeezed tomato. My face is totally red as happens whenever I get too tired, and my whole face and my feet are swollen. At the end, I become like a tomato myself while I am following them.[1]

Over the next few days, I spent time interviewing women who used the company's tomato sauce, and seeking out the tomato sauce we produced in Turkey on Japanese supermarket shelves. But, after interviewing Japanese women, it turned out they bought the same brands of tomato sauce from the supermarket, but they were produced in Italy and tomato paste from Turkish tomatoes was in warehouses rather than in supermarkets. In effect, it seems that 'Turkish' tomatoes are not viewed as 'good' enough to enter Japanese households. Instead, catering companies or 'low grade' foreign restaurants purchase them.

So, while I was heading to one of Tokyo's most touristic spots – 'Akihabara' with the hope of finding a Turkish kebab shop to locate the destination of 'our' tomatoes, I was thinking millions of things: how could I tell the women workers back in Turkey that people in Japan prefer Italian tomatoes to ours? I was remembering how women working on the Japanese production line would flaunt their position over other women workers in the factory, because of their role in producing for the Japanese market. They were different and 'better' than other workers. Çavuş's words were echoing in my mind, 'be serious, we are not playing here. Those tomatoes go to Japan. Show them that "we" [implying the "Turkish nation"] have the best tomatoes. You don't want to shame us, do you?' I remembered how we would clean for hours when the representatives from a

Japanese company came to the factory on one of their regular visits. We even had to clean the streets outside the factory gates. I remembered how the forewoman sent me to another line, where tomato sauce for a national supermarket was produced, because my uniform was not clean enough. How proud landowners were of themselves because they were 'chosen' to plant for the Japanese, how women on the land enjoyed the idea that they ate the same tomatoes as the Japanese. But, as it turns out, they do not, or at least people in Japan do not eat Turkish tomatoes in their homes. And, in a Turkish kebab shop in Tokyo, these tomatoes, that were held in such high esteem at the Turkish factory, are in fact used by Kurdish workers to make tomato sauce for *döner kebabs* intended to be consumed by migrants, tourists or Japanese people from low-income groups. And this is how the story of 'local' Turkish tomatoes connects the Japanese 'global' tomato production in this book: via a Kurdish worker in a Turkish kebab shop in Tokyo.

Ali, the young Kurdish employee in the Turkish kebab shop in Tokyo, explained this to me by saying that the 'Chinese come to eat here, the South Koreans come, they are migrants just like us and like us, they try to save money. Sometimes, young Japanese women come, as they like me [laughing here, and implying that young women visit the shop solely because of his attractiveness]. Students and tourists come'.[2]

Apparently, I should have taken 'the identity of tomatoes' more seriously; here I underestimated that tomatoes become the representatives of 'us', their producers; tomatoes are also inscribed within ethnicity and class as well as gender. Turkish tomatoes cannot compete with Italian tomatoes in the Japanese supermarkets because of the higher prestige attached to the latter. Finding an answer to the question of why richer countries like Japan prefer Italian to Turkish tomatoes could be the objective of another research. But for now, with this book, we know that when someone touches a tomato on the land, in the factory or in their homes, which are the places we cannot name, they create themselves as well as us. This chapter, our last stop, is the where I will remind this creation process.

## *Same story across and within differences*

This book did not tell us an unknown story; looking at how attempts to integrate local agriculture and food industries into the global economy have affected rural populations and how constructions of, and the availability of, women's labour shape and are shaped by the interaction between the global economy and local dynamics is not a novel thing to do. But this book would have aimed to say something 'more' – not 'new' – than what is already said about the gender in global food production until now, mainly with its method. Method here does not only refer the research technics but also the way of locating the main actors of global food production into the study as well as the reason and hope of the study.

This book has written to keep my promise to the people in the study. They want me to tell their stories to others and I did it. In doing so, hopefully, the book has also managed to contribute the scholarly literature, thanks to its main arguments:

1. In order to understand the interaction between 'local' and 'global', it is necessary to deploy locally developed terms derived from lived experiences.
2. Global capital capitalizes the familial features.
3. Global production relies on mainly unpaid or poorly paid work by women through its cooperation within the familial ideology, as well as the state's support.
4. Contrary to the suggested in the literature, femininity is not always seen as productive in the global production.
5. Masculinities and femininities are shaped and shape by the division of labour within the labour process.
6. People, regardless of gender, invest actively in the construction of masculinities and femininities, although this supports the emergence and application of control over female actors.

In terms of contributing the enormous literature on global production, particularly on women's work, the book is just a sip of water – as women in this study see their life for men – and this put me in a very difficult position in terms of concluding that the book said something 'more'. Maybe I could have just said that nobody has worked with the women who are in this study, working in tomato production and processing for a Japanese company in Turkey, and hence everything the book has told about 'more' to the literature. But, we know that contributing something 'more' to the literature does not actually refer to the differences of place, people or things in terms of their different context or the results of what do differences cause in terms of social, economic and political contexts or vice versa. Rather saying something the 'same' across and within those differences leads us to say something 'more' sociologically, and consequently we could have a chance to talk about being human, and particularly for this study; being 'women', even more specifically 'being gendered'. In this sense, the book has sought the connections between what has been done in the literature until now and in which ways I can make connections between these by focusing on connections themselves such 'global' and 'local', 'women' and 'men', 'Turks' and 'Kurds', 'old' and 'young', 'researcher' and 'participants' and so on. Here the intention was not handled those as and within binaries instead intervening relations. To focus on these as relations could have been possible, thanks to working and talking with women and men, through 'witnessing' their lives. However, I must admit that different methodologies and approaches might have led to different conclusions than those I have drawn because the way we do research transforms and is transformed by our understanding of the social world. It is important, therefore, to bear in mind that no set of conclusions can be right or wrong in and of themselves.

Drawing on one case study, I have explored the gendered relations in global tomato production and processing in western Turkey. I suggest that by looking at this 'specific' case, we can see the similarities and differences between this particularity and other people have drawn generally, and, in doing so, develop a 'comprehensive' theory about how production and reproduction reinforce each other and about how intersectional patriarchy works in tomato production and processing in Turkey as part of a global commodity chain.

I also want to suggest that the methods I used make empathy possible. Empathy does not merely mean trying to understand someone's position from the points at which we stand in our lives. If we tried to do this every time, we would come to conclusions based on our own subjectivity without necessarily understanding people's conditions, and ultimately, we would not understand the whole subject of our inquiry. The only possible inference of this way of looking would be statements like 'if I were you'. On the other hand, in order to generate empathy and thus make understanding possible, we must experience the conditions that 'others' face even if this is not always completely possible because of our differences. Without seeing the payslip addressed to you that shows how little you have earned in comparison to your huge bodily effort, without tomatoes entering your dreams or without developing an eye infection because of tomato dust, or feeling grateful just for the existence of clean drinking water, it is difficult to 'comprehend' the meaning of tomato work for its workers.

Living and witnessing the lives of women workers also make it possible to reveal the malleable and various forms of masculinity governing femininity – which I conceptualize as intersectional patriarchy – since close observation and a deep focus are vital to reveal the ways in which gender relations are becoming unfixed. For instance, my findings suggest that daughters and mothers become closer in transitional patriarchy. Older women begin to see their daughters as their future 'protector' instead of their sons, and as a result daughters are more highly valued and seen as more 'masculine'. In a similar vein, women from the landowning family do not have as much confidence as Kurdish women that they will become mothers-in-law in an extended household due to the changing structure of production relations. This pushes them closer to their husbands rather than their sons. Moreover, in order to see the mutual changes in the relations of production and reproduction, a close look is necessary because the dynamics of those relations are constantly shifting. Furthermore, the possible forms of resistance cannot be easily grasped without the application of qualitative methods, as the mode of resistance, in reality, is actually quite different from what we expect when we define resistance without having a deep understanding of women's own strategies. Besides, most of the time women themselves do not think or say that they are resisting – culturally women's resistance is not desirable so they do not like to see themselves as resisting. The intersectional forms of the gendered division of labour are also hidden, both at the workplace and in homes when we look at them through defined gender roles.

Knowing people in the study better also enables them to know you and your work better. The people in the study always knew that I was doing research but they did not put its subject into the same words I have. 'Knowing'[5] the same thing but stating them differently has always been an issue between them and me. The women I worked with did not know the Global South and Global North division in the organization of global food production, and they did not identify the Global South as a producer of labour-intensive products and as a consumer (Friedmann 1995). They did know that Japan is a new and increasingly demanding customer of tomatoes in Turkey but did not know that tomatoes are highly attractive for researchers working on global food chains (Barndt 2002), labour (Torres 1997) and economic sociology (Harvey et al. 2002). They did not know that the current Turkish government has proposed two important legislations, the Seed Law (2006), which constrains farmers from using their own seeds, and the Land Law (2007), which refers to 'land consolidation'. Furthermore, it looks to integrate its agro-food industry into global food production patterns; rather, they know that they cannot use their local seeds anymore and they cannot divide their lands even because of inheritance. As such, small farmers are leaving the villages increasingly and continuously and women have begun to work in food factories, which have become important alternatives.

People in the study did not know that I build this research on the tradition of feminist commodity chain analysis, which has been proposed by Ramamurthy (2004) as an alternative approach to global commodity chain analysis (GCCA), which emphasizes the location of both rich and poor countries within the unequal but integrated international economy as the source of economic problems in the regions of the Global South (Gereffi and Korzeneiwicz 1994). This is done by claiming that GCCA is gender blind (Bair 2005; Collins 2014; Dunaway 2014; Ramamurthy 2000, 2004, 2014) and has masculine undertones (Ramamurthy 2004). Instead, Ramamurthy (2004: 40) identifies feminist commodity chain analysis as

> a method for researchers (1) to pinpoint and investigate the different nodes of a global chain in which women are key agents, (2) to understand how gender and sexual ideologies structure social relations and code value in the production and consumption of commodities, and (3) to track value is created, extracted, and distributed in commodity circuits so as to accomplish the social production of labour and capital.

Women of the study knew that I was trying to understand what being a woman or man means on the land, in the factory and at home; how this is important in shaping their relations and organizing what we did at work. They did not know that Ramamurthy (2004) states that feminist commodity chain analysis does not only look at how value is added in the production process, but it is also attentive towards tracking globalization in daily lives, experiences and the imaginaries of people. As such, I tried to understand their dreams and struggles. They had never heard about intersectionality, but they knew that 'being an older woman is different from being a younger woman' (A young seasonal migrant woman, 15 September 2013). They do not know that along with other feminist scholars (Collins 2014; Dunaway 2014; Dedeoğlu 2014), I see the household as a kernel unit of analysis within a global commodity chain, but they believe that family is the centre of their life, is in the centre of when they work or when they are at home. These people never see what Friedmann (1995) writes: 'Changes in women's and men's roles in the family are a local counterpart to the global changes in the political economy of food' (1995: 49). Yet, they feel that tomatoes have changed their family life.

In the following sections I will review what women of the study know about it and what I have learned from them. I first focus on the changing patterns of women's work when situated within the context of global capitalism; then I will approach how it shapes and is shaped by local dynamics via intersectional forms of the gendered division of labour on the land, in the factory and at home, then demonstrate the ways in which workers generate both consent and resistance, and finally highlight the interweaving of production and reproduction relations.

## Intersectional forms of the gendered division of labour

The book identifies gendered division of labour in three different spheres: agriculture, manufacturing and in the home. It proposes that the gendered division of labour is best understood by the application of the concept of 'intersectional patriarchy'.

'Intersectional patriarchy' to the way that different masculinities are constructed through the intersectionality of gender, class, ethnicity, age and education in various and malleable ways within the division of labour, their power over femininities and their association with particular patriarchal household structures. In Chapter 7, the book addressed the role of *el âlem* in supporting this system of male governing and operating intersectional patriarchy. *El âlem* as a mode of social control refers to a group of unidentified people who you believe will talk about and pass judgement on the appropriateness of your behaviour. It simultaneously refers to a group of identifiable people who decide on the appropriateness of your behaviour according to requirements of *el âlem*'s unidentifiable members. Gendered social control makes masculine dominance over femininity possible and persistent in rural Turkey and this is constructed through the fluid and various intersections of gender, class, ethnicity, age and education which themselves construct and are constructed within the division of labour in the labour process. Before continuing this discussion, here I would like to reprise the broader patterns of the division of labour in relation to global capital in Turkey and the chapters of the book that preceded this one.

In Chapter 2, I provided background information on the changing patterns of rural life in Turkey over the last thirty years, providing insight into how rural women's employment has been affected by these changes. Mass migration to urban areas since the 1970s increased the precariousness of rural women's employment, leading them to work mostly in the home, or in family-owned small textile firms known as *atölye*. While this is relevant to the women who migrated to urban areas, for women who stayed in rural communities, being an unpaid family worker remains the main occupational position. Today, majority of women working in agriculture are unpaid family workers. Although rates of women's employment and their numeric domination of agricultural labour have not changed significantly in the past thirty years, in the last fifteen years women's agricultural work has become more precarious and difficult as a result of the neoliberal economic policies. According to the reports of the 'occupational health and safety association' (İSGM 2014), 23 per cent of worker fatalities occurred amongst agricultural labourers in 2014.

As we have seen at several points in this book, the regulations imposed by the Turkish state, such as restricting the use of local seeds (Seed Law) or the minimum amount of land someone has to have (Land Law), result in an effective land grab, whereby the lands of smallholders are transferred into the hands of big landowning families. As emphasized, the only way to become a bigger farmer within tomato production is by increasing your stake in the system. In this sense, although most farmers in Turkey are still not big landlords, they have begun to produce large amounts by renting the lands of others who have been 'forced' to stop cultivating their small plots of land. In Chapter 6, which looked at women factory workers, we saw that in the region in which this study took place, the people who were effectively forced off their land had to move to the towns to look for factory work. On the other hand, farmers who have stayed on the land have tried to find the cheapest labour force possible in order to expand their business; in order to do this, they have sought the cooperation of Kurdish migrant seasonal workers. Kurdish migrant workers become the most profitable option for them not only because of their acceptance of low wages but also because of their acceptance of the group performance-based payment system.[4] In the following, I talk about how the book has revealed the interrelated effects of these changes on the gendered division of labour.

## *Gendered class and ethnicity in the division of labour on tomato land*

Employing Kurdish workers does not change the appearance of the gendered division of labour on tomato land at planting time. In the spring, most of the time, the women occupy the tomato fields by themselves; they plant tomato seedlings all day without seeing any men. This is because men come to the land before the women's work starts in order to prepare the land by ploughing it and setting up the irrigation systems. They then leave as soon as these tasks are complete. However, this rigid division between the sexes is not associated with overt class divisions in the organization of labour in the planting season. At planting time, women from the landowning family, Kurdish seasonal workers and local women workers work together. Women from the landowning family take two roles on the land, as both workers and managers, since although they do the same job as other workers they also assume a managerial position. We met Fatma who most readily embraced her managerial position. Based on this, it is unsurprising that she was seen as the 'man of the group' even though there were no 'actual' men around. Others perceived her in this way because she is slow to tire, has considerable physical strength, knows how to control others and can drive both cars and tractors. In addition to her 'masculine' personal traits, her ability to perform masculinity on the land is bound up with the intersection of her class as a member of landowning family, her ethnicity as a Turk and her age as the oldest woman from the landowning family who still works on the land. Those intersections apparently feed her 'masculine' personal traits. None of the Kurdish women on the land perform masculinity, even though the gangmaster's wife is on the land as a *çavuş* (forewoman) and also has considerable strength and is slow to tire, though these traits for her are not sufficient to perform masculinity. Performing masculinity is associated with being powerful, and being powerful on the land for Kurdish migrant women workers, especially when someone from the landowning family is around, does not seem to be possible.

On the other hand, although Fatma's 'manly woman' character is desirable on the land so as she can organize work, she becomes the target of the agent of patriarchy, *el âlem*, as soon as she leaves the workplace. Her driving, which enables workers to leave the land when there are no men available to pick them up, is applauded, but once she returns to the village, her ability to drive suddenly becomes inappropriate. She has to stop driving at the entrance to the village because she cannot drive past the men's coffeehouse without being criticized by the *el âlem*. As a social control mechanism, *el âlem* demonstrates how everyone including men and women, young and old, has a stake in the patriarchy. Everyone can have some power over someone occupying a different role. So, while Fatma has control over workers' labour on the land, she loses her power as soon as she arrives outside the men's coffeehouse where she suddenly becomes a *gelin* – daughter-in-law – of the landowning family. Outside the coffeehouse, the *el âlem* does not allow her to be a 'man-like woman' because there are enough men around. These malleable power hierarchies demonstrate how *el âlem* as well as patriarchy are flexible and this flexibility is discussed as a reason for the persistence of patriarchy. When everyone gets something from it, they are eager to perpetuate it.

While the application of the concept of *el âlem* explains why patriarchy persists, the question of how it persists is explained by emphasizing the intersectional formations of masculinity and femininity, which are reproduced via the gendered division of labour, as seen in the case of Fatma. While Fatma has a right to be masculine on the land as a member of the landowning family, for other workers, being masculine is not an option. On the other hand, Fatma also uses femininity as a means to control the workers. These attempts were quite clear in Chapter 4. For example, when she interrupted the argument between local workers and Kurdish workers about the Turkish–Kurdish conflict, she humiliated the other women by accusing them of talking about politics 'just like men'. Here, she acted as a member of *el âlem*, which in rural Turkey condemns any interest that women may show in politics. In this way the term *el âlem*, which, when translated, simultaneously captures 'others' and 'everyone' and functions as a way of disciplining and controlling behaviour based on perceived and imagined norms. The gangmaster's wife also adopted the use of the term *el âlem*. She is effectively a middle woman in the planting season and works to increase worker productivity. We saw that this justified her control over workers by emphasizing her need to protect the reputation of the group for being hardworking; otherwise she said 'people' would talk about how they were lazy and this would decrease their chances of being employed in the same region again. Those 'people' to whom she referred are also (the) *el âlem*.

Unlike during the planting season, at harvest time Kurdish men are also on the land and they replace the women from the landowning family. Therefore, in Chapter 5, we saw how the gendered division of labour intersects with ethnicity and age. As the group performance–based system eliminates the necessity of direct managerial supervision during harvest time, the male workers have some control over their labour. In this case, we saw that the oldest member of the group, Yahya, took this control into his own hands by using his higher position in the familial hierarchy to organize the labour process by assigning and allotting specific tasks. Most of the workers were eager to follow what Yahya proposed as their primary focus was on producing greater outputs. The basis of Yahya's division was physical strength, which subsequently led to a division of labour based on age and gender. Tomato picking is physically labour intensive and thus more output can be guaranteed by people who have more strength than others. Indeed, the tasks of young women are deemed to be the least important as they require minimal physical strength.

However, we saw that young women's elimination from tasks requiring more physical power such as shaking the tomato roots does not prevent the men who do this task from perceiving themselves as doing a woman's job. Here, the difference between this task – uprooting tomato plants – and the only male task of the tomato picking – carrying the full bags to the tractors – is that relatively older or physically stronger women can be assigned the former task, but assigning women to the latter is almost impossible. Therefore, the pride of the men who are given the task of carrying the sacks to the tractors is clearly visible, as they are happy to be given a task that 'fits' with their masculinity.

Here, the study found another chance to discuss intersectional patriarchy as a result of the starkly contrasting views of two groups of Kurdish men. One of these groups believed that they were 'doing a woman's job because they are Kurdish', whereas the second believed that they were 'doing a man's job because they are Kurdish'. Based on the former statement, being Kurdish is feminized; in the latter, it is masculinized. Here we can see how men in the second example are masculinized through the intersection of gender, ethnicity as well as age. This is because carrying the sacks to the tractors is strictly the work of younger males due to the physical strength required. In this way, such emphasized masculine traits in addition to the way in which work is organized with the oldest male, Yahya, allow for masculinity to be performed. Moreover, these traits also allow those masculine workers to hold power over other workers. For this group, Kurdish ethnic identity is masculinized in order to exert control over the workers. In order to make them proud of their work, the idea that only Kurdish men can carry the sacks because of their sheer strength in comparison to Turkish men is constructed. This shows us how ethnicity is intertwined with gender whereby ethnicity itself becomes gendered. This maps onto our discussion of class in the previous section. Moreover, these also show us that people can change their positions from masculinity and femininity, but femininity and masculinity are always present in a hierarchical relationship. In the present binary, the hierarchical positions of these categories do not change. When something or someone is subordinated it becomes feminized, and they are seen to be doing a woman's job and vice versa.

When we consider the processes of masculinization and feminization of the Kurdish ethnic identity, it is also evident that it is actually specific tasks that are feminized and masculinized as well as ethnic identity. Both men and women can change their position within masculinities and femininities. However, the femininity and/or masculinity of tasks remains the same. Indeed, the workers who have the closest physical interaction with the tomatoes are feminized, whether by planting the seedlings, sorting tomatoes on the assembly line or making tomato sauce at home. Feminization increases as direct engagement increases. The final tasks, both on the land – carrying the tomatoes to the tractors – and in the factory – carrying the tomatoes to the warehouses – belong to men and never to women. Even within the scope of the men's jobs, the tasks are more feminized and less prestigious depending on how much direct contact workers have with the tomatoes. This is because masculinities and femininities are not attached to people, but to the way people behave or, even, to material things such as tomatoes, rural work, assembly lines and so on. People who exercise authority are seen as masculine, even if they are women, and people who follow commands are seen as feminine, even if they are men. This clearly restricts changing the meaning of femininity to include wielding authority.

### Gendered 'Kemalism' and education in the division of labour in the factory

The chapter on work in the factory clearly evidenced the gendered nature of specific tasks. This was shown when we saw how women were masculinized when they were assigned tasks in the warehouse. Tasks in the warehouse require physical strength, and if there are no men available for this task, the management has to employ women. Although the general manager admits that he prefers employing men in the warehouse, the factory management managed to modify 'women' to 'fit' masculinity by deploying the gendered ideologies of Kemalism. We saw how the image of 'Anatolian Women', who are physically strong, hardworking and always shoulder to shoulder with men, was re-constituted on the shop floor by the management and by women workers to normalize their 'masculine' actions. Here, trying to find a justification for these women's 'absurd' position it is necessary to convince (the) *el âlem* that women working in the warehouse are not challenging social norms and conventions. The women who work on the tomato sorting lines constitute (the) *el âlem* for the women working in the warehouse. The former group argue that working in the warehouse is not appropriate for women as it makes the women there 'wild' and 'masculine'. This social judgement of what is proper and what is not reproduces the social control of the *el âlem*. Indeed, the women in the warehouse fear this judgement and therefore strive to contribute to the reconstruction of the Anatolian woman image in the warehouse.

As discussed, physical strength is not the only determinant of the gendered division of labour; education is also important. We saw how the Kemalist regime uses education as a tool to organize labour on the shop floor. The management assumes that 'educated women' are less feminine and they put them in the machine sections. They also do not hesitate to assign more educated women to tasks where they may come into contact with male workers. This is because they 'trust' their educated daughters to know how they should behave in every circumstance, including not flirting on the shop floor. Here, again, it is possible to see the construction of femininity through the intersection of gender, age and education within the division of labour in the shop floor. (The) *el âlem* also endorses this by underlining the assumption that educated women do not constantly think about flirtation.

Chapter 6 is also important as it challenges the assumption that femininity is necessarily constructed as a desirable feature of factory labour. In contrast to the construction of productive, 'docile' femininity often associated with global manufacturing chains, the chapter shows how constructions of femininity draw on local histories, including political dogma, and may draw their continuing resilience from political attachments. It not only demonstrates how the reconstruction of masculinities and femininities on the shop floor is bound up with managers' political ideologies, but also shows how the tension between political ideologies has an impact on women workers' experiences in the shop floor.

### *'Hierarchy of masculinity' in the division of labour at homes*

The division of labour in women's homes is mostly bound up with their labour in the factory or on the land. The conditions of their paid work shape and are shaped by what women do in their homes. When we look at the homes of the landowning families, we can see that Recep (Turkish), who is the eldest male of the third generation who live in the household and is the most 'masculine' individual, manages all of the financial resources. We can also see that the post-menopausal mothers-in-law assume the management of all domestic tasks. The common features of the above are the management of masculinity. Power in patriarchal structures is more available to masculine actors, and in the 'hierarchy of masculinity' within households, after older males, older women (primarily the mothers-in-law) come second mainly as a result of the belief that post-menopausal women lose their femininity and are thus more like men. Although this does not give post-menopausal women sexual freedom, as the menopause is seen as the end of the period during which one needs to be protected because they are seen as asexual, the menopause nonetheless gives women the opportunity to see themselves on a more equal footing with men, and in this way, their age enables them to climb the ladder of the familial hierarchy. Women also benefit from the status of their husbands in the masculinity hierarchy.

Ascending the hierarchy of masculinity decreases the work they do both in the household and on the land. In this sense, the only thing a mother-in-law does is cook. The answer to the question of why they cook instead of hiring a domestic servant once again raises ideas that surround the concept of *el âlem*. In western rural Turkey, hiring a domestic servant is seen as shameful for women. *El âlem* would say 'what kind of women are they?' – *bunlar nasıl kadın?* – which suggests that they are not 'proper' women because they are not proper housewives doing all the domestic tasks themselves. Indeed, hiring a domestic worker would be likely to provoke the ire and gossip of (the) *el âlem*; women would literally 'fall upon the tongue of (the) *el âlem*' (*el âlemin diline düşmek*). This shows how *el âlem* is not only about protecting men's *namus* – honour related to the 'purity' of female members of family – by protecting women's sexuality, but it is also about protecting women's reputation as 'proper housewives'. In this way, *el âlem* also controls women's labour. Therefore, while mothers-in-law in the landowning families are responsible for cooking, their grandchildren (the youngest of the four generations in the household) are mostly responsible for cleaning and assisting with the cooking whilst their mothers, work on the land.

In the case of Kurdish workers, we should look both to their shacks during their seasonal work in rural Turkey and to their homes in their hometowns during the winter in order to see a more complete picture of the household division of labour. As discussed in Chapter 7, along the same lines as the landowning family, in the hierarchy of masculinity, mothers-in-law also occupy the second most prestigious position within the home. This placement in the familial hierarchy releases them from the need to migrate for seasonal work. When the younger generations return from seasonal work, however, their daughters-in-law become responsible for all domestic tasks, including their mother- and father-in-law's care. In the case of Kurdish mothers-in-law, their chance to perform 'masculinity' is very much bound up with how many sons they have borne, whereas with the landowning family this is not as pronounced. Reaching menopause is not enough to warrant equality with men; indeed for these women, they must reach menopause only after a sufficient period of fertility – one that is measured by the number of sons that a woman has had. This 'earned masculinity' gives them a chance to control both their sons and daughters-in-law's labour and sexuality.

As far as the gendered division of labour in the homes of factory workers is concerned, we can see how their labour in the factory depends on their mothers-in-law's or daughters' labour in the home. This dependency on the labour of the mother-in-law to take care of the children prevents women workers from escaping the experience of the extended patriarchal family structure. Although most of them move to towns with their nuclear families, they still maintain very close connections with their villages, which are mostly in the same region, as their mothers-in-law care for their children when they work at the factory. At that point, the daughters of those women gain greater importance. This is because they can do domestic tasks in the home including caring for their younger siblings. In this way, the number of daughters one has decreases women factory workers' dependency on their mothers-in-law. In turn, daughters are also masculinized by their mothers who work in the factory by underlining their increasing similarity with men as a result of their education. Women say that (the) *el âlem* take pity on women who do not have daughters. This is because young women are increasingly able to earn and control money through paid work. This makes them even more 'manly' than men, according to many women in the factory. This, however, does not relieve them of the dual burden of domestic work and paid work. Here, it is important to note that much like Fatma, women factory workers who are masculinized by their paid work cannot perform this masculinity in the home. Indeed, they do not perform masculinity in the home until they reach their post-menopausal age. This situation is also supported by the positions occupied by mothers-in-law because, thanks to their daughters-in-law or grandchildren, they become less associated with domestic tasks as they get older and, consequently, become more masculine.

In light of this, we can draw the same conclusions as those made in the section about the land and the factory. Although people can move between masculine and feminine categories, this is nonetheless bound up with the intersection of their gender, class, ethnicity and age. It is clear therefore that femininity or masculinity of the domestic tasks themselves is not subject to change. Across space and time, tomato picking has not led to social mobility or heightened prestige, and neither has washing the dishes. Being a man or a woman, Kurdish or Turkish, young or old can be both an advantage and a disadvantage in different places and in different social contexts. Working with tomatoes however, remains a constant – the meanings involved in tomato production remain static. This stasis prevails even if living conditions and working conditions differ depending on social setting, as with tomato production in Mexico (Torres 1997). In this context, we see that although the way of picking tomatoes and gendered division of labour on the tomato land change, gendering of the tasks does not change, even if their ingredients change. Kurdish men who make the most effective workers since Yahya redesigned the picking routine by using washing-up bowls to shake the tomatoes into, and which men lift more easily, continue to believe that they are doing women's job, even if they do it differently than women.

## *'Family' and 'ideology' as tools for both control and resistance*

Why and how do we sustain this 'unsustainable' system? The people's answer in the study speaks to the contribution of this study: their familial relations. People working in tomato production and processing most often do what they do in the workplace in order to meet their family commitments and support their family members, and most of the time they work in a way which their familial relationships construct and they are constructed through it. The generation of consent and possible forms of workers' resistance, therefore, could be understood by deploying the concept of 'family' and also 'ideology' as tool of the management. I will respectively look them on the land and then in the factory.

### *Familial control vs familial resistance*

The 'family' acts as the chief mechanism in shaping tomato production in a capitalist way. The interweaving of kinship relations with the intersection of gender, class, ethnicity and age organizes the labour process on the tomato land. Here, the important point was the deployment of family at one and the same time for control by management – it can also be applied by workers to control other workers in the group performance payment system – and for resistance by workers.

Kurdish migrant families are persuaded to work in poor conditions on the tomato land, as this is the only work in which families can draw upon women's and children's labour. It is not possible for Kurdish women to work in paid work 'alone' without direct supervision from male members of the family. Most of the Kurdish women (with one exception, as she is continuing her high school education) in this study noted that they have never gone to the market, hospital or another village to visit their relatives alone or in an all-female group. This is not too different for the women from the landowning family. In the landowning family's case, the women also stated that they had never been to public places alone with the exception of those who were pursuing their secondary education. The difference between these groups, however, is that the women from the landowning family can be in public places as a group of women from the same family. Therefore, both for women from the landowning family and for the Kurdish seasonal women workers, agriculture becomes the only viable option for their labour. However, unlike their Kurdish counterparts, the local women can work anywhere in the region as long as they are with other women in a group consisting of their family and neighbours. In such cases, it is permissible for these women to work alongside men. Kurdish women, on the other hand, cannot work with men unrelated by blood or marriage. For this reason, they require female-only workplaces or a place where they can work only with men from their own family. Tomato work has become the only work in western Turkey where Kurdish women can work in all-female or extended family groups. Work to produce other agricultural commodities such as peppers, watermelons, melons and olives does not offer the same opportunities to Kurdish families as they are only produced for national markets and there is thus no great demand for 'cheaper' labour.[5] As seen, the landowning family uses the kinship relations of Kurdish families to organize and to manage the labour process as well as using their own kinship relations for the very same reasons.

Kurdish migrant workers, just as the landowning family, use their families to sustain capitalist relations of production. Tomato production gives them a chance to capitalize their own familial relations in the workplace. In other words, they come to capitalist tomato land as 'who they are' and they do not need to change at all. On the contrary, they know that they are the ones whom the capitalists seek. So, this is a form of automatic cooperation with capital; both sides accept each other as who they are and indeed, both sides even seek each other out. Workers embrace capitalist production as it gives them profit and they themselves become capitalists and thus do not hesitate to capitalize their familial relations. For instance, we saw that workers are eager to adopt the group performance payment system as it gives them more income and they already have a shared budget in their extended families. Another striking example of this can be seen in Yahya's and his wife Zarife's harsh attitudes towards other workers and the pressure they put upon them to increase their speed and, hence, their productivity. As they occupy higher positions in the familial hierarchy thanks to their age, their control of other workers is largely accepted. This is especially evident in Yahya's case as the eldest male worker.

On the other hand, workers also use their family as a means of resistance. As highlighted, there is no effective union for agricultural workers in Turkey. As a result of this, rural workers depend on their family for acts of solidarity. As we have seen, family becomes a 'natural' form of organized labour under the management of a 'natural' leader, the eldest male worker in the family. So, we saw that they often threatened the landowning family with wildcat strikes and work stoppages. The most striking gain of the workers in this study was seen at the beginning of Chapter 4, during planting time, when the workers forced the landowning family to employ younger women and give them daily wages. The workers were clear that if the landowning family did not pay the teenage women workers, they would stop work altogether. As it was the beginning of the season, the workers were aware that they would easily be able to find alternative work, whereas the landowners would not be able to hire new labour with such ease. However, as we saw, as the season wore on, this threat began to lose its clout. This was because the landowning family had already sold the majority of the tomatoes to the factory and they knew that local workers could pick the remaining tomatoes. Time pressure owing to the likelihood of rain decreased as the season wore on. So, as seen at the end of Chapter 5, workers' familial resistance was not as effective as before and the landowning family succeeded in dividing the workforce and sacking non-compliant workers. Here, these divisions were also bound up with the conflicts in the familial relations of the workers.

## *'Kemalist control' vs 'religious resistance'*

The gendered ideologies of Kemalism are used to organize women's labour in Red tomato-processing factory. By perpetuating the three Kemalist categories of 'Religious Women', 'Educated Daughters of the Republic' and 'Anatolian Women' on the shop floor, the factory offered the workers familiarity with hegemonic ideologies. As emphasized, consent was generated in a way that mirrored the way in which Kemalism generated the consent of Turkish citizens before losing its hegemony in the 2000s. As Kemalism has a modern-Western core, the factory is proud of being the most modern and Westernized factory in the region, and even, in Turkey. In order to uphold its reputation for being the most favoured company by workers as well as by consumers, it pays its workers regular wages, which are higher than any other factory, it encourages workers to join their union and it offers the best food and transportation options. Therefore, women cooperate with the factory, as they also believe that this is the best option they have in the region.

However, this does not automatically persuade them to work on the shop floor. This only makes it possible for them to come as far as the factory gates. Once within the factory gates, however, the 'Backward Religious Women' are controlled very strictly, as these are the workers that the Kemalist factory regime trusts the least and is most suspicious of for their unwillingness to sustain the factory regime. The factory management justifies its strict control by claiming that those 'Backward Religious Women' can only understand and, even, enjoy draconian disciplinarian practices. The factory managers assume that harsh discipline is what these 'backward' women experience in their home lives. They believe that as they are brow-beaten by their husbands and vote for the AKP, they deserve harsh treatment and strict surveillance. The women we met clearly show that they do not support or respond well to harsh discipline. However, there is little desire for resistance among the workers and, indeed, that the managers are confident in their belief that no organized resistance will occur. Women working on the sorting lines think that the treatment they receive is simply part of the way things are and that there is nothing to be done about it other than praying to God. Apart from praying to women try to take longer breaks and go on slowdowns as a means of revolt.

On the other hand, as has been illustrated in the case of the 'Daughters of the Republic' who work in the machine section and the 'Anatolian Women' working in the warehouse, there is no need to resist as they are 'enjoying' their position as the most 'privileged' workers of the factory. They become a privileged group and are masculinized by the factory regime. By applying the gender categories of Kemalism, the factory makes the 'Daughters of the Republic' less 'feminine' by means of their 'education'; educated women take on 'masculine' values and attributes compared to their less well-educated sisters. In addition to this, the regime masculinizes 'Anatolian Women', by emphasizing their physical strength. As 'masculine' actors it is not surprising that they cooperate with the management. This was very clear in the example from my fieldwork diary. Although I stopped the line due to my carelessness, neither the forewoman nor managers punished me, as they believed that someone with my educational background could not possibly be careless. It is clear that management thinks that in the machine section, the workers do not need to be strictly controlled, as the machines effectively control them.

In their case, it is not the machines, but their daily quotas that act as an effective disciplinary method. As with the 'Educated Daughters of the Republic', the managers believe that they do not *need* to strictly monitor and discipline the trustworthy 'Anatolian Women'. Not surprisingly, in these circumstances, both of these groups of women are eager to cooperate with Kemalist capitalism. This mirrors the conditions of Turkish society beyond the factory gates where 'backward religious' people are seen as undesirable by Kemalists. However, as the book reminded us, this has been undergoing a rapid change in Turkey, as many so-called backward groups are now pursuing higher education and thus deconstructing the hegemonic categories of 'the Educated Daughters of the Republic'. For the time being, the factory has chosen to ignore these developments and changes in the fabric of Turkish society. However, choosing to ignore such changes has already had severe consequences for the strength of traditionally Kemalist political parties electorally,[6] and it can be assumed that the factory could have difficulties in sustaining the same management principles in controlling its labour in the near future.

## Interweaving the relations of production and reproduction

This [the determining factor in history], again, is of a twofold character: on the one side, the production of the means of existence, of food, clothing and shelter and the tools necessary for that production; on the other side, the production of human beings themselves, the propagation of species. The social organisation under which the people of a particular historical epoch and a particular country live is determined by both kinds of production: by the stage of development of labour on the one hand and of the family on the other. The lower the development of labour and the more limited the amount of its products, and consequently, the more limited also the wealth of society the more the social order is found to be dominated by kinship groups. (Engels 1972: 36)

Like many other feminist studies on women's labour, the above quotation, one of Engels's most quoted, was the departure point of this book in terms of emphasizing the mutual interdependence of the relations of production and reproduction. Here – in the case of rural tomato production and processing – I conceptualize reproduction relations as 'kinship relations' that 'produce' and 'are produced' by the total conditions of production, including the reproduction of labour and its narrower concept of human reproduction (Mackintosh 1984).[7] By following the movement of women's labour from the tomato lands to their homes and the tomato factories, I seek to reveal how the relationships between the 'development' of labour (from the land to the factory) and the 'development' of family (the transition from an extended rural family structure to a 'nuclear', 'urban' family structure) are interlocking; they are fluid and mutually entangled. As evidenced by the bulk of discussion in the body of my book, it is clear that the boundaries between home and workplaces blur and, in some cases, overlap. People live to work and work to live. One of the clearest examples of this is when Kurdish families explained to me the importance of having a son in order to continue to live and work as they do now. This was also evident in how both male and female Kurdish workers underlined kinship marriage as a necessity to sustain their lives and working conditions as they are now. Melek is very clear that she cannot do seasonal work with a 'stranger', *elti*. Osman's story about his previous lover, who was neither Kurdish nor part of the same extended family, also showed us the link between the relations of production and reproduction. In this case, Osman's mother warned him that he would not be able to find work if he married a stranger because, if he did, he would have to leave the village as it would not be possible for a bride, *gelin*, from outside the extended family to live and work with the extended family she marries into.

These examples can be expanded by also focusing on the landowning family and factory workers. Strikingly, the landowning family continues to live in one dwelling as a four-generational patrilineal family. This is because splitting their inheritance would effectively lead to the end of their livelihood; this leaves them with no option but to preserve and increase their landholdings by living under one roof as an extended family. Working together is not enough to control each other's access to resources, so as we have seen, they also live within the same building in order to control each other's spending. In the case of the women factory workers, they were compelled to move to the town closest to their village of origin because they remained dependent on their mother-in-law's labour for childcare. The factory manager's household type is also closely associated with employment. His 'Kemalist' home – as he claimed – does not surprise us, especially when we think about his position in the Kemalist factory.

These connections make it possible to discuss the similarities and differences between the positions people occupy in the family and in their place of work. The similarity in generating the consent of workers and of brides was discussed in the book. While workers were eager to 'produce' for the profit of capital, Kurdish women were eager to 'produce' for the sake of their 'family' and the continuation of their patriarchal kinship relations and to secure their status as future 'mothers-in-law'. The differences here are quite clear. While Kurdish workers and factory workers do not believe that they can one day wield the same power as landowners or managers, brides know that they will one day become mothers-in-law.

Here, there is a link between Burawoy's theory of manufacturing consent and Kandiyoti's theory of bargaining with patriarchy which highlights the similarity between the creation of consent amongst both Kurdish women in their extended patriarchal families and amongst workers in the US factories Burawoy (1979) studied. As discussed in several places in the book, Burawoy (1979) defined the concept of 'consent' as an outwardly voluntary acceptance of capitalist production relations and put it at the centre of labour process analysis in contemporary society. He showed that 'coercion' was not the chief mechanism behind the reproduction of relations of production, but workers were persuaded to collaborate in the pursuit of their employers' profits voluntarily via the construction of 'consent' on the shop floor. This voluntary acceptance and collaboration with capital is similar to women's voluntary acceptance of the patriarchal reproduction relations at home and their collaboration with their mothers-in-law as a way of bargaining with patriarchy. Burawoy demonstrates that workers were eager to 'produce' for the profit of capital and, in a similar way, Kurdish women were eager not only to 'produce' for the sake of their 'family' and the continuation of their patriarchal kinship relations but also to ensure their future status as 'mothers-in-law'.

However, in contrast with what Burawoy (1979) stated on the basis of his study of factory workers in the United States, the chief mechanism in the construction of Elif's consent in accepting and contributing to those patriarchal relations was still 'coercion'. Burawoy (1979) did not take into consideration the identities workers bring with them to work, especially aspects of their external consciousness and orientations with respect to gender. Therefore, he concluded that 'consent' can be created in 'hegemonic' regimes rather than 'despotic' ones, but as I argue here, the opposite can occur. Although in the case of 'Kurdish extended patriarchal relations' the main mechanism is 'coercion', there is still 'consent' to sustain this form of patriarchy, as the women know that they will benefit from it in the future.

In the case of agricultural workers, the way of creating consent is different. The tension between these workers and landowners is higher when workers do not have any hope of gaining authority themselves. Therefore, resistance is more common amongst agricultural workers than brides at home or factory workers even though agricultural workers have more need of the money they make to survive than do factory workers. Here, the difference between factory workers and agricultural workers is important. Although factory workers also do not have to be promoted, they create consent by mirroring the gendered ideologies of Turkish politics, 'backward traditional' women by 'coercion', and the other ones – Daughters of the Republic and Anatolian Women – by incorporation. Here, ideology makes the differences, and it also interweaves with ethnicity. In the Kurdish workers' case, their resistance also manifests in a specific form against 'Turkish' landowners, not just 'landowners' in general, as they – landowners and workers – both see each other as representatives of an 'other threatening group'.

Despite the limited prospects for workers, they nonetheless embrace capitalist production because it offers them some profit and power, and in this way, they themselves become capitalists. This is also the case in family relations. Both men and women become 'patriarchs' and there is a prospect of some future gain in terms of power for all. This similarity is important when pointing out the similar operations of capitalism and patriarchy, as they are the two interweaving systems that underpin this study. I hope that by demonstrating the similarities between patriarchy and capitalism, I have also been able to highlight the ways in which they interweave and, in this way, contribute to feminist theory on this question (Collins 2014; Clallend 2014; Dunaway 2014; Hartmann 1981).

## What the book has said

This book mainly contributes to labour process theory by integrating reproduction relations with global production analysis. I base this on my agreement with Thompson and Smith (2009), who argue that we urgently need to develop labour process theory in order to understand global production. The necessity of refreshing labour process theory comes from the crucial importance of understanding the reasons why and the ways in which workers do their work as well as focusing on the places in which production and reproduction occur. So, I claim that through focusing on the 'local' as a place where production and reproduction occur as well as showing the interweaving of those relations as both reasons for and ways of workers' generating consent, this study has managed to refresh labour process theory as a kernel of global commodity chain analysis.

This study takes a somewhat different focus than many other feminist studies of women's roles in global production. While they too may incorporate a focus on the relation between production and reproduction relations, they mostly concentrate on 'new factory workers' with rural backgrounds – but this provides us with insight into just one part of the operation of capitalism and patriarchy (as well as the transformation of rural life) (Lee 1998; Ngai 2005; Wolf 1994). However, this book looks at who fills the spaces in agriculture that are left when the process of industrialization begins. In so doing, it offers a fuller picture of the functioning of capitalism in relation to reproduction relations by showing the transformation of families and their incorporation into production relations and vice versa. Ramamurthy (2004) emphasizes the necessity of underscoring the relationship between agriculture and industry in order to understand the operation of global production chains in the cotton industry. She looks at the link between production and consumption using the relation between agriculture and industry. Here, however, I have tried to show the link between agriculture and industry by looking at the link between production and reproduction. I have looked not only at how global production affects the women's production and reproduction relations, but also at how these in turn affect global production. Focusing on these linkages rather than the link between production and consumption (although I still consider this to be beyond the main objective of this study) makes it possible to analyse the effect of the local in global production. This is because the focus on the relationship between production and reproduction relations reveals the differences and transformations inside the local more clearly, and consequently as we understand the local more fully, we can understand its connection with the global more fully.

The study has used the term 'intersectional patriarchy' to understand the social relations in the 'local' by depending on the local itself. When feminists said that they gave up using the concept of patriarchy (Acker 1989; Gottfried 1998; Pollert 1996; Rowbotham 1981), their reasons were that patriarchy is an abstract and reductionist (to biology) concept; it neither captures the malleable nature of gender relations nor does it offer us a chance to see the interweaving relations of gender and class. In contrast, I have suggested that through using the term 'intersectional patriarchy' this study overcomes these critics, at least for this context. By emphasizing (the) *el âlem* as a reproducer of patriarchy, I hopefully concretize the concept of patriarchy. Besides, it prevents patriarchy from being biologically reductionist as everyone can exercise some power in the patriarchal structures and I noted this as a reason for the persistence of patriarchy. Moreover, by also showing how patriarchy sustains and is sustained through the intersections of other inequalities, mainly of class, ethnicity and age, I have tried to capture the interweaving of gender and class. I have also argued that masculinities are themselves constructed by the intersectionality of gender, class, ethnicity, age and education in various and malleable ways within the division of labour in tomato production. In addition, the book demonstrates how similar material conditions of work can lead to the overlapping of some elements of hegemonic masculinity (e.g. affinity with machines in both rural and Kemalist patriarchies) and, as a result, similarities between patriarchies. Indeed, intersectional patriarchy gives us a chance to examine similarities and differences between patriarchies other than those explored in the book and shows how the forms taken by patriarchy and masculine domination are dependent upon gendered divisions of labour within production.

## What could be hoped from tomatoes

> When I saw the tomato paste we produced on the shelf, I was surprised how ordinary it looks: it is just like others. It is just a 5 kg. tomato paste. I feel myself immensely sad when I think that people will not know how this tomato paste came here; how people migrate to make it possible; how they love and hate each other while doing it; how they imagine Japan and the people who eat these tomatoes.[8]

What would have happened if consumers knew that people become seasonal cooks to make this tomato paste that is now standing on a shelf in a warehouse in Tokyo, that they escape from their mothers-in-law thanks to these tomatoes or that they become dependent on their mothers-in-law because of these tomatoes? What would happen if consumers knew that *Hazal* is able to talk with her boyfriend, thanks to cooking for the workers of this tomato paste? This book did provide the answers to this but it was written just for the sake of hope: knowing the production process in a global food chain may eventually lead people to be more human friendly, more local and more ethical when buying alternatives. At least the literature believes that when consumers obtain information about the production process, they demand a more ethical one (Balsiger 2014). To make this hope lively, the book offered more stories than numbers, as it believes that consumers need to know the lives, struggles, as well as the hopes and dreams of its producers.

If the hope of change for better – ethical and equal – and the way of getting this hope are with people's own stories and their daily life experiences, then these are the main things that make this book feminist. Further, focusing on tomatoes as analytical tool in order to explore the interweaving relationships between production and reproduction relations is the reason the analysis of the book is intersectional. Endeavouring on what people in the study refer to as their family, working together and/or working for it enabled the book to explore how the different intersections of gender, class, ethnicity and age play different roles in creating the consent of workers to work for others.

If Turkish tomatoes would not have been produced for Japan and other 'far away' countries, there would not be this amount of demand for tomatoes by factories in Turkey, which increases the working hours and changes payment system. *Ayşe*'s mother would not have the night shift, *Pınar*'s family would not migrate, *Fatma* would not have to protect seeds. These are of course probabilities and they could happen anyway, but in different forms and within different worlds. Nonetheless, in this world, changes in tomatoes are the reason that makes all these happen, and mainly women's work is the common factor that makes all these tomatoes happen.

# NOTES

## Chapter 1

1. This is what one of the women with whom I worked on the land for this study, whose name is also Emine, asked me to call my study. By saying 'our', she is referring to the fact that she, I and another woman from the landowning family all share the name Emine. When we were talking about my study, I explained that I was writing about how we work on the land, what we talk about and so on. Then, I was asked what it was that I was writing, whether I was writing something like a story. To this, I replied that I was writing a kind of story. Then, Emine, a Kurdish worker, asked me to call my study 'Emine's story, our story'. I have permission from her to use her real name. She wished to keep her name as it is. I used pseudonymous for the names of the other Emines. There are two real Emines inside the book: one is I, the researcher, and the other one is a Kurdish worker.
2. My grandparents have migrated from Bosnia and live in rural Turkey. My parents are also involved in agriculture but not as the main source of their income. They live in a city which is located in a close distance to the village where my extended family lives, so they can regularly visit them and work on the land as unpaid family workers when workforce is necessary. I will, therefore, tell the story of ordinary Emines as one of them. As for the other millions of Emines in Turkey, they could have been given the name for different reasons, perhaps to carry the name of the prophet's mother or to be named after a grandparent.
3. Here I mean 'Turkist radical nationalists' (Bora 2003: 445).
4. In 2003, as a result of the European Integration Process, the ban on giving Kurdish names to Turkish citizens as well as names in other languages, such as in Circassian languages, was lifted. However, as the new law only allows people to give their children names with Turkish letters, Kurds – who have different letters in their alphabet – are still not able to give all Kurdish names to their children.
5. Over the past few years there has been a constant rise in girls' schooling rate in Turkey. According to TÜİK (2019a), the schooling rate of five-year-olds has increased to 75.2 per cent in 2018 from 67.2 per cent in 2015. As the report suggests, there is no gender difference in the schooling rate of children. The rate for secondary school attendance is even higher for girls (93.6 per cent) than boys (92.9 per cent). This difference can be explained by noting that more boys have worked as a child worker than girls (TÜİK, 2019a). Although there is no gender difference in the schooling rate, geographical differences are still valid in terms of continuing the education. For instance, according to EUROSTAT (2020), the rate of early leavers from education is the highest in Southeast Anatolia by 47.8 per cent in 2019. Although there is a decline trend, Turkey still has the highest rate, 32.5 per cent, of early leavers from education comparing with European countries (Member and candidate countries of European Union).
6. *Cicianne* and *küçükanne* are the words used by other children in the extended rural family to call their '*yenge*'. These words can be directly translated as 'sweet mother'

and 'little mother'. By applying these words, the distinctiveness of the mother figure in the nuclear family is blurred within the extended family structure.
7   Fieldwork notes, 13 May 2013, Bursa.
8   Fieldwork Notes, 22 September 2013.
9   There are no official statistics for forced marriage in Turkey. However, based on research in eastern and southeastern Anatolia, Women for Women's Human Rights, WWHR (2004) have found that 50.8 per cent of women in these regions are married without their consent. These are the latest statistics that I could find in 2019.
10  This is a pseudonym; there are two different Emines in the landowning family from different generations. However, here I have changed one of the women's names to Emine whose name is actually not Emine. She also has a different pseudonym in the main body of the text to prevent confusion, as I already have two Emines.
11  Until 1997, compulsory education in Turkey was five years.
12  Fieldwork Notes, 8 May 2013.
13  I wrote her name here as Emine, but this is a pseudonym. In the main body of the text and in real life, she has a different name. My intention is to emphasize that Emine is a very common name among those women who share a very similar background and stories with each other. In the factory, I met four Emines.
14  Fieldwork Noes, 14 September 2014.
15  See Şen (2014) for a detailed analysis about continuous migration from the Black Sea region. Recent statistics of the Turkish Official Institute also show that settlements on the Black Sea coast have a significant decline in population (TÜİK 2017b).
16  Sarıgıl (2012) defines *Laz* as 'a distinct ethnic group of Caucasian origin, mostly living at the eastern end of Turkey's Black sea shore in coastal lowlands' (269). 'However it must be noted that not all people from Black Sea Region belong to this ethnic group'.
17  Fieldwork Notes, 14 September 2014.
18  JDP could be used to refer The Justice and Development Party. However, I keep the AKP because the party is internationally known as it is.
19  Ironically, the wife of the current Turkish President, Emine Erdoğan, is yet another of the millions Emines in Turkey. Her husband, Recep Tayyip Erdoğan, was previously the prime minister of the AKP government and has been the president of Turkey since 2014. Erdoğan does not hesitate to emphasize this sameness with 'ordinary' citizens to maintain his majority. Even more ironically, the fact that I am writing this book, as an ordinary Emine, is partly due to the fact that the same ruling party has opened new state universities in almost every Turkish city and, as a result, has been able to send more students and academics abroad to continue their postgraduate studies than ever before.
20  Here it is noteworthy to say that the neoliberalization of Turkish agriculture has not mushroomed with the AKP's governance. This has been an ongoing process since the 1980s (Aydın, 2010). However, AKP government has a power to apply these economic policies heavily without interruption since 2002.
21  *El âlem* refers to a group of unidentified 'real' and at the same time 'imaginary' people – to whom speakers refer when explaining why it is necessary for them to do this or that. *El âlem ne der* – what will the *el âlem* say? –it is a commonly used expression to refer to what other people think. *El âlem* is both an abstract and concrete concept. It can designate someone who acts like the *el âlem* by judging you according to social norms. On the other hand, you may feel forced to give up doing something you want to do because of what you fear the *el âlem* may say. The difference between concrete and abstract *el âlem* might be clarified more with the common expression *el âlem için yaşamak*, which can be directly translated as living for the *el âlem*. It refers

to prioritizing the thoughts you perceive others to have of you when you make a decision about something. When someone does something of which the el âlem do not approve, and she or he and their family is talked about by the el âlem, the idiom for this kind of situation is *el âlemin diline düşmek* (falling on the *el âlem's* tongue). It means that people – *el âlem* – in general (other villagers, for example) are gossiping about what a certain individual has done.

22  I would like to state my three reasons for insisting on using the term 'patriarchy'. Firstly, almost all scholars, even those who avoid using the term, agree that the term must be reserved for specific historical structures, namely patrilocal extended households, in which senior males hold authority (Acker 1989; Gottfried 1998; Pollert 1996). Many of the women I worked with still live in rural extended family structures of this type, while most of the others, who no longer live in extended households, have experienced living in them at some point in their lifetime. My second reason lies in Walby's (2011) statement that the term 'patriarchy' means the same as the phrase 'gender regime' (104). This she defines as 'a set of inter-connected gender relations and gendered institutions that constitutes a system' (Walby 2009: 301 cited in Walby 2011: 104). Walby says that although both concepts refer to gender inequalities, she drops patriarchy, as there is 'a tendency for the term "patriarchy" to be misinterpreted' (ibid.). Dropping the term is not an option for my research, since I need the political sharpness of patriarchy (Acker 1989) to reveal the structures that lead one of the women in this study to say that 'our life is a sip of water in their eyes' – implying both men and the state.

23  There are also other scholars who have tried to link patriarchy and intersectionality, although they do not necessarily name the concepts. For instance, Bozzoli's (1983: 149) concept of a patchwork-quilt of patriarchies refers to 'a system in which forms of patriarchy are sustained, modified and even entrenched in a variety of ways depending on the internal character of the system in the first instance'. Walby's work (1990) can also be considered as an attempt to link patriarchy and intersectionality because she tackles the articulation of gender with class and ethnicity. However, her forms of patriarchy do not depend on the intersections of these inequalities but on changes in the relations between and within six structures: the 'patriarchal mode of production, patriarchal relations in paid work, patriarchal relations in the state, male violence, patriarchal relations in sexuality, and patriarchal relations in cultural institutions' (20). Fiorenza, on the other hand, proposes the concept of 'kyriarchy' (1992: 7) instead of patriarchy to analyse interlocking structures of domination. Kyriarchal power, she says, 'operates not only along the axis of gender but also along those of race, class, culture and religion. These axes of power structure the more general system of domination in a matrix like fashion, or in what Bell Hooks calls the interlocking systems of oppression' (Fiorenza 1992: 123).

24  'Speak like a man' is a Turkish idiom – *adam gibi konuşmak* – which refers to good and 'proper' communication.

25  Fieldwork Diary, 14 May 2013.

26  By story, I refer to enacting women's own subjectivity, their coping mechanisms and parts of their work, daily lives or life stories.

## *Chapter 2*

1  The majority of the women in this study completed their compulsory education (all of the Turkish women and more than half of the Kurdish women). Moreover, all of them know how to read and write Turkish, with the exception of one Kurdish woman.

2   See Önderman (2018) Türkiye'de Paranoid Ethos (Paranoid Ethos in Turkey) for a detailed discussion about how paranoia shapes the socio-political arguments in Turkey.
3   This is the last part of a student oath; it was compulsory to recite this each morning, in every school, at all levels of the education system (from primary to high school), in both state and private schools until 2012.
4   One day each week during my fourth grade in primary school, my friend and I read the oath using a microphone to the other students, who then repeated it.
5   Bora (2003) usefully identifies the types of nationalism in Turkey as Atatürk Nationalism, Kemalist Nationalism, Liberal Neonationalism and Turkist Radical Nationalism. Here I do not follow this classification and refer the Kemalist nationalism as an umbrella term. While doing this, I rely on Bora's explanation showing that all types of nationalism giving weight on different features and attainments of Kemalist ideology.
6   For a detailed discussion about women's place in the construction of nationalist discourses, see Altınay (2013), Kandiyoti (1991) and Yuval-Davis (1997).
7   For a detailed discussion about 'modernity' and Kemalism in Turkey, see Bozdoğan and Kasaba (1997). In this volume, Kandiyoti examines the sexuality, family relations and gender identities that are central to discourses about Turkish modernity. Here I am only able to offer a limited discussion about Kemalism. It deserves more attention and detail.
8   Anatolia refers to the geographical location known in antiquity as Asia Minor. The region is surrounded by the Black Sea, the Mediterranean Sea and the Aegean Sea. Kemalists intentionally emphasize and encourage the use of the term 'Anatolia', as they want to draw attention to Turkey's pre-Islamic heritage.
9   Based on these discussions in Turkish scholarly literature, I highlight the three contrasting images of women in Kemalist ideology to examine the gendered factory regime in Chapter 6. The first image is educated 'Daughters of the Republic', the second one is wise 'Anatolian Women' and the third is 'Backward Religious Women'. These images are perceived in the same way by Kemalist ideology and the factory manager. Here it is important to note that I do not claim that all Kemalists see religious women as backward, especially nowadays, his was a prevalent discourse in the 1990s and 2000s, especially by urban elite.
10  Here, I refer to immigration from rural villages to big cities. According to Keyder and Yenal (2013), this trend has begun to shift in recent years and people are beginning to move to towns – *kasaba* – rather than big cities.
11  The creation of shanty towns as a result of mass migration into urban areas from the 1960s onwards transformed the landscape of Turkey's largest cities. Although the establishment of new slum areas, *gecekondu mahellesi*, has now slowed to a halt and many of the largest *gecekondular* (plural) have now become established as boroughs in their own right, with legal and political recognition, it is also important to note that as a result of gentrification and booming house prices, many former *gecekondu* are now being replaced by luxury high-rise apartment buildings in the inner cities. This has led to accusations of social cleansing. Moreover, the *gecekondu* communities displaced by rapid economic growth in Turkey's big cities have often been forcibly evicted to high-density social housing on the outskirts of big cities and often to areas where there is limited access to social amenities such as schools, shops, public transport, health centres and employment.

12 For a detailed discussion about the mass immigration from rural to urban in Turkey in the 1960s and 1970s, see Karpat (1976), Keleş (1983).
13 The novel *A Strangeness in My Mind* (2015) by Orhan Pamuk beautifully portrays rural migrants' experiences in Istanbul from the 1970s to 2000s.
14 Tribes formed through kinship and ruled by a feudal *ağa*. Moral and political codes imposed by the *aşiret* are understood to supersede the law. Some tribes number in the tens of thousands and have an impact on local politics in their regions. Although the power of the *aşiret* is decreasing, it is still a social phenomenon predominantly affecting some of the Kurds in Turkey.
15 The novel *Mehmed My Hawk* by one of Turkey's most renowned novelists, Yaşar Kemal, 1955 (2013), offers an important account of this agrarian system, which is known as *Ağalık*, wherein the local landowner or *Ağa* controls the lands.
16 *Hemşeri* and *hemşericilik* can enable us to understand more about the supportive networks of Turks. However, among Kurds, *aşiret* could be more appropriate to understand these relationships.
17 This is highly popular in traditional Turkish and Kurdish cuisine. In Turkish cuisine, it is mostly consumed on occasions like '*gün*', especially in the region where this study takes place. Among the Kurdish workers in the study, it is one of the main dishes that they bring to the land, as it is so easy to prepare. Although the ingredients used vary depending on the region, adding tomato paste, spring onions, lemon juice, parsley or lettuce to pre-prepared bulgur wheat usually makes *kısır*. Its simplicity derives from the fact that bulgur does not need to be cooked and is ready to be eaten once the bulgur has been steeped in boiling water.
18 This is the generic name for filled pastries. It is made by rolling out filo pastry (*yufka*) and is usually filled with cheese, potato, mince or spinach. Making *börek* requires more time when you make your own *yufka*. Buying pre-made pastries decreases the value of *börek*, as well as the value of 'being a woman' among the women I worked with.
19 *Çeyiz* refers to the cost of a new bride setting up a home. It usually includes furniture, white goods and kitchen equipment, as well as homemade lace tablecloths and tea towels that have often been made overtime and throughout a woman's youth. Female members of the family and the bride herself often create the items themselves that make up the *çeyiz*. The contents of a bride's *çeyiz* vary significantly by region. For example, in the region in which this study was undertaken, while the bride's family purchases bedroom and living room furniture, for Kurdish women, this was not the case. The Kurdish women in the study told me that the groom's family buys everything for their *çeyiz*.
20 This still plays a major role in the life of Kurdish citizens. For instance, in the last three months of 2015, the last year of my fieldwork, many Kurds living in the southeastern parts of the country have had to migrate to western Turkey because of the continuous conflict, including some of the people with whom I worked on the land during my fieldwork.
21 According to TÜİK (2017b)'s latest statistics, İstanbul is no longer the only city to take most of the immigrants.
22 There is no direct translation of this idiom in English. Nonetheless, it is widely used in the Turkish language and is used when you want to thank someone for everything they have done for you and to seek their forgiveness. The term has religious origins, as Muslims believe that you will be punished in the afterlife if you breach another person's rights. Therefore, a person can 'force' you to say that you will forgive them in a case where *your rights* have been breached by another (*Hakkımı helal ettim*).

For instance, on the land when the landowning family forced workers to work for more than they earned, they told them to please *hakkını helal et*! In this way, the landowning family assuaged their guilt as God 'bore witness' to the 'fact' that the workers had consented and forgiven the landowning family for their actions.

23  Koç (2001) emphasized the role of a series of articles in the popular press (*Güneş* Newspaper) in 1985. The 'atelier homes' (atölye evler) project was linked to the prime minister at the time, Turgut Özal.
24  People who migrate from the Balkans (Bulgarian Turks, Bosnians, Albanians) or other ethnicities, such as Circassians, create their own supportive networks. However, their networks cannot be translated as kinfolk support or *hemşericilik* because their support networks are primarily generated on the basis of ethnicity.
25  I largely use the term 'kinfolk' to refer to the *aşiret* system adopted by ethnic Kurds.
26  'Imagined community' is Anderson's concept (2006) and refers to the nation. However, here I use the term to refer to supportive networks of 'similar' groups, such as Kemalists, feminists and sociologists.
27  Praying for someone else because of the kindness or care they have shown you. *Hayır duası* is the only thing that some women receive for their unpaid labour. Elders give *hayır duası* for their *gelin* as she looks after them. My mother's neighbours gave her *hayır duası* for working in their *atölye* in busy periods without pay. Mostly, a son should make some financial contribution to his parents to get *hayır duası*; for a bride however, this is related to unpaid care work and domestic labour.
28  See Keyder and Yenal (2013) for the extra things farmers have been doing in rural areas to continue their livelihoods there.
29  Caliphate – *halifelik* – refers to the governing of a geographical region by a caliph – *halife* – who is the successor of the Prophet Muhammad and the leader of all Muslims. Since the sixteenth century, sultans – governors and leaders of the country – of the Ottoman Empire were also the caliphs of other Muslims. Only the son of a sultan could become a caliph.
30  *Anayasa mahkemesi* is Turkey's constitutional court. It is also Turkey's Supreme Court. It was established in 1962 following a military coup in 1960 to judicially review laws passed by the Turkish Parliament. Although it was established to control the Parliament by reducing its power and to ensure that all laws were made in accordance with the Constitution, whether or not its outcomes lead to greater 'fairness' remains the subject of debate. This is particularly pertinent given current Turkish politics.
31  In 2018, Turkey has been turned from a parliamentary to the presidential republic with a referendum which was held in 2017, and 51.41 per cent of the voters chose the presidential republic. This result shows the political polarization of the country. AKP won the referendum by the support of Nationalist Movement Party (MHP). In this system, president is the head of government and also the state. S/he can also be the leader of political party.
32  According to TÜİK (2019a) in Turkey the youth unemployment rate is 24.5 per cent. This ratio is even higher for young women: 31.7 per cent. Employment rate, on the other hand, is 32.6 per cent for the young workforce and 45.9 per cent for the whole population. It is, therefore, difficult to mention 'social neoliberalism' of AKP today (2020). Cihan Tuğal's book *The Fall of the Turkish Model* (2016) offers a comprehensive debate about the problems of 'Islamic liberalism'.
33  Rural population is consisted not only of the villages but also rural towns. That is why the ratio of rural population is higher than that of villages.

## Chapter 3

1. For instance, at the press conference on 3 May 2017, they (Vladimir Putin and Recep Tayyip Erdoğan) announced that the relations between the countries would go back to normal and to expect tomato exports (NTV 2017).
2. *Dayı* means maternal uncle and *başı* means headman. The direct translation refers to the most senior of the maternal uncles. This can be considered as an interesting reflection on the relationship between women workers and their male 'agents'. The factory does not work with *dayıbaşı* to recruit workers, but landowning families need to contact a *dayıbaşı*.
3. This is a pseudonym. I call the factory 'Red' because when I picture the factory, the first colour that comes to my eyes is 'Red'.
4. Fieldwork Notes, 29 April 2013.
5. The factory manager uses the terms 'peasants' and 'farmers' interchangeably because he sees peasants as just farmers. Farmers often do so too. As discussed in the previous section, this is related to the rapid transformation in rural settlement patterns in Turkey. Moreover, being a peasant not only refers to an occupation, but also includes one's lifestyle, beliefs, values and so on. As discussed in more detail in Chapter 6, the founding ideology of the Turkish Republic, Kemalism, in some cases celebrates rural settlements, but also sees all things rural as 'backward, conservative and religious'. Although Mustafa Kemal Atatürk did say good things about peasants, such as 'peasants are the leaders of the people', in reality, it divided the rural population into two: wise Anatolian republicans and backward, traditional and religious people. Thus, this led to the idea of 'being rural' essentially becoming a pejorative term. Calling someone a peasant is a means to humiliate them. For example, when somebody behaves inappropriately, depending on the context, one might say, 'Are you a peasant?' Linking peasantry and inappropriate behaviour is also one of the consequences of the mass rural to urban migration in the 1970s.
6. Fieldwork Notes, 18 September 2014.
7. See Chapter 2.
8. Fieldwork Notes, 29 April 2013.
9. Hatice, Fieldwork Notes, 8 March 2014.
10. Mehmet, Fieldwork Notes, 8 March 2014.
11. Fieldwork Notes, 8 March 2014.
12. Fieldwork Notes, 10 March 2014.
13. They had a really big fight with the landowning family at the end of the picking season because of 'money'. This fight, its reasons and consequences are explained later.
14. Hatice's family has been migrating to Bursa every year for the past fifteen years.
15. Fieldwork Notes, 9 March 2014.
16. Osman, Fieldwork Notes, 7 September 2013.

## Chapter 4

1. I am aware that using the term 'landowners wives', 'daughters' etc. implies I am comfortable defining the relationships of the women I worked with according to their relations with men. Whereas this appears to contradict the overtly feminist approach and methods of this book, women workers on the land often define themselves according to their relationship to men and in the absence of a more appropriate collective noun I have used terms such as 'landowners' wives'.

2   When I use the term 'landowning family', I am referring to a single extended landowning family. There are four generations of this family.
3   Researcher, Fieldwork Diary, 8 May 2013.
4   Fieldwork Notes, 9 May 2013.
5   Researcher, Fieldwork Diary, 13 August 2013.
6   Researcher, Fieldwork Diary, 13 May 2013.
7   'Cross-class' marriages are common in the western rural Turkey – both of my two aunts were seasonal workers on my uncles' lands when they met. It could be different among Kurds under the *aşiret* system, where the priority is to marry someone from one's own kinship group.
8   Before Kurdish families were employed, workers from around the villages, which are known as 'forest villages', were employed seasonally around the region, as in their villages there were no commercial agricultural lands. With the capitalization of agriculture, this trend is no longer observable, as it requires more workers and longer working hours. Nezahat – ethnically Turkish – was one of those seasonal workers, who also lived in the shacks for a season before the Kurdish families arrived.
9   Fieldwork Notes, 4 May 2013.
10  Fieldwork Notes, 7 May 2013.
11  Here, I do not refer to a registered, official marriage as polygamy in Turkey is illegal.
12  Fieldwork Notes, 11 May 2013.
13  Fieldwork Notes, 31 April 2013.
14  Fieldwork Notes, 14 May 2013.
15  Researcher, Fieldwork Diary, 15 May 2013.
16  Here, I reiterate that this marriage would be a religious marriage that would not be officially registered. In Islam, a *nikah* is a formal marriage contract. Whilst a *nikah* is not recognized as legally binding by the Turkish state, it is common for couples to have both a wedding registered by the state and a *nikah*. Although the practice of polygamy is illegal and most clergy are overseen by the state through the *diyanet* (religious authority), there are imams who are not overseen by the *diyanet* and will perform polygamous marriage ceremonies.
17  Fieldwork Notes, 1 September 2013.
18  Fieldwork Notes, 6 May 2013.
19  When the number of children registered at small village primary schools fall below ten, the schools are shut down. Although compulsory education spans twelve years and the state is committed to ensuring school access through school bus schemes, these schemes are often poorly overseen: poor control over school bus drivers, who often do not arrive to collect schoolchildren in the mornings, mean that schoolchildren in more remote villages are unable to attend. Although villagers do complain, local authorities do not generally hear these complaints. As a result of this, many families from smaller villages move to larger towns for the sake of their children's education.
20  *Abla* is also a way of showing respect to older women.
21  Researcher, Fieldwork Diary, 12 May 2013.
22  Fieldwork Notes, 12 May 2013
23  Women in the village use this phrase where this study was conducted for the evening visits to different neighbourhoods. After dinner, most of the men in the village go to the coffee house – *kahve* – and women go each other's houses. Watching TV together, drinking tea and gossiping are the main activities during the evening.
24  Fieldwork Notes, 13 May 2013.

## Chapter 5

1. I discuss the reasons for her absence in the picking time in Chapter 7
2. Fieldwork Notes, 26 August 2013.
3. Fieldwork Diary, 19 July 2013.
4. This is a bazaar mostly appealing to villagers who wish to sell their homemade products and purchase small goods. They are common in the village towns. 'Peasants', especially women, from nearby villages, come and sell their handmade products at these markets. Buying or renting a stall is not necessary. Mostly, the customers of the bazaar are people living in the town and working in the factories, as they do not have enough money to buy these products at a supermarket, but also do not have enough time to make them for themselves. The products typically include tomato sauce, tomato *purée*, pepper *purée*, varieties of homemade pasta, cheese and eggs. Women from the same village sell their products in the same area of the bazaar, and there is no rigid class division among the women who come to sell their products; it is still possible to see women from very big landowning families alongside the women from landless families. However, things are changing and women from rich families have begun to stay away. The oldest and youngest women from the families are the most suitable for the job. Among Kurdish seasonal workers, only young men – in their mid-teens – are seen as suitable for this job.
5. Fieldwork Diary, 8 September 2013.
6. Fieldwork Notes, 22 August 2013.
7. Fieldwork Notes, 15 September 2013.
8. Delaney's work on Turkish rural is called 'The Seed and The Soil' (1991), which uses the same metaphor to understand the organization of rural relations.
9. Researcher, Fieldwork Diary, 19 August 2013.
10. Songül, Fieldwork Notes, 30 August 2013.
11. Researcher, Fieldwork Notes, 5 September 2013.
12. Researcher, Fieldwork Diary, 12 August 2013.
13. Fieldwork Notes, 12 August 2013.
14. *El âlem* is an Arabic term that directly translates into 'the world'. Both in Turkey and in the Arabic-speaking world, the term is used to refer to 'the people' or the populace in the broadest sense. It is a term that is often used to refer to what is thought of one group of people by another. It is sometimes used to refer to the other in a pejorative way.
15. Fieldwork Notes, 18 August 2013.
16. Researcher, Fieldwork Diary, 17 August 2013.
17. Fieldwork Notes, 11 September 2013.
18. Researcher, Fieldwork Diary, 24 September 2013.

## Chapter 6

1. Reports (TÜİK 2017b) indicate that 21.6 per cent of the population is living under the poverty line in Turkey (stated for 2016). Official reports are not available for the statistics in 2020. However, the unions (in this case Türk-iş and Disk) claim that today this rate is far more higher. The statistics on recent unemployment figures stated in Chapter 2 supports the claims of the unions.

2   From 2003 to 2013 14,269 workers have lost their lives in workplaces in Turkey (İSİG 2014). The recent reports of İSİG (2017, 2018, 2019) demonstrate a constant trend in the numbers of workplace deaths: in 2017 at least 2006 workers; in 2018 at least 1923 workers; and in the first ten months of 2019 at least 1477 workers have lost their lives.
3   I am aware that using the term 'mechanical monster' lends weight to a negative interpretation of factory work. It reflects, however, the views of the majority of my key informants who expressed negative views of factory work in terms of working conditions and the environment, particularly inside the plant. Most of them stated that they found the factory too claustrophobic, too loud, too hot and too dirty. Neither they nor I would deny the economic and social advantages of factory work but these advantages are not always enough to create a 'positive' interpretation of factory work. Despite this, women work in the factory because it provides them with jobs.
4   Researcher, Fieldwork Diary, 18 August 2014.
5   A 'living wage' is set by the Turkish state. All women in the factory receive the same money. There is no gender wage gap, and the material differences between workers lie in working conditions – levels of autonomy, types of contracts and the way they are treated – which are mostly shaped by Kemalist gender categories and are used by the factory as a way of managing women's labour.
6   Salzinger (2003: 5).
7   Fieldwork Notes, 16 September 2014.
8   This debate deserves more attention and detail. The history of CHP offers different eras which the party gets closer to left and contrary. Here, however, I could only give some brief knowledge for reader to understand how people in the study perceive Kemalism, CHP and their relationship with left-wing politics.
9   Here DİSK (Confederation of Progressive Trade Unions of Turkey) should be noted. Disk was established in 1967 and it is still an active and 'opponent' union. When Disk was established, Türk-İş was the only confederation, so Disk was organized against it (Algül 2015). In Red factory, women workers do not know about Disk or even Türk-İş which they registered in. I, therefore, offer a discussion about union (Türk-İş) as in their lives.
10  When I say Islamist capital, I refer to the capitalists who have closely aligned themselves with 'moderate' Islamic ideology. I am saying 'moderate' here intentionally, as Tuğal (2009) demonstrates that the AKP's neoliberal economic policies lead to the absorption of liberal economic ideals by political Islam, and this converts 'radical Islamists' to 'moderate' ones. As he points out, the dream of the Islamic state does not exist anymore amongst the residents of the neighbourhood, as they are satisfied with the governing of the state. Tuğal (2009) shows how the discussions amongst the men in the local coffee houses often begin with Islam and the concept of the Islamic state but quickly transform into conversations about money and economics. In his later work, Tuğal (2016) also discusses the falling of the Islamic liberalism in Turkey.
11  By 'Anatolian Women', I refer to the women who work permanently in the warehouse throughout the year. The Kemalist factory regime implicitly constructs the women warehouse workers as amongst the women Kemalism terms 'Anatolian Women' because of their ability to cope with difficult working conditions and long hours.
12  Fieldwork Notes, 16 September 2014.
13  Researcher, Fieldwork Diary, 25 August 2014.
14  My sister drew the pictures for the book, according to my instructions, because I am not able to use professional drawing programme, as for Figure 6.1, nor do I have

the artistic drawing skills required for Figure 6.2 or 6.3. I took photos of the factory during my fieldwork with the permission of the factory manager. However, he requested that I should not use the actual photos but drew the images instead.
15  Fieldwork Notes, 10 September 2014.
16  Fieldwork Notes, 18 September 2014.
17  Mustafa Kemal Ataturk was a chief commander during the Freedom War (1919–23), afterwards founding the Turkish Republic and becoming its first president. Almost all members of first Turkish Parliament (1920) were commanders and/or military officers. Army, therefore, is in the heart of Kemalism (Bora 2003).
18  Secular people have increasingly begun to associate those adjectives with conservative people in Turkey by saying that conservative groups continue to support the AKP despite their increased authoritarianism, fraud and oppression.
19  Fieldwork Notes, 16 September 2014.
20  Fieldwork Notes, 16 September 2014.
21  Fieldwork Notes, 23 August 2014.
22  *Survivor* is a popular TV show around the world, in which people try to live on a remote island without using any consumer goods.
23  Researcher, Fieldwork Diary, 3 September 2014.
24  Researcher, Fieldwork Diary, 22 August 2014.
25  Fieldwork Notes, 2 September 2014.
26  Fieldwork Notes, 1 September 2014.
27  Fieldwork Notes, 18 September 2014.
28  Researcher, Fieldwork Dairy, 30 August 2014.
29  Fieldwork Notes, 18 September 2014.
30  Fieldwork Notes, 14 September 2014.
31  Fieldwork Notes, 12 September 2014.
32  Fieldwork Notes, 16 September 2014.
33  Researcher, Fieldwork Diary, 16 September 2014.
34  Fieldwork Notes, 13 September 2014.
35  Women in the warehouse perceive the job as permanent, although it is not a permanent job officially, rather a series of contracts.
36  However, politically it could be argued that secularism has been seen as embodied by main religious political actors of the Turkey (Kuru 2007; Turam 2006). Here, I continue to refer to these two counter-ideologies as secularism and Islamism, as this is how the workers and managers of Red perceived this difference, as do many other citizens of the country.

## Chapter 7

1  The Turkish language does not have a definite article, so *el âlem* is not directly translated as 'the *el âlem*'. However, in certain contexts 'the *el âlem*' in English better captures its meaning when I refer to an identifiable group of people.
2  As stated periodically throughout this book, there is an ongoing tension between conservative and secular citizens of Turkey. When Mardin introduced this concept in 2007 in an interview (accessible from: http://www.rusencakir.com/Prof-Serif-Mardin-Mahalle-havasi-diye-bir-sey-var-ki-AKPyi-bile-dover/749) for a newspaper article about his book *Religion, Society and Modernity in Turkey* (2006),

the opposition media used it to emphasize a 'pressure' exerted by the conservative population – with the presumption that the latter are primarily AKP supporters – against the lifestyles of secular citizens. The concept has received greater attention in the media than the academy, and is typically associated with the AKP's conservative ideology. Mardin has tried to clarify that the concept has historical roots in Turkish society and its existence is not directly related to the AKP's conservative ideology or policies, but his efforts have not prevented the concept from being associated with the demonizing of non-conservative Turkish citizens. Toprak et al. (2009) have noted that *mahalle baskısı* (neighbourhood pressure) is on the rise in Turkish society, especially in small Anatolian cities with regard to religious practices. Social taboos against the non-observance of Ramadan are an example of this phenomenon.

3   When the concept was particularly popular during 2008, my mother and I were watching a TV programme in which different scholars were discussing what 'neighbourhood pressure' meant. Given her profile, my mother – rural, uneducated – shares an affinity with the people in this study, and she asked me with surprise why they did not specifically use the phrase *el âlem ne der* – 'what will el âlem say?'
4   Fieldwork Notes, 14 September 2013.
5   Having control over someone is understood in daily life in Turkey as a right to have a say about someone else's life – *söz söyleme hakkı*. It refers to the 'right' to pass judgement or make a decision about what the other should do in a given context and it can also include the right to issue punishment if the individual is not deemed to act 'appropriately'.
6   In the Turkish language, this judgement is more rigid than the mere appropriateness of behaviour; (the) *el âlem* have the right to talk about the 'rightness' or 'wrongness' of your behaviour. According to my friends on the fields, the same applies in Kurdish (kurmanci).
7   Fieldwork Notes, 16 September 2013.
8   Gelin is the direct translation of a 'bride'. It is used to refer to the daughter-in-law on the day of her wedding and thereafter. Similarly, *Damat, the Turkish word for 'groom'*, is used for the son-in-law on the day of wedding and thereafter.
9   Fieldwork Notes, 5 May 2013.
10  Nezahat, Fieldwork Notes, 14 May 2013.
11  Nezahat, Fieldwork Notes, 24 August 2013.
12  Fieldwork Notes, 4 May 2013.
13  Fieldwork Notes, 12 May 2013.
14  Nurhan, Fieldwork Notes, 16 August 2013.
15  In the countryside, this is used to tease people about unexpected and so-called modern behaviour from a rural woman. This is especially the case for women who migrate to towns and cities and later return to visit their village. Using accessories associated with being urban, such as sunglasses and straw hats, or changing one's accent is among the main reasons for teasing a woman for being *sosyete*. Men are not the targets of such teasing, as their adoption of 'modern' culture is more accepted by the *el âlem*.
16  Fieldwork Notes, 19 September 2013.
17  Fieldwork Notes, 27 September 2013.
18  Fatma, Fieldwork notes, 14 September 2015.
19  Fieldwork Notes, 15 August 2013.
20  Fieldwork Notes, 7 May 2013.

21 *Tandır* means an outdoor earthenware oven and a type of bread. *Tandırs* are mostly used to bake bread. The bread made in this oven is called *tandır ekmeği* – *tandır* bread – but women in the study simply call it *tandır* for short. *Tandır* is a vital part of Kurdish cuisine. Every day, the woman who stays at home is responsible for making *tandır* for the family members working on the land.

22 See Küçükkırca (2015) for the housing conditions of Kurdish seasonal workers across Turkey.

23 When some of the other workers around the region (not those I worked with during the season) saw me on the tomato fields, they complained about the newspapers' photographers who continually took photos of them. One of them asked, 'Do you also have a camera? I do not know how many photos they took of our children. We are too famous. Don't talk with me if you will take photos.'

24 Fieldwork Notes, Melek, 22 September 2014.

25 Fieldwork Notes, 24 September 2014.

26 Fieldwork Notes, 26 September 2014.

27 Researcher, Fieldwork Diary, 29 August 2013.

28 The official statistic institute in Turkey (TÜİK 2012) also supports my findings from the field with regard to the reasons for kin-based marriage. According to TÜİK (2012) 51.3 per cent of people in southeastern Anatolia who married with their kin state that they accept kin marriage because of knowing the familial roots of her/his partner. As many as 19.1 per cent of the informants of the survey said that in kin marriages; the mother and father-in-law are more respected by bride and groom.

29 The same report (TÜİK 2012) shows that in southeastern Anatolia 29.3 per cent of women who married their kin married their *amcaoğlu*. This is the biggest category of marriages between kinfolk.

30 Fieldwork Notes, 30 September 2013.

31 Fieldwork Notes, 22 August 2013.

32 Fieldwork Notes, 22 August 2013.

33 Fieldwork Notes, 29 September 2013.

34 The word *kaynana* derives from *kayınvalide* in Turkish. It is used to refer to both the mother of a bride and the mother of a groom. However, if a woman does not get on well with her mother-in-law, she is more likely to use the word *kaynana* than she is *kayınvalide*. While the word *kayınvalide* connotes 'respect' and some distance, *kaynana* includes negative associations. On the other hand, the usage of *kayınvalide* instead of *kaynana* is also associated with being more 'modern', 'urban' and 'educated'. It is safe to say that most educated urban women prefer to use *kayınvalide*, especially when they speak in public.

35 Researcher, Fieldwork Diary, 5 March 2014.

36 Researcher, Fieldwork Diary, 16 September 2013.

37 Fieldwork Notes, 9 March 2014.

38 Fieldwork Notes, 29 August 2013.

## Chapter 8

1 The construction of new buildings, especially those built by the TOKİ (Housing Development Administration of Turkey), and especially apartments and shopping centres, is criticized by opponents of Turkey's current government. One of the largest protests in Turkish history, which occurred recently in Gezi Park in 2013, aimed to prevent the demolition of a park and the construction of a new shopping centre in one of

the most important centres in İstanbul. It could easily be said that this attitude towards new buildings has become a symbol of politics for some of the government's opponents.
2   Fieldwork Notes, 16 September 2014.
3   Fieldwork Notes, 16 September 2014.
4   Abadan-Unat (1986: 186) calls household structures where conjugal families live in *separate dwellings* but their budgets are not separated fully the 'functionally extended family'. Here, I prefer to describe these households as 'trying to be a nuclear family' as I want to emphasize the viewpoint of the brides of these families. In either case the boundaries of the household can be understood as including parents-in-law and the son's nuclear family even though these families do not share a dwelling.
5   Fieldwork Notes, 15 September 2014.
6   Fieldwork Notes, 13 September 2014.
7   Fieldwork Notes, 14 August 2014.
8   Fieldwork Notes, 17 September 2014.
9   Fieldwork Notes, 14 September 2014.
10  *Görümce* is another rival facing a *gelin* in the extended family structure. Most of the time, the main complaints of a *gelin* are about the way her *görümce* and *kaynana* jointly criticize her treatment of her children or her attitudes towards her husband (e.g. spoiling the children and not being respectful towards her husband), as well as about their gossiping and thus controlling the *gelin*'s monetary expenditure.
11  Fieldwork Notes, 11 September 2014.
12  Fieldwork Notes, 3 September 2014.
13  Fieldwork Notes, 22 August 2014.

## Chapter 9

1   Researcher, Fieldwork Diary, 20 May 2015.
2   Fieldwork Diary, 22 May 2015.
3   In this research, I use the term 'knowing' to refer to a state of affairs of thinking, feeling and experiencing.
4   However, as pointed out, Syrian refugees have increasingly become rural workers because of their acceptance of working with lower wage and the ending the 'reconciliation process' in 2015, which proposed to work towards an agreement between the Turkish state and the PKK to reach a 'peace process'. The AKP has lost the support of Kurds (not of all of them but with an important numbers) when HDP (People's Democratic Party) entered the parliament and lost its majority in June 2015. The coalition government could not be formed, the election has been repeated and the AKP has won the majority in November 2015. In 2017, the constitution has been changed by the AKP and the support of nationalist party (MHP). In this way, Turkish Republic became a presidency from a parliament and Recep Tayyip Erdogan became the first president in Turkey in 2018.
5   At this point, it is important to note that the distribution of Kurdish seasonal family workers shows parallels with the demands of global production. Kurds work on the north coast of Turkey to pick nuts (Duruiz 2015), which are exported in huge quantities to Russia, the Middle East and Europe. On the south coast of Turkey, Kurds work to pick oranges, which are exported to Russia, whereas in central Anatolia and the west, Kurdish seasonal workers produce onions and tomatoes for export.

6 CHP (the main opposition party and known as Kemalist) has attempted to abandon this discourse gradually over years by placing itself to the centre. The winning of mayoral election in Istanbul and Ankara in 2019 could be seen as a result of these attempts.
7 Mackintosh (1984) did not define the reproduction of relations as I do here. Rather, she offered a discussion of two concepts, the reproduction of labour and of human reproduction. She highlighted that the reproduction of labour includes many tasks that are undertaken in the spheres of production, and thus there is no way to divide those two spheres. Moreover, she highlighted the concept of human reproduction, which is included in the concept of reproduction of labour, chiefly concerning the relations of marriage and kinship in society. I would like to concentrate on the same points with those concepts underlined.
8 Researcher, Fieldwork Diary, 22 May 2015.

# REFERENCES

Abadan-Unat, N. (1978), 'The Modernization of Turkish Women', *Middle East Journal*, 32 (3): 291–306.
Abadan-Unat, N. (1986), *Women in the Developing World: Evidence from Turkey*, Denver: University of Denver Press.
Abadan-Unat, N. (1991), 'Educational Reforms on Turkish Women', in N. Keddi and B. Baron (eds), *Women in Middle Eastern History: Shifting Boundaries in Sex and Gender*, 177–94, New Haven: Yale University Press.
Acar, F. (1993), 'Women and University Education in Turkey', *Higher Education in Europe*, 18 (4): 65–77.
Acker, J. (1989), 'The Problem With Patriarchy', *Sociology*, 23 (2): 235–40.
Acker, J. (1990), 'Hierarchies, Jobs, Bodies: A Theory of Gendered Organizations', *Gender and Society*, 4 (2): 139–58.
Acker, J. (2006), 'Inequality Regimes Gender, Class and Race in Organizations', *Gender and Society*, 20 (4): 441–64.
Adaman, F., Buğra, A. and İnsel, A. (2009), 'Social Context of Labor Union Strategy: The case of Turkey', *Labor Studies Journal*, 34 (2): 168–88.
Agricultural Economic and Policy Development Institute (TEPGE) (2014), *Domates ve Domates Salçası, Durum ve Tahmin 2012/2013*, Ankara.
Ainsworth, S., Batty, A. and Burchielli, R. (2013), 'Women Constructing Masculinity in Voluntary Firefighting', *Gender, Work and Organization*, 21 (1): 37–56.
Akın, C. R. and Danışman, F. (2011), *Bildiğin Gibi Değil: 90'larda Güneydoğu'da Çocuk Olmak*, İstanbul: Metis.
Algül, S. (2015), *Türkiye'de Sendika-Siyaset İlişkisi: Disk (1967-1975)*, İstanbul: İletişim.
Altınay, G. A. (2013), *Vatan, Millet, Kadınlar*, İstanbul: İletişim.
Anderson, B. (2006), *Imagined Communities: Reflections on the Origin and Spread of Nationalism*, London: Verso.
Arat, Y. (1997), 'The Project of Modernity and Women in Turkey', in S. Bozdoğan and R. Kasaba (eds), *Rethinking Modernity and National Identity in Turkey*, 95–112, Seattle: University of Washington Press.
Arat, Y. (1998a), *Türkiye'de Modernleşme ve Ulusal Kimlik*, İstanbul: Tarih Vakfı Yurt Yayınları.
Arat, F. Z. (1998b), 'Educating the Daughters of Republic', in Z. Arat ed., *Deconstructing Images of the Turkish Women*, 157–83, London: Macmillan.
Arat, F. Z. (2010), 'Opportunities, Freedoms and Restrictions: Women and Employment in Turkey', in C. Kerslake, K. Öktem, and P. Robins (eds), *Turkey's Engagement with Modernity*, 165–89, London: Palgrave Macmillan.
Aydın, Z. (2005), *The Political Economy of Turkey*, London: Pluto Press.
Aydın, Z. (2010), 'Neo-liberal transformation of Turkish Agriculture', *Journal of Agrarian Change*, 10 (2): 149–87.
Bair, J. (2005), 'Global Capitalism and Commodity Chains: Looking Back, Going Forward', *Competition and Change*, 9 (1): 158–80.

Balsiger, P. (2014), *The Fight for Ethical Fashion: The Origins and Interactions of the Clean Clothes Campaign*, London: Routledge.

Barndt, D. (2002), *Tangled Routes: Women, Work and Globalization on the Tomato Trail*, Lanham, MD: Rowman and Littlefield Publication.

Barrientos, S. and Kritzinger, A. (2004), 'Squaring the Circle: Global Production and the Informalization of Work in South African Fruit Exports', *Journal of International Development*, 16: 81–92.

Barrientos, S. and Perrons, D. (1999), 'Gender and the Global Food Chain: A Comparative Study of Chile and the UK', in H. Afshar and S. Barrientos (eds), *Women, Globalisation and Fragmentation in the Developing World*, 150–73, London: Macmillan.

Barrientos, S., Dolan, C. and Tallontire, A. (2003), 'A Gendered Value Chain Approach to Codes of Conduct in African Horticulture', *World Development*, 31 (9): 1511–26.

Başlevent, C. and Onaran, Ö. (2004), 'The Effect of Export-Oriented Growth on Female Labor Market Outcomes in Turkey', *World Development*, 32 (8): 1375–93.

BBC (2015), *Kürt İşçilerin Terk Ettiği Beypazarı'nda Neler Yaşandı?* [online] available https://www.bbc.com/turkce/haberler/2015/09/150908_beypazari_saldirilar [accessed 19 April 2020].

Beechey, V. (1979), 'On Patriarchy', *Feminist Review*, 3: 66–82.

Behar, R. (1995), 'Introduction: Out of Exile', in R. Behar and D. Gordon (eds), *Women Writing Culture*, 1–33, London: University of California Press.

Behar, R. and Gordon, A. D. (eds) (1995), *Women Writing Culture*, London: University of California Press.

Beşikçi, İ. (1969), *Doğu Anadolu'nun Düzeni*, Development Studies Association Annual Conference, Ankara: E Yayınları.

Beşpınar, F. U. and Topal, C. (2018), 'Interplay of Gender Subtext and Local Culture in the Organizational Logic: The Case of a Textile Factory in Turkey', *Community, Work and Family*, 21(3): 292–309.

Bora, T. (2003), 'Nationalist Discourses in Turkey', *South Atlantic Quarterly*, 102 (2/3): 433–51.

Boratav, K. (2004), *Tarımsal Yapılar ve Kapitalizm*, Ankara: İmge.

Boserup, E. (1970), *Women's Role in Economic Development*, London: George Allen and Unwin Publishing.

Bott, E. (2010), 'Favourites and Others: Reflexivity and the Shaping of Subjectivities and Data in Qualitative Research', *Qualitative Research*, 10 (2): 159–73.

Bozdoğan, S. and Kasaba, R. (1997), 'Introduction', in S. Bozdoğan and R. Kasaba (eds), *Rethinking Modernity and National Identity in Turkey*, 3–15, Washington DC: University of Washington Press.

Bozzoli, B. (1983), 'Marxism, Feminism and South African Studies', *Journal of Southern African Studies*, 9 (2): 87–96.

Bradley, H. (1996), *Fractured Identities: Changing Patterns of Inequality*, Cambridge: Polity Press.

Bradley, H. and Healy, G. (2008), *Ethnicity and Gender at Work: Inequalities, Careers and Employment Relations*, London: Palgrave Macmillan.

Braverman, H. (1974), *Labor and Monopoly Capital: The Degradation of Work in the Twentieth Century*, New York: Monthly Review Press.

Buğra, A. and Özkan, Y. (2012), 'Modernization, Religious Conservatism and Female Employment through Economic Development in Turkey', in A. Buğra and Y. Özkan (eds), *Trajectories of Female Employment in Mediterranean*, 91–114, London: Palgrave Macmillan.

Buğra, A. and Savaskan, O. (2012), 'Politics and Class: Turkish Business Environment in the Neoliberal Age', *New Perspectives on Turkey*, 46: 27–63.
Buğra, A. and Yakut-Cakar, B. (2010), 'Structural Change, the Social Policy Environment and Female Employment in Turkey', *Development and Change*, 41 (3): 517–38.
Burawoy, M. (1979), *Manufacturing Consent: Changes in the Labor Process under Monopoly Capitalism*, Chicago: University of Chicago Press.
Burawoy, M. (1985), *The Politics of Production*, London: Verso.
Cemal, N. (2012), *Tekel'in Elleri: Mücadele ve Yordam*, İstanbul: H20.
Çağatay, N. and Berik, G. (1990) 'Transition to Export-led Growth in Turkey: Is There a Feminization of Employment?', *Review of Radical Political Economics*, 22 (1): 115–34.
The Chamber of Agricultural Engineers (ZMO) (2014), *Türkiye' de Domates ve Domates Salçası Üretimi ve Dış Ticareti*, Ankara.
Chant, S. (1991), *Women and Survival in Mexican Cities: Perspectives on Gender, Labour Markets and Low-income Households*, Manchester: University of Manchester Press.
Chant, S. (1997), *Women-headed Households: Diversity and Dynamics in the Developing World*, Houndmills, Basingstoke: Macmillan.
Chant, S. and McIlwaine, C. (1995), *Women of a Lesser Cost: Female Labour, Foreign Exchange and Philippine Development*, London: Pluto.
Chant, S. and McIlwaine, C. (2009), *Geographies of Development in the 21st Century: An Introduction to the Global South*, Cheltenham: Elgar.
Chant, S. and McIlwaine, C. (2016), *Cities, Slums and Gender in the Global South: Towards a Feminised Urban Future*, London: Routledge.
Chatterjee, P. (2001), *A Time for Tea*, Durham: Duke University Press.
Clelland, D. (2014), 'Unpaid Labor as Dark Value in Global Commodity Chains', in W. Dunaway ed., *Gendered Commodity Chains: Seeing Women's Work and Households in Global Production*, 72–90, California: Stanford University Press.
Cockburn, C. (1983), *Brothers: Male Dominance and Technological Change*, London: Pluto Press.
Cockburn, C. (1985), *Machinery of Dominance: Women, Men and Technical Know-How*, London: Pluto Press.
Cockburn, C. (1991), *In the Way of Women: Men's Resistance to Sex Equality in Organisations*, Basingstoke: Macmillan Publishing.
Collins, J. (2014), 'A Feminist Approach to Overcoming the Closed Boxes of the Commodity Chain', in W. Dunaway ed., *Gendered Commodity Chains: Seeing Women's Work and Households in Global Production*, 27–38, California: Stanford University Press.
Connell, R. (1987), *Gender and Power: Society, the Person and Sexual Politics*, Cambridge: Polity in association with Blackwell.
Cravey, J. A. (1998), *Women and Work in Mexico's Maquiladoras*, Boston: Rowman and Littlefield Publishers.
Crenshaw, K. (1989), 'Demarginalizing the Intersection of Race and Sex: A Black Feminist Critique of Antidiscrimination Doctrine, Feminist Theory, and Antiracist Politics', *University of Chicago Legal Forum*, 139–67.
Crenshaw, K. (1991), 'Mapping the Margins: Intersectionality, Identity Politics, and Violence against Women of Color', *Stanford Law Review*, 43 (6): 1241–99.
Çakır, R. (2008), *Türkiye Tartışıyor 1: Mahalle Baskısı*, İstanbul: Doğan Kitap.
Çınar, E. M. (1991), 'Labour Opportunities for Adult Females and Home-Working Women in İstanbul, Turkey', Los Angeles: University of California, The G.E. von Grunebaum Centre for Near Eastern Studies, Working paper 2.

Çınar, E. M. (1994), 'Unskilled Urban Migrant Women and Disguised Employment: Home-working Women in Istanbul, Turkey', *World Development*, 22 (3): 369–80.

Dedeoğlu, S. (2010), 'Visible Hands – Invisible Women: Garment Production in Turkey', *Feminist Economics*, 16 (4): 1–32.

Dedeoğlu, S. (2012), *Women Workers in Turkey: Global Industrial Production in İstanbul*, London: I.B. Tauris.

Dedeoğlu, S. (2014), 'Patriarchy Reconsolidated: Women's Work in Three Global Commodity Chains of Turkey's Garment Industry', in W. Dunaway ed., *Gendered Commodity Chains: Seeing Women's Work and Households in Global Production*, 106–18, California: Stanford University Press.

Delaney, C. (1991), *The Seed and the Soil*, California: University of California Press.

Dixon, J. (2002), *The Changing Chicken: Chooks, Cooks and Culinary Culture*, Sydney: New South Wales University.

Dunaway, W. ed. (2014), *Gendered Commodity Chains: Seeing Women's Work and Households in Global Production*, California: Stanford University Press.

Durakbaşa, A. (1998), 'Kemalism as Identity Politics in Turkey', in Z. F. Arat ed., *Deconstructing Images of 'the Turkish Women'*, 139–57, London: Macmillan Press.

Duruiz, D. (2015), 'Embodiment of Space and Labour: Kurdish Migrant Workers in Turkish Agriculture', in Z. Gambetti and J. Jongerden (eds), *The Kurdish Issue in Turkey*, 289–308, London: Routledge.

Ecevit, Y. (1991), 'Shop Floor Control: The Ideological Construction of Turkish Women Factory Workers', in N. Redclift and T. M. Sinclair (eds), *Working Women: International Perspectives on Labour and Gender Ideology*, 56–75, London: Routledge.

Eisenstein, Z. ed. (1979), *Capitalist Patriarchy*, New York: Monthly Review Press.

Elson, D. and Pearson, R. (1981), '"Nimble Fingers Make Cheap Workers": An Analysis of Women's Employment in Third World Export Manufacturing', *Feminist Review*, 7 (Spring): 87–107.

Engels, F. (1972), *The Origin of the Family, Private Property and the State*, London: Lawrence and Wishart.

Eraydın, A. and Erendil, A. (1999), 'The Role of Female Labour in Industrial Restructuring: New Production Processes and Labour Market Relations in the İstanbul Clothing Industry', *Gender, Place and Culture*, 6(3): 259–72.

Erdogan, E. (2016), '"I Pray for the Factory to Continue Earning Money": The Familial Factory Regime of the 'Sun' Food Factory in Turkey', *Feminist Review*, 113: 68–84.

EUROSTAT (2020), 'Early Leavers from Education Training by Education and Sex', [online] available https://ec.europa.eu/eurostat/tgm/table.do?tab=table&init=1&language=en&pcode=tgs00106&plugin=1 [accessed 24 April 2019].

Fenster, T. (1999), 'Space for Gender: Cultural Roles of the Forbidden and the Permitted', *Environment and Planning D: Society and Space*, 17: 227–46.

Fernandez-Kelly, P. M. (1983), *For We are Sold, I and My People: Women and Industry in Mexico's Frontier*, Albany: State University of New York Press.

Fiorenza, E. (1992), *But She Said: Feminist Practices of Biblical Interpretation*, Boston: Beacon Press.

Firestone, S. (1971), *The Dialectic of Sex*, London: Paladin.

Foucault, M. (1991), *Discipline and Punishment*, London: Penguin Books.

Friedmann, H. (1995), 'The International Political Economy of Food: A Global Crisis', *International Journal of Health Services*, 25 (3): 511–38.

Friedmann, H. (2004), 'Remaking "Traditions": How We Eat, What We Eat and the Changing Political Economy of Food', in D. Barndt ed., *Women Working the NAFTA Food Chain*, 35–61, Toronto: Sumach Press.

Fuentes, A. and Ehrenreich, B. (1983), *Women in the Global Factory*, Boston: South End Press.

Gereffi, G. and Korzeniewicz, M. (eds) (1994), *Commodity Chains and Global Capitalism*, Westport, CT: Greenwood Press.

Göle, N. (1991), *Modern Mahrem*, İstanbul: Metis.

Göle, N. (1997), 'The Quest for the Islamic Self within the Context of Modernity', in S. Bozdoğan and R. Kasaba (eds), *Rethinking Modernity and National Identity in Turkey*, 81–95, Seattle: University of Washington Press.

Glucksmann, M. (1982), *Women on the Line*, London: Routledge.

Glucksmann, M. (1990), *Women Assemble: Women Workers and the New Industries in Inter-war Britain*, London: Routledge.

Gordon, D. (1995), 'Border Work: Feminist Ethnography and the Dissemination of Literacy', in R. Behar and D. Gordon (eds), *Women Writing Culture*, 373–90, London: University of California Press.

Gottfried, H. (1998), 'Beyond Patriarchy? Theorising Gender and Class', *Sociology*, 32 (3): 451–68.

Gündüz-Hoşgör, A. and Smith, J. (2008), 'Variation in Labor Market Participation of Married Women in Turkey', *Women Studies International Forum*, 31: 104–17.

Gürel, B. (2011), 'Agrarian Change and Labour Supply in Turkey, 1950–1980', *Journal of Agrarian Change*, 11 (2): 195–219.

Haraway, D. (1988), 'Situated Knowledges – The Science Question in Feminism and the Privilege of Partial Perspective', *Feminist Studies*, 14 (3): 575–99.

Harding, G. S. (1986), *The Science Question in Feminism*, Milton Keynes: Open University Press.

Hartmann, H. (1981), 'The Unhappy Marriage of Marxism and Feminism: Towards a More Progressive Union', in L. Sargent ed., *Women and Revolution: A Discussion of the Unhappy Marriage of Marxism and Feminism*, 1–43, Boston: South End Press.

Harvey, M., Quilley, S. and Beynon, H. (2002), *Exploring the Tomato: Transformation of Nature, Society and Economy*, Cheltenham: Edward Elgar Publishing.

İlkkaracan, İ. (2012), 'Why so Few Women in the Labor Market in Turkey?', *Feminist Economics*, 18 (1): 1–37.

İlyasoğlu, A. (1998), 'Islamist Women in Turkey: Their Identity and Self-Image', in Z. F. Arat ed., *Deconstructing Images of 'the Turkish Women'*, 241–63, London: Macmillan Press.

İncirlioğlu, O. E. (1998), 'Images of Village Women in Turkey: Models and Anomalies', in Z. F. Arat ed., *Deconstructing Images of 'the Turkish Woman'*, 199–225, London: Macmillan Press.

Kabeer, N. (1994), *Reversed Realities: Gender Hierarchies in Development Thought*, London: Verso.

Kabeer, N. (2000), *Power to Choose: Bangladeshi Women and Labour Market Decisions in London and Dhaka*, London: VERSO.

Kadioglu, A. (1994), 'Women's Subordination on Turkey: Is Islam Really the Villain?', *Middle East Journal*, 48 (4): 645–60.

Kandiyoti, D. (1985), *Women in Rural Production Systems: Problems and Policies*, Paris: UNESCO.

Kandiyoti, D. (1987), 'Emancipated but Unliberated? Reflections on the Turkish Case', *Feminist Studies*, 13 (2): 317–38.
Kandiyoti, D. (1988), 'Bargaining with Patriarchy', *Gender and Society*, 2 (3): 274–90.
Kandiyoti, D. ed. (1991), *Women, Islam and the State*, London: Macmillan.
Kandiyoti, D. (1995), 'Patterns of Patriarchy: Notes for an Analysis of Male Dominance in Turkish Society', in S. Tekeli ed., *Women in Modern Turkish Society*, 306–18, London: Zed Books.
Kandiyoti, D. (1996), *Cariyeler, Bacılar, Yurttaşlar: Kimlikler ve Toplumsal Dönüşümler*, İstanbul: Metis.
Kandiyoti, D. (1997), 'Gendering the Modern: On Missing Dimensions in the Study of Turkish Modernity', in S. Bozdogan and R. Kasaba (eds), *Rethinking Modernity and National Identity in Turkey*, 113–32, Seattle: Washington University Press.
Karpat, K. (1976), *The Gecekondu: Rural Migration and Urbanization*, New York: Cambridge University Press.
Keleş, R. (1983), *100 Soruda Türkiye'de Kentleşme Konut ve Gecekondu*, İstanbul: Gerçek Yayınevi.
Kemal, Y. (2013), *İnce Memed*, Ankara: YKY.
Keyder, C. and Yenal, Z. (2011), 'Agrarian Change under Globalization: Markets and Insecurity in Turkish Agriculture', *Journal of Agrarian Change*, 11 (1): 60–86.
Keyder, C. and Yenal, Z. (2013), *Bildiğimiz Tarımın Sonu: Küresel İktidar ve Köylülük*, İstanbul: İletişim Yayınları.
Koç, Y. (2001), 'Eve Is Verme', *Türk İş Dergisi*, Aralık 2000–Ocak 2001.
KONDA. (2018), *Seçmen Kümeleri: Ak Parti Seçmenleri*, İstanbul.
Kondo, D. K. (1990), *Crafting Selves: Power, Gender and Discourses of Identity in a Japanese Workplace*, London: University of Chicago Press.
Kuru, A. (2007), 'Passive and Assertive Secularism: Historical Conditions, Ideological Struggles, and State Policies toward Religion', *World Politics*, 59: 568–94.
Küçükkırca, A. İ. (2015), 'The Transformation of the Private Home of Kurdish Seasonal Workers', in Z. Gambetti and J. Jongerden (eds), *The Kurdish Issue in Turkey*, 309–30, London: Routledge.
Kümbetoğlu, B., User, İ. and Akpınar, A. (2010) 'Unregistered Women Workers in the Globalized Economy: A Qualitative Study in Turkey', *Feminist Formations*, 22 (3): 96–123.
Leavy, L. P. (2007), 'The Feminist Practice of Ethnography', in S. Nagy, H. Biber and L. P. Leavy (eds), *Feminist Research Practice*, 187–219, London: Sage.
Lee, K. C. (1998), *Gender and the South China Miracle: Two Worlds of Factory Women*, Berkeley: University of California Press.
Lessinger, J. (1990), 'Work and Modesty: The Dilemma of Women Market Traders in Madras', in Leela Dube and Rajni Palriwala (eds), *Structures and Strategies*, 129–50, New Delhi: Sage.
Lordoğlu, K. (1990), *Eve İş Verme Sistemi İçinde Kadın İşgücü Üzerine Bir Alan Araştırması*, İstanbul: Friedrich Ebert Vakfı.
Mackintosh, M. (1984), 'The Sexual Division of Labour and the Subordination of Women', in K. Young, C. Wolkowitz and R. McCullagh (eds), 2nd ed., *Of Marriage and the Market: Women's Subordination Internationally and Its Lessons*, 3–18, London: Routledge.
Makal, A. and Toksöz, G. (eds) (2012), *Geçmişten Günümüze Türkiye'de Kadın Emeği*, Ankara: Ankara Üniversitesi Yayınevi.

McBride, A., Hebson, G. and Holgate, J. (2015), 'Intersectionality: Are We Taking Enough Notice in the Field of Work and Employment Relations?', *Work, Employment and Society*, 29(2): 331–41.

Marcus, G. (1995), 'Ethnography in/of the World System: The Emergence of Multi-sited Ethnography', *Annual Review of Anthropology*, 24: 95–117.

Mardin, Ş. (1991), *Türkiye de Din ve Siyaset Makaleler I*, İstanbul: İletişim.

Mardin, Ş. (2006), *Religion, Society and Modernity in Turkey*, New York: Syracuse University Press.

Marx, K. (1990), *Capital: The Critique of Political Economy Volume I*, London: Penguin Classics.

McBride, A., Hebson, G. and Holgate, J. (2015), 'Intersectionality: Are We Taking Enough Notice in the Field of Work and Employment Relations?', *Work, Employment and Society*, 29(2): 331–41.

McCall, L. (2005), 'The Complexity of Intersectionality', *Signs*, 30 (3): 1771–800.

Mernissi, F. (1985), *Beyond the Veil: Male-Female Dynamics in Modern Muslim Society*, London: Routledge.

Merton, R. (1988), 'Some Thoughts on the Concept of Sociological Autobiography', in Matilda White Riley ed., *Sociological Lives: Social Change and the Life Course, Volume 2*, 17–21, Newbury Park, CA: Sage.

Mies, M. (1982), *The Lace Makers of Narsapur: Indian Housewives Produce for the World Market*, London: Zed Books.

Millet, K. (1977), *Sexual Politics*, London: Virgo.

Mills, C. W. (2000), *Sociological Imagination*, London: Oxford University Press.

Ministry of Development (TCKB) (2012), *Onuncu Kalkınma Planı 2014*, Ankara.

Ministry of National Education (MEB) (1983), *Meb Mevzuat: Milli Eğitim Temel Kanunu*, Ankara.

Mitchell, J. (1975), *Psychoanalysis and Feminism*, Harmondsworth: Penguin.

Moghadam, M. V. (2003), *Modernising Women: Gender and Social Change in the Middle East*, London: Lynne Rienner Publishers.

Mohanty, C. (1984), 'Underwestern Eyes: Feminist Scholarship and Colonial Discourse', *Boundary*, 12 (3): 333–58.

Nash, C. J. (2008), 'Re-thinking Intersectionality', *Feminist Review*, 89: 1–15.

Ngai, P. (2005), *Made in China: Women Factory Workers in a Global Workplace*, Durham [NC]: Durham University Press.

Nichols, T. and Sugur, N. (2004), *Global Management, Local Labour: Turkish Workers and Modern Industry*, New York: Palgrave Macmillan.

NTV (2017), 'Erdoğan Putin Görüşmesi Sonrası Açıklama', [online] available https://www.ntv.com.tr/dunya/erdogan-putin-gorusmesi-sonrasi-aciklama,unbddcn5kUyhNdxIBN6lYA [accessed 24 April 2019].

Oakley, A. (1974), *The Sociology of Housework*, New York: Pantheon Books.

Ong, A. (1987), *Spirits of Resistance and Capitalist Discipline*, Albany: SUNY Press.

Önderman, M. (2018), *Türkiye'de Paranoid Ethos*, İstanbul: Vakıfbank Kültür Yayınları.

Öniş, Z. (2006), 'Globalisation and Party Transformation: Turkey's Justice and Development Party', in P. Burnell ed., *Globalizing Democracy: Party Politics in Emerging Democracies*, 122–40, London: Routledge.

Öniş, Z. (2012), 'The Triumph of Conservative Globalism: The Political Economy of the AKP Era', *Turkish Studies*, 13 (2): 135–52.

Özuğurlu, M. (2011), *Küçük Köylülüğe Sermaye Kapanı: Türkiye'de Tarım Çalışmaları ve Köylülük Üzerine Gözlemler*, Ankara: Nota Bene.

Pahl, J. (1989), *Money and Marriage*, London: Macmillan.
Pahl, J. (1995), 'His Money, Her Money: Recent Research in Financial Organisation in Marriage', *Journal of Economic Psychology*, 16 (3): 361–76.
Pamuk, O. (2015) *A Strangeness in My Mind*, E. Oklap trans., New York: Faber and Faber.
Patil, V. (2013), '"From Patriarchy to Intersectionality": A Transnational Feminist Assessment of How Far We've Really Come', *Signs*, 38 (4): 847–67.
Pearson, R. (1998), 'Nimble Fingers Revisited: Reflections on Women and Third World Industrialisation in the Late Twentieth Century', in C. Jackson and R. Pearson (eds), *Feminist Visions of Development: Gender, Analysis and Policy*, 171–88, London: Routledge.
Pearson, R. (2000), 'All Change? Men, Women and Reproductive Work in the Global Economy', *European Journal of Development Research*, 12 (2): 19–37.
Phillips, A. and Taylor, B. (1980), 'Sex and Skill: Notes towards a Feminist Economics', *Feminist Review*, 6: 79–88.
Pilgeram, R. (2007), '"Ass-kicking" Women: Doing and Undoing Gender in a US Livestock Auction', *Gender, Work & Organization*, 14 (6): 572–95.
Pillow, W. (2003), 'Confession, Catharsis or Cure? Rethinking the Uses of Reflexivity as Methodological Power in Qualitative Research', *International Journal of Qualitative Research in Education*, 16 (2): 175–96.
Pollert, A. (1981), *Girls, Wives, Factory Lives*, London: Macmillan Press.
Pollert, A. (1996), 'Gender and Class Revisited; or the Poverty of Patriarchy', *Sociology*, 30 (4): 639–59.
Rainnie, A. (2013), *Global Destruction Networks*, Labour and Waste, Rutgers University: International Labour Process Conference, no. 31.
Ramamurthy, P. (2000), 'The Cotton Commodity Chain, Women, Work and Agency in India and Japan: The Case for Feminist Agro-Food Systems Research', *World Development*, 28 (3): 551–78.
Ramamurthy, P. (2004), 'Why Is Buying a "Madras" Cotton Shirt a Political Act? Feminist Commodity Chain Analysis', *Feminist Studies*, 30 (3): 734–69.
Ramamurthy, P. (2014), 'Feminist Commodity Chain Analysis: A Framework to Conceptualise Value and Interpret Perplexity', in W. Dunaway ed., *Gendered Commodity Chain Analysis: Seeing Women's Work and Households in Global Production*, 38–54, California: Stanford University Press.
Ran, H. N. (2007), *Memleketimden İnsan Manzaraları*, İstanbul: YKY.
Rowbotham, S. (1981), 'The Trouble with Patriarchy', in M. Barrett, S. Bruley, G. Chester, M. Millman, S. O'Sullivan, A. Sebestyen and L. Segal (eds), *No Turning Back*, 72–9, London: The Women's Press.
Salzinger, L. (2003), *Genders in Production: Making Workers in Mexico's Global Factories*, Berkeley: University of California Press.
Salzinger, L. (2004), 'Revealing the Unmarked: Finding Masculinity in a Global Factory', *Ethnography*, 5 (1): 5–27.
Sancar, S. (2012), *Türk Modernleşmesinin Cinsiyeti*, İstanbul: İletişim Yayınları.
Sarıgıl, Z. (2012), 'Ethnic Groups at "Critical Junctures": The Laz vs. Kurds', *Middle Eastern Studies*, 48(2): 269–86.
Sarıoğlu, E. (2013), 'Gendering the Organization of Home-based Work in Turkey: Classical versus Familial Patriarchy', *Gender, Work and Organization*, 20(5): 479–97.
Sarıoğlu, E. (2016), 'New Imaginaries of Gender in Turkey's Service Economy: Women Workers and Identity Making on the Sales Floor', *Women Studies International Forum*, 54: 39–47.

Selwyn, B. (2012), *Workers, State and Development in Brazil*, Manchester: Manchester University Press.
Stanley, L. (1993), 'On Auto/Biography in Sociology', *Sociology*, 27(1): 41–52.
Stanley, L. and Wise, S. (1991), 'Feminist Research, Feminist Consciousness and Experiences of Sexism'. in M. M. Fonow and A. J. Cook (eds), *Beyond Methodology: Feminist Scholarship as Lived Research*, 265–84, Indianapolis: Indiana University Press.
Stewart, A. (2015), *Gender, Law and Justice in a Global Market*, Cambridge: Cambridge University Press.
Strohmeier, M. and Yalçın-Heckmann, L. (2013), *Kürtler: Tarih, Siyaset, Kültür*, İstanbul: Tarih Vakfı Yurt Yayınları.
Subaşı, N. (2008), 'Mahalleyi Baskıyla Hatırlamak', in T. Takış ed., *Şerif Mardin Okumalar*, Ankara: Doğu-Batı Yayınları.
Sugur, N. and Sugur, S. (2005), 'Gender and Work in Turkey: Women Workers in the Textile Industry in Bursa', *Middle Eastern Studies*, 41 (2): 269–79.
Şen, M. (2014), 'Trabzon'dan İstanbul'a Göç Edenlerin Sosyo-ekonomik Analizi', *Çalışma Dünyası*, 2 (3): 46–61.
Tekeli, Ş. (1990), 'The Meaning and Limits of Feminist Ideology in Turkey', in F. Özbay ed., *Women, Family and Social Change in Turkey*, 139–60, Bangkok: UNESCO.
Thompson, P. (1989), *The Nature of Work*, London: Palgrave: Macmillan.
Thompson, P. and Smith, C. (2009), 'Labour Power and Labour Process: Contesting the Marginality of the Sociology of Work', *Sociology*, 43 (5): 913–30.
Toksöz, G. (2007), *Women's Employment Situation in Turkey*, Ankara: International Labour Office.
Toksöz, G. (2011), 'One Step Forward, Two Step Backward' from Labour Market Exclusion to Inclusion; A Gender Perspective on Effects of the Economic Crisis in Turkey', in N. Visvanathan ed., *The Women, Gender and Development Reader*, 306–17, London: Zed Books.
Toprak, B., Bozan, İ., Morgül, T. and Ve Şener, N. (2009), *Türkiye'de Farklı Olmak: Din ve Muhafazakârlık Ekseninde Ötekileştirilenler (Mahalle Baskısı Raporu)*, İstanbul: Metis.
Torres, G. (1997), *The Force of Irony: Power in the Everyday Life of Mexican Tomato Workers*, Oxford: Berg.
Tuğal, C. (2009), *Passive Revolution: Absorbing the Islamic Challenge to Capitalism*, Stanford, CA: Stanford University Press.
Tuğal, C. (2016), *The Fall of Turkish Model: How the Arab Uprisings Brought Down Islamic Liberalism*, London: Verso.
Turam, B. (2006), *Between Islam and the State: The Politics of Engagement*, Stanford, CA: Stanford University Press.
Turkish Official Gazette (2006), *Tohumculuk Kanunu* (Seed Law) [online] available http://www.resmigazete.gov.tr/eskiler/2006/11/20061108-1.htm [accessed 24 April 2019].
Turkish Official Gazette (2007), *Toprak Kanunu* (Land Law) [online] available http://www.resmigazete.gov.tr/eskiler/2007/02/20070209-1.htm [accessed 24 April 2019].
Turkish Republic Central Bank (TMCB) (2012), *Foreign Direct Investment Inflows to Food Manufacturing*, Ankara.
Turkish Statistical Institute (TÜİK) (2011), *İstatistik Göstergeler 1923–2011*, Ankara.
Turkish Statistical Institute (TÜİK) (2012), *İstatistiklerde Kadın 2012*, Ankara.
Turkish Statistical Institute (TÜİK) (2013), *Hanehalkı İşgücü İstatistikleri*, Ankara.
Turkish Statistical Institute (TÜİK) (2014a), *Seçilmiş Göstergelerle Mardin 2013*, Ankara.
Turkish Statistical Institute (TÜİK) (2014b), *İstatistiklerle Türkiye 2014*, Ankara.
Turkish Statistical Institute (TÜİK) (2014c), *Toplumsal Cinsiyet Araştırması*, Ankara.

Turkish Statistical Institute (TÜİK) (2015), *İl ve ilçelere göre il/ilçe merkezi, belde/köy nüfusu ve yıllık nüfus artış hızı*, Ankara.
Turkish Statistical Institute (TÜİK) (2016), *Tarımsal İşletme Yapı Araştırması*, Ankara.
Turkish Statistical Institute (TÜİK) (2017a), *Nüfus Kütüklerine Kayıtlı En Çok Kullanılan 50 Kadın ve Erkek Adı*, Ankara.
Turkish Statistical Institute (TÜİK) (2017b), *İstatistiklerle Türkiye*, Ankara.
Turkish Statistical Institute (TÜİK) (2018), *Hanehalkı İş Gücü Araştırması*, Ankara.
Turkish Statistical Institute (TÜİK) (2019a), *İstatisklerle Çocuk 2019*, Ankara.
Turkish Statistical Institute (TÜİK) (2019b), *Hanehalkı İş Gücü Araştırması*, Ankara.
The Union of Exporters of Fresh Fruit and Vegetables (YSMİB) (2017), *Değerlendirme Raporu Mayıs 2014*, Mersin.
The Union of Chambers and Commodity Exchanges of Turkey (TOBB), (2014), *Sanayi Kapasite Raporu İstatistikleri*, Ankara.
The United Nations Refugee Agency (UNHCR), *Fact Sheets Turkey*, November, 2019.
Walby, S. (1986), *Patriarchy at Work: Patriarchal and Capitalist Relations in Employment*, Cambridge: Polity Press.
Walby, S. (1990), *Theorizing Patriarchy*, Oxford: Basil Blackwell.
Walby, S. (2009), *Globalization and Inequalities: Complexity and Contested Modernities*, London: Sage.
Walby, S. (2011), *Future of Feminism*, Cambridge: Polity Press.
West, C. and Zimmerman, H. D. (1987), 'Doing Gender', *Gender and Society*, 1 (2): 125–51.
West, C. and Zimmerman, D. (2009), 'Accounting for Doing Gender', *Gender and Society*, 23 (1): 112–22.
Westwood, S. (1984), *All Day, Every Day: Factory and Family in the Making of Women's Lives*, London: Pluto Press.
White, J. (2004), *Money Makes Us Relatives: Women's Labour in Urban Turkey*, Austin: University of Texas Press.
White, J. (2012), *Muslim Nationalism and the New Turks*, New Jersey: Princeton University Press.
Whitehead, A. (2009), 'The Gendered Impacts of Liberalisation Policies on African Agriculture Economies and Rural Livelihoods', in S. Ravazi ed., *The Gendered Impacts of Liberalisation; Towards 'Embedded Liberalism'*, 37–62, Oxon: Routledge.
Williams, S. (2013), *Globalization and Work*, London: Polity.
Wolf, D. (1994), *Factory Daughters: Gender, Household Dynamics and Rural Industrialization in Java*, Berkeley: University of California Press.
Women for Women's Human Rights (WWHR) (2004), *Gender Discrimination in the Turkish Penal Code Draft Law*, İstanbul.
Worker Health and Work Safety Assembly (İSİG) (2014), *2014 Yılı İş Cinayetleri Raporu*, Ankara.
Worker Health and Work Safety Assembly (İSİG) (2017), *2017 Yılı İş Cinayetleri Raporu*, Ankara.
Worker Health and Work Safety Assembly (İSİG) (2018), *2018 Yılı İş Cinayetleri Raporu*, Ankara.
Worker Health and Work Safety Assembly (İSİG) (2019), *2019 Yılı İş Cinayetleri Raporu*, Ankara.
Wright, C. and Madrid, G. (2007), 'Contesting Ethical Trade in Colombia's Cut-Flower Industry: A Case of Cultural and Economic Injustice', *Cultural Sociology*, 1 (2): 255–75.

Wright, M. (2006), *Disposable Women and Other Myths of Global Capitalism*, London: Routledge.

Vera-Sanso, P. (1995), 'Community, Seclusion and Female Labour Force Participation in Madras, India', *Third World Planning Review*, 17 (2): 155–67.

Yalçın-Heckmann, L. (2012), *Kürtlerde Aşiret ve Akrabalık İlişkileri*, İstanbul: İletişim.

Yalman, G. and Bedirhanoğlu, P. (2010), 'State, Class and the Discourse', in A. Saad-Filho and G. Yalman (eds), *Economic Transitions to Neoliberalism in Middle-income Countries: Policy Dilemmas, Economic Crises, Forms of Resistance*, 108–25, London: Routledge.

Yeates, N. (2014), 'Global Care Chains: Bringing in Transnational Reproductive Laborer Households', in W. Dunaway ed., *Gendered Commodity Chains: Seeing Women's Work and Households in Global Production*, 175–208, California: Stanford University Press.

Yeğen, M. (1996), 'The Turkish State Discourse and the Exclusion of Kurdish Identity', *Middle Eastern Studies*, 32 (2): 216–29.

Yuval-Davis, N. (1997), *Gender and Nation*, London: Sage.

Yuval-Davis, N. (2006), 'Intersectionality and Feminist Politics', *European Journal of Women's Studies*, 13 (3): 193–209.

# INDEX

**Boldface** locators indicate illustrations.

Ağalık 24, 174 n.15
agricultural work/workers 16, 35, 44, 49, 60, 111, 154–5, 163, 167
agriculture 154
   capitalization of 19, 34, 51, 139, 177 n.7
   death of small farmers 34, 42
   and industry 168
   liberalization of 34
   mechanization of 23, 29
   transformation process 58
   women 35, 39, 49, 154
agro-food industry 39, 153
*aile (family)* 47, 112. *See also hane* (household); landowning family
AKP. *See* Justice and Development Party (AKP)
*akşam oturması* 60
*Anadolu Kadını. See* 'Anatolian Women'
Anatolia 24, 173 n.8, 182 n.28
'Anatolian Women' 21, 86, 93, 158, 164, 173 n.9, 179 n.11
   tomato sorting lines 97
   union 88
   in warehouse 106–8, 158, 164
*anayasa mahkemesi* 32–3, 175 n.30
Anderson, B. 175 n.26
*aşiret* system 23–4, 112, 174 n.14, 174 n.16, 175 n.25, 177 n.6
Atatürk, Mustafa Kemal 15, 20, 31, 82, 87, 94–5, 140, 145, 176 n.4, 179 n.16
Atatürk nationalism 20, 87, 173 n.5
*atölye* (ateliers) 29–30, 154, 175 n.23, 175 n.27
awarding or punishing workers 56, 101, 164

Backward Religious Women 82, 86, 88, 92, 110, 163–4, 173 n.9
Bangladeshi women's factory 73
Barndt, D. 39

Bedirhanoğlu, P. 31
Behar, R. 12
Bentham's panopticon 99
Berik, G. 84
Beşpınar, F. U. 84
Beynon, H. 40
biologically reductionist 8, 168
Bora, T. 20, 173 n.5
Boratav, K. 24
Boserup, E. 25
Bozzoli, B. 172 n. 21
Braverman, H. 69
Buğra, A. 87
Burawoy, M. 65, 104, 166
bureaucratic authority 32

Çağatay, N. 84
Caliphate (*halifelik*) 20, 31, 175 n.29
capitalist 65, 69
   families 79
   production 16, 42, 49, 53, 63, 67, 161–2, 167
   tomatoes turn workers into 79
capitalization of agriculture 19, 34, 51, 139, 177 n.7
*Çavuş* (sergeant) 55, 97–8, 100–2, 104, 149, 156
*çeyiz* (dowry) 26, 116, 174 n.19
Chant, S. 112, 114
chronic immiseration 120
*cicianne* 170 n.6
Çınar, E. M. 29
Circassians 175 n.24
classic neo-liberalism 33
classic patriarchy 120, 128
compulsory education 3, 26, 171 n.10, 172 n.1, 177 n.14
Confederation of Progressive Trade Unions of Turkey (DİSK) 179 n.9

Confederation of Turkish Trade Unions (Türk-İş) 88, 179 n.9
Connell, R. 9
consent 63, 65, 79, 104, 137, 154, 161, 163, 166–7, 169, 175 n.22
contract farming 15, 35, 40–1, 121
corporate nationalism 36, 43
Cravey, J. A. 8
Crenshaw, K. 8

*dayıbaşı*'s family 52–3, 55, 57, 64–5, 70–2, 77, **128**
  extended family 67–8, 78
  familial labour force 44–7
death of small farmers 34, 42
Dedeoğlu, S. 8, 30
division of labour 9, 43, 49, 51, 67, 69, 79, 83, 120, 129, 143, 151, 168
  gender and ethnic **50** (*see also* gendered division of labour)
'doing gender,' concept of 83
domestic femininities 85
domestic intersectionality 9
domestic labourer 2, 8, 175 n.27
drip irrigation method 51
Dunaway, W. 7
Durakbaşa, A. 21, 106

Ecevit, Y. 84
economic and political instability (Turkey) 30–2
'Educated Daughters of the Republic' 21, 86, 91–2, 98, 102, 104–6, 110, 164, 167, 173 n.9
*el âlem* 7, 9, 16–17, 25, 74, 154, 156, 171 n.21, 178 n.14, 180 n.1, 181 n.6
  conceptualizing households and family 111–12
  controls women's labour 160
  enemies of rural women 120
  and family honour 114–15
  Kurdish seasonal migrants 128–36
  landowning family **119**
  *mahalle baskısı*, conception 113–14
  modern culture 181 n.14
  Muslim order 113
  normative order 114
  patriarchal family in the village 120–8
  persistence of intersectional patriarchy 115–19, 156, 168
  pluralities of 112–13
  power of 136–7
  social order 113
*el âlem için yaşamak* 118
Elson, D. 83
*elti* 120, 124, 129–33, 145, 165
emancipation 109–10
Emines (Turkey) 4–5, 14, 170 n.1
emphasized femininity 60
Erdoğan, E. 1–5
Erdoğan, Recep Tayyip 32, 39, 99, 136, 171 n.17, 183 n.3
ethnicity 8, 10, 12, 61, 65–6, 79, 110, 116, 150, 155–8, 167, 172 n.21
European Integration Process 170 n.4
EUROSTAT 170 n.5
*Exploring the Tomato* (Harvey, Quilley & Beynon) 40
export-oriented growth model 84
extended patriarchal households/family 65, 121, 129, 133, 135, 139, 160, 166

factory work/workers 4, 6, 12–13, 16, 55, 64–6
  and agricultural workers 167
  homes of 160
  landowning family and 165
  negative interpretation of 178 n.3
  purchasing decisions 64
  resources within extended family 145–7
  subcontracting employment firms 81
  women as 84–5, 97, 139–40, 143, 155, 160–1, 166, 179 n.9
*The Fall of The Turkish Model* (Tuğal) 175 n.32
familial control *vs.* resistance 161–3
familial labour force 44–7
familial labour relations (tomato picking)
  Autumn 77–8
  capitalist tomato production process 79
  factory workers 64–6
  oldest couple, managing workers 67–71
  young men 76–7
  young women workers 71–4
  youngest women 74–6

family and ideology 161
farmers 12, 43, 47, 176 n.4
　conditions of agreement 15, 40–2
　as contracting farms 121
　death of small 34, 42
　Kurdish workers and 66
　producing seeds 69, 153
　registered seeds 34
　small-scale 23, 42
　unpaid workers 143
female tomato land 49–52
femininity/feminization 9–11, 49, 84, 147, 151–2, 158
　agricultural work 44
　constructions of 159
　to control workers 156
　emphasized 60
　within household **117**
　images of women (Kemalist factory) 83–6
　masculine dominance 154
　and modernism 109, 140
　trope of productive 83
feminist commodity chain analysis 153
feminist ethnography 11–14
Fenster, T. 114
Fiorenza, E. 172 n.23
*The Force of Irony* (Torres) 40
'forest villages' 177 n.8
Friedmann, H. 154

Gecekondulaşma 23
gender 8–10, 12, 66, 69, 76, 79, 83, 168, 172 n.21. *See also* gendered division of labour; gendered labour (tomato planting)
　changes on relations 147–8
　and global production 5, 16, 39
　labour processes 6
*Gendered Commodity Chains* (Dunaway) 7
gendered division of labour 9, 43, 143–5
　in the factory, Kemalism and education 158–9
　hierarchy of masculinity 159–61
　intersectional forms 152, 154–5
　on tomato land 155–8
gendered labour (tomato planting)
　controlling young workers', obsession 52–5

inequalities of female 49–52
Kurdish seasonal worker 56–8
middle women 55–6
'resentful' local worker 58–61
tomato-growing stages **50**
Gereffi, G. 5
global capital 5–6, 29–30, 34, 43, 151, 154
global commodity chain analysis (GCCA) 5–7, 153, 167
　commodities 5
　global capitalized labour 6
　global production 53
　labour process theory 167
　mobile ethnography 6
　multi-sited ethnography 5
　people's labour 5
　reproduction 7
　social welfare rights 5
　tomato production, labour 7
Global North, intersectionality 8, 153
global production 16, 27, 109, 151, 167–8, 183 n.5
　devaluation of femininity 83–6
　GCCA 5, 53
　local and 151
Global South 44, 153
Göle, N. 20
*görümce* 145–7, 183 n.10
group performance-based payment system 43, 53, 58, 65, 129, 155, 157, 162

*hane* (household) 112, 120, 172 n.22, 182 n.4
　conceptualizing 111–12
　hierarchy of masculinity 118, **118**, 137, 159
　Kemalist 139
　patriarchy, types **117**
　transitional 139
　women-headed 114
Harvey, M. 40
Hebson, G. 8
hegemonic nationalism 36
Holgate, J. 8
homeworking project 27–30
honour 111, 114–15, 118, 160
honour killings (*namus cinayeti*) 115–16
honourable and safe workplace 30, 85

household structures 7, 9, 16, 111, 113, 120, 139, 154, 183 n.4
hybrid seeds 51

imagined community 30–1, 140, 175 n.26
immigration 23, 173 n.10
import subsidized growth model 84
inequalities 7–8, 87, 168, 172 n.22, 172 n.23
of female tomato land 49–52
inferior bearers of labour 83, 108
Institute of Turkish Official Statistics (TÜIK) 1, 29, 170 n.5, 175 n.32, 182 n.28
intersectional patriarchy 7–11, 16–17, 111, 117, 136, 152, 154, 168, 172 n.23
el âlem and 115–19
subcontracting and 109–10
Islamic liberalism 175 n.32, 179 n.10
Islamist Welfare Party (*Refah Partisi*) 32
Istanbul 174 n.21, 182 n.1
Bağcılar 22, 24
relationship with family 30
social transformation 32
ungrateful residents 22–7

Justice and Development Party (AKP) 4, 32–3, 81, 94, 98–9, 164, 171 n.18, 171 n.19, 180 n.2, 183 n.4
and cooperative nationalism 34–6
neoliberal economic policies 179 n.10
political Islam and women's work 32–4
reconciliatory politics 36
rule (2002–20) 19
social neoliberalism and 32, 33, 175 n.32

Kabeer, N. 8, 56, 73
Kandiyoti, D. 9, 128, 135, 166, 173 n.7
Karpat, K. 23
Kavakçı, Merve 31
*kaynana* 120, 124, 133–6, 182 n.34
Kemal, Yaşar 174 n.15
Kemalism 87, 109, 113, 176 n.5, 179 n.8, 180 n.17
and education in factory 158–9
femininity 109, 147
and Kemalist patriarchy 140
and modernity 91, 109, 173 n.7

political Islam and 16
rivals in 92–3
and unionization 87–8
and women 19–22, 83–6, 179 n.11
Kemalist control *vs.* religious resistance 163–4
Kemalist ideology 14–15, 19, 173 n.5, 173 n.9
egalitarian 21, 110
femininities 82
gendered factory regime 82, 86–7
images of women in 83–6, 108, 173 n.9
Kemalist nationalism (Atatürk nationalism) 20, 173 n.5
Kemalist patriarchy 16, 139, 147
changes on gender relations 147–8
*el âlem* 139
Kemalist factory manager 140
Kemalist/opponent (factory manager) 140–2
Kemalist tomato-processing factory. *See* Red (tomato-processing factory)
Keyder, C. 35, 173 n.10
Kılıçdaroğlu 136
kinship relations 8, 23–4, 30, 112, 120, 131–2, 136, 140, 161–2, 165–6, 184 n.7
Koç, Ali 87
Koç, Y. 28–9, 175 n.23
Korzeniewich, M. 5
*küçükanne* 170 n.6
'Kurdish problem' in Turkey
'feudal' agrarian systems 24
Kurdish nationalism 26
migration 23–4
PKK 26–7
urbanization 24
women's employment 25–6
Kurdish seasonal migrant workers 2, 6, 15–16, 36, 40, 43, 49–50, 56–8, 63–4, 127, 155, 162, 178 n.4, 183 n.5
Mardin (hometown) **44**
patriarchal homes of 16, 128–36
undignified 66
kyriarchy, concept of 172 n.23

*Labour and Monopoly Capital* (Braverman) 69

labour process 6–7, 15, 151
  agricultural 49
  control over 69, 81
  division of labour 151, 154
  gendering 83
  and human reproduction 184 n.7
  intersectional patriarchy in 9, 79
  key concepts 79
  mechanical monster 82
  payment system 65, 68, 162
  theory 167
land consolidation 153
Land Law 34, 153, 155
landowners 9, 15, 36, 47, 49–50, 121,
  129–33, 135, 150, 163, 166–7, 174
  n.15, 176 n.1
landowning family 4, 24, 46, 50, 52, 78,
  **119**, 171 n.10, 175 n.22, 176 n.2
  as capitalists 65
  kinship relations 162
  managing labour process 63
  mothers-in-law as cooks/fashion
    designer 125–8, 160
  'resentful' local worker 58
  women in 58–60, 63, 111
  workers and 52, 54–5, 64, 65–6
*Laz* 3, 171 n.16
Leavy, L. P. 12
Lee, K. C. 8
Liberal Neonationalism 173 n.5
liberalization of agriculture 34
'living wage' 179 n.5
Lordoğlu, K. 29

Mackintosh, M. 184 n.7
Madrid, G. 42
*mahalle baskısı* (neighbourhood pressure)
  113, 181 n.2, 181 n.3
*mal* 112
Marcus, G. 6
Mardin (Kurdish migrant workers) 6, 44,
  **44**
  unemployment 44
Mardin, S. 113, 180 n.2
Marx, K. 81–2
Marxism 81
masculinity(ies) 17, 79, 83, 151, 156, 158
  governs femininity 109, 152
  hegemonic 9, 11, 47, 77, 84, 168

hierarchy in division of labour 159–61
  within household **117**
  intersectionality 10, 79, 148, 154
  public face of the family 47
  in rural households, hierarchy **118**, 119
mass migration 23, 154, 173 n.11
Mazıdağı 44, 56
McBride, A. 8
McIlwanie, C. 112
mechanical monster 81–2, 90, 92, 109,
  178 n.3
Mernissi, F. 113, 114, 118–19
middle-class femininities 21, 85
Moghadam, M. V. 114
multi-sited ethnography 5

*namus* 115, 160
Nash, C. J. 8
nationalism 20
  AKP and cooperative 34–6
  corporate 36, 43
  hegemonic 36
  Kemalist 20, 173 n.5
  types of 173 n.5
neoliberalism 33, 175 n.32
Nezahat (workers' favourite) 54–5, 119,
  125–7, 177 n.7
Ngai, P. 8
'Nimble Fingers' 83

Öcalan, Abdullah 36
official feeling 36–7
Öniş, Z. 33, 94

paid employment/workers 19, 25–30,
  34–5, 65, 112, 146, 151, 159, 161–2,
  172 n.23
Pamuk, Orhan 174 n.13
*Partiye Karkeren Kurdistan* (Kurdistan
  Workers Party (PKK)) 2
  international powers 26
  peace process 36, 183 n.4
  Turkish Army and 23, 26, 29, 31
Patil, V. 8–9
patriarchal family in the village
  budget control 121–3
  extra man of the family 123–5
  mothers-in-law as cooks/fashion
    designer 125–8

patriarchal honour 114
patriarchy 74, 100, 172 n.22
  and capitalism 167
  classic 120, 128
  and family 30, 85
  forms of 120
  and intersectionality (*see* intersectional patriarchy)
  Kemalist (*see* Kemalist patriarchy)
  pluralities of 112–13
  theory of bargaining 166
  theory of manufacturing consent 166
  transitional (*see* transitional patriarchy)
  types of **117**
peace process 36, 183 n.4
Pearson, R. 83
peasant market (*köylü pazarı*) 67
peasants 24, 32, 41–2, 54, 140, 176 n.5, 178 n.4
People's Democratic Party (HDP) 36, 183 n.4
Phillips, A. 83, 108
piece rate system 66–7, 74
piece work payment system 65, 69
Pilgeram, R. 83
Pillow, W. 13
populism 20
postmodern coup 32
production and reproduction 5, 7, 16, 30, 111, 119, 139, 152, 154, 165–9
'proper woman' 50, 60
Putin, Vladimir 39

Quilley, S. 40

Ramamurthy, P. 153, 168
Ran, Nazım Hikmet 106
reconciliation process 36, 183 n.4
Red (tomato-processing factory) 40–2, 111, 140–1, 143, 163, 176 n.3, 179 n.9
  'Anatolian Women' in warehouse 106–8
  'Daughters of Red Republic' 103–6
  external environs of plant **93**
  images of women 83–6
  machines 102–3
  mechanical monster 81–2
  production line to stop 103–4
  rivals in Kemalism 92–3
  subcontracting and intersectional patriarchy 109–10
  tomato sorting lines (*see* tomato sorting lines)
  vision of managers 86–92
reflexivity 12–13
registered seeds 34, 42
*Religion, Society and Modernity in Turkey* (Mardin) 113, 180 n.2
Republican People's Party (CHP) 87, 179 n.8, 184 n.6
republicanism 20
'resentful' local worker 58–61
revolutionism 20
rule of the father 7
Rural Union of Brazil (STR) 53

Salzinger, L. 10, 13, 83, 86
Sarıgıl 171 n.16
Sarıoğlu, E. 85
Savaşkan, O. 87
schooling rate 170 n.5
scientific management 68–70, 79
seasonal work/workers 1–2, 4, 15, 36, 45, 47, 49, 55–8, 60, 66, 78, 89, 92, 98, 105, 107, 111, 129, 133–6, 155, 160, 165, 177 n.7, 178 n.4, 183 n.5
secularism 20, 31, 87, 180 n.36
secularist hegemony 32
Seed Law 34, 153, 155
Selwyn, B. 53
*şeref* 115–16
sexual hierarchy 8
small-scale farmers 23, 41–2
social neoliberalism and AKP 32, 33, 175 n.32
sociological autobiography 15
sociological imagination 15
*sosyete* 124, 181 n.15
statism 20
Stewart, A. 7
*A Strangeness in My Mind* (Pamuk) 174 n.13
subcontracting employment firms 29–30, 81, 85, 88, 90, 106–7, 109–10

*tandır* 129–33, 182 n.21
*Tangled Routes* (Barndt) 39

Taylor, B. 83, 108
Taylorism 69
Taylorist principles 69
tomato picking, workers 16, 42, 65, 75, 157. *See also* familial labour relations (tomato picking)
tomato planting, labour 15
tomato-processing factory. *See* Red (tomato-processing factory)
tomato sauce 7, 67, 93–4, 102–3, 149–50, 158, 178 n.4
tomato sorting lines
  break times 100–2
  *çavuş*'s perspective 97–8
  for diced tomatoes 93
  first and second part 94–5, **96**
  quality difference 94
  religious women's and Kemalist control 98–9
  third part 95, **96**
  for tomato sauces 93
  upper and lower production lines **97**
tomatoes production 1–2, 17, 39–40
  capitalist 16, 67, 79, 161
  *dayıbaşı* and familial labour force 44–7
  farmers 43, 155
  final stage of 76–7
  hierarchy of masculinity 118, **118**
  in Mexico 161
  social actors of 65, 133
  tomato agreement, conditions 40–2
  women workers 39, 43–4, 49, 113
Topal, C. 84
Toprak, B. 181 n.2
Torres, G. 40
transitional patriarchy 16, 139, 147, 152
  changes on gender relations 147–8
  *el âlem* 139
  factory women workers and nuclear home 143
  gendered division of labour 143–5
'trope of productive femininity' 83
Tuğal, C. 32–4, 36, 175 n.32, 179 n.10
Turkey. *See also* 'Kurdish problem' in Turkey
  and *dayıbaşı* 10
  fieldwork sites **6**
  *gecekondu mahellesi* 173 n.11

  regions of **22**
  schooling rate in 170 n.5
Turkish Central Bank 34
Turkish-Kurdish conflict 59, 156
Turkish Official Dictionary (TDK) 114
Turkist Radical Nationalism 173 n.5

unemployment rate 22, 33, 44, 175 n.32, 178 n.1
United Nations High Comissioner for Refugees (UNHCR) 10
unpaid workers 15, 49, 115, 143, 147, 151, 154, 170 n.2, 175 n.27
urban women's employment 135

Virtue Party (*Fazilet Partisi*) 31–2

Walby, S. 172 n.22, 172 n.23
wealthy landowning family 24
West, C. 83
Westwood, S. 90
White, J. 8, 30, 135
Women for Women's Human Rights (WWHR) 171 n.9
*Women Writing Culture* (Behar & Gordon) 12
women's labour 6, 8, 27, 106, 135, 150, 152, 155–6
  changing patterns 19
  *el âlem* 158, 160
  family to manage 85
  fieldwork diary 51, 59
  homeworking 29
  Kemalist factory regime 85
  low-skilled categorization 84
  on machines 88, 100, 105, 109, 110
  and male agents 176 n.2
  management 16, 158, 179 n.5
  patriarchy 8, 29
  rural 19, 36, 44
  on sorting lines 86, 97, 99, 107, 110, 164
  in tomato-processing factory 140–1, 143, 149, 163, 179 n.9
  transitional households 139, 143
  unpaid 154
  in the warehouse 107–8, 158

young 71–4
youngest 74–6
women's subordination 8
working-class femininities 85
workplace deaths 179 n.2
Wright, M. 42

Yalman, G. 31
Yenal, Z. 35, 173 n.10
Yuval-Davis, N. 8

Zimmerman, H. D. 83

CPSIA information can be obtained
at www.ICGtesting.com
Printed in the USA
LVHW080009160422
716296LV00021B/1189